# Operational Research

## S.S. Cohen

Senior Lecturer in Mathematics
Polytechnic of Central London

## Edward Arnold

5/198?
math

© S.S. Cohen 1985

First published in Great Britain 1985 by Edward Arnold (Publishers) Ltd, 41 Bed___ ___,
London WC1B 3DQ

Edward Arnold, 300 North Charles Street, Baltimore, Maryland, U.S.A.

Edward Arnold (Australia) Pty Ltd, 80 Waverley Road, Caulfield East, Victoria 3145, Australia

Cohen, S.S.
    Operational research.
    1. Operations research
    I. Title
    001.4'24      T57.6
    ISBN  0-7131-3528-X

To Ruth, Philip, Elouise, Aaron and Jonathan

Printed by Butler & Tanner Ltd
Frome and London

# Preface

There is a growing awareness amongst managers that quantitative methods can help them in the planning and execution of their business activities. Operational Research is the name given to a collection of such techniques and many management courses include it as a part of their curriculum. There is, however, a lack of textbooks which are suitable for non-mathematicians in this area and so, as a lecturer experienced in and sympathetic with the needs of such students, I have attempted to provide one.

This book has been written to give a fairly numerate but not necessarily mathematical reader the capability to implement many of the ideas of operational research. It contains no calculus or advanced algebra and each topic is illustrated by worked examples with numbers in them instead of the more usual symbols. It is hoped that the reader will find it easier to learn in this way than by studying a more abstract theoretical text.

Towards the end of every chapter there is a short computer program written in the BASIC language. This enables the reader to computerise, on even the smallest of machines, some of the techniques he or she is learning to perform by hand. The programs have been designed in what specialists would derisively call an 'unstructured' way. I apologise to the specialists but I have done this deliberately so that the programs are short and therefore easier to type into the computer. They can be ignored by readers if they wish as they are not meant to contribute to an understanding of operational research. These programs are included simply to show how computers are used to implement the subject, a use which becomes essential when there is a mass of data or many calculations to be performed.

Each chapter ends with a summary of the topics covered within it, a section on suggestions for further reading, and a collection of problems with answers. The problems not only give the reader practice in the methods described but also indicate the variety of situations in which they can be applied.

It is the intention that the combination of worked examples, summary, further reading and problems will allow the reader to identify and then utilise the material he or she wants without necessarily reading the whole book or even a whole chapter. There is a comprehensive index containing all the key words used in the book to facilitate its use for reference purposes. The text should then function like a general practitioner and offer methods of solution for the more common problem situations while referring the reader to specialist sources in the section on further reading for the less common, possibly more advanced, applications.

I acknowledge with thanks the numerous discussions I have had with my colleagues Dr K. Darby-Dowman and Dr D. Emery on the subject matter and methods of presenting it. I also thank my wife, Ruth, for advising me on how a non-mathematician reacts to mathematical ideas.

SSC 1984

# Contents

# 1 Introduction

'What is the use of a book', thought Alice, 'without pictures or conversations?'—*Alice in Wonderland* by Lewis Carroll.

Operational Research is the science of planning and executing an operation to make the most economical use of the resources available. The operation can be as simple as making a cup of coffee or as complicated as scheduling the movements of a fleet of oil tankers around the world. It can be a project which will be undertaken only once, like the construction of a particular building, or a regularly repeated activity like the weekly ordering of stock in a shop. In each case the manager has to organise labour, equipment and materials in order to achieve a certain objective, usually the maximisation of profit. Operational Research techniques attempt to model such real-world systems, either on paper or in a computer, so that their performance can be optimised with respect to an appropriate set of criteria.

The history of Operational Research is not a long one although its origins can be traced back to the Industrial Revolution. Most of the ideas were not developed until the Second World War when the British and American Armed Forces found themselves mounting large scale operations many thousands of miles from their home bases. It became necessary to study the logistics of moving quantities of men, weaponry, vehicles and supplies over long distances in a coordinated fashion. Even in the fighting itself a mathematical approach was used to find the optimum military strategies.

After the war, many of the techniques developed were adopted by multinational companies, who were themselves beginning to grow, to organise their large, but this time peaceful, projects. Even the methods employed to make the purely tactical decisions were given the name 'Games Theory' and taken to model the competitive behaviour of firms marketing similar products. The post-war boom in international trade, the advanced technology of production processes and the increased use of computers all stimulated the growth of Operational Research. It has now become an important discipline in its own right rather than merely being another topic within mathematics or statistics.

The mention of computers should not deter the reader who is unfamiliar with them. The use of a computer in Operational Research becomes necessary only when a problem involves a large amount of data or many calculations and the methods themselves are often used without the aid of a computer. There are, however, some elementary mathematical concepts which have general relevance to the subject. These are covered in the remainder of this chapter while Chapter 6 deals with the essential ideas of probability needed for Chapters 7–13.

## Mathematical Models

All scientific understanding of the real world is achieved by means of models. Meteorologists have theories about the behaviour of the weather which enable them to use observed data to make forecasts of temperatures and pressures. Doctors believe that certain symptoms indicate the presence of specific illnesses in accordance with a 'cause and effect' model they have of the way the human body functions. In fact, a scientific advance can occur only when an existing model, representing the culmination of all previous knowledge in a given area, fails to explain some newly observed phenomenon. The model is then amended in the light of the new findings and taken to be 'true' until fresh contradictory evidence emerges and the whole cycle is repeated. Scientific method is the process of making observations or designing experiments in order to refute existing models and provide information for creating new ones.

Some branches of science deal with qualities rather than quantities. For example the theory of evolution is a qualitative model used in biology to explain certain properties or characteristics observed amongst animal and plant populations. Operational research, however, is concerned mainly with quantities and so the models encountered in it are quantitative mathematical ones. These usually consist of formulae or other techniques for giving a numerical description of a system's status. For example, suppose that a tyre manufacturer knows that there are about 19 million motor vehicles in use in the United Kingdom. He is told by a motoring organisation that 32% of these vehicles have owners who live in rural areas which are liable to heavy snowfalls. Taking into account spare wheels and heavy lorries, he believes that each vehicle uses an average of 5.2 tyres at any one time and therefore predicts that the total potential market for snow tyres is $19 \times 0.32 \times 5.2$ million, which is 31.6 million tyres. This simple model of the size of the market for snow tyres gives a prediction which may or may not be borne out by subsequent events. It may prove necessary to modify the model if the prediction is found to be wrong but, provided the manufacturer is aware of its limitations, it can give useful management information before any marketing takes place.

The word **system** is used throughout this book to denote that part of the real world which is of interest in a particular problem and is therefore being modelled. It is a vague term which must be taken in the context of the underlying situation, although at the end of the book, in Chapter 13, we shall reconsider it.

The art of mathematical modelling is to identify those quantities associated with a system which provide essential management information about the system. These are then linked mathematically to each other and to as few other variables as possible to form a model describing how the system behaves. The objectives of the exercise are important in this as they affect the choice of the variables of interest. For example, two people can be observing the same system, say, a bus. The first person, a transport manager, records the times of its arrival and departure at the various stages of its journey. The second person, a maintenance engineer, is possibly interested in the fuel consumption and the wear on the tyres. Each man has a completely different model of the bus in his mind because their objectives in studying it, and so the quantities they measure, are not the same.

The model itself may or may not reflect a degree of 'cause and effect' between the variables in the real system. While scientists do look for evidence of causality in the universe, and of course any such knowledge does help us to build a model, the only important thing as far as operational research is concerned is that we obtain an accurate numerical description of the way the system behaves. This description can result from a purely mathematical relationship which does not imply cause and effect, for example, the number of admissions to mental hospitals per year in a country can be predicted from the number of television receivers sold there. This is merely a consequence of the fact that the numbers are both related to the population size and so one is an indicator of the other; it does not imply that watching television drives you crazy! This very example is discussed further in the section on Correlation and Regression in Chapter 12 on Forecasting.

The use of worked examples in the treatment of the various topics in this book should help in the identification of an appropriate model for a given situation. Of course, the reader who has a specific problem to solve may not find an example which corresponds to it exactly. In practice a certain amount of ingenuity is required to formulate a problem in such a way that it resembles a stereotype and can then be solved by a known technique. For instance, in a flash of inspiration, Johannes Kepler, in the 17th century, realised that he could account for the observed motion of the planets by assuming a model in which they all rotated about the sun in elliptic orbits. This allowed him to cast the problem in terms of the geometry of the ellipse, which was well known to him, and hence derive his three laws of planetary motion.

We shall study the different types of mathematical models used in operational research under two main headings, **deterministic** and **stochastic.** Those in the first category attempt to establish exact mathematical relationships between the variables concerned. Whenever this task is too difficult and complicated, as it is in analysing the tossing of a coin allowing for wind speed, force of toss etc., it may be possible to build a stochastic model. These use probabilities in one way or another to describe the average, rather than the precise, behaviour of the system.

There are other types of mathematical models and in Chapter 12 on Forecasting we build a statistical model based solely on data observed in the real system. This kind of empirical rather than theoretical modelling is used in economics, for instance, where our understanding of the mechanisms linking the variables of interest is poor.

It should be emphasised that the models of operational research are to be regarded as management forecasting tools and not as completely infallible predictors of the future. Sometimes a key factor has been omitted from the calculation or some assumption about the system ceases to be true and the model then becomes inadequate. Our results are only as good as the accuracy of the assumptions upon which they are based.

## Methods of Analysis

There are several ways in which mathematics is used to analyse the models found in operational research. Sometimes a formula can be derived which enables us to calculate the quantities of interest directly. Such formulae can provide a quantitative comparison of different strategies, so that the cheapest or quickest can be found. Some deterministic models do not give rise to formulae but are solved by means of **algorithms.** These are step-by-step procedures like a recipe for baking a cake. Often the algorithm generates a sequence of possible solutions with each one being better in some sense than the previous one. The model is solved by repeating the process until no further improvements can be made. Algorithms are used in Chapters 2 to 5.

When there are no appropriate formulae or algorithms available for the analysis of a model then the method of simulation might be used. This is a 'playing through' of the system on paper or in a computer to see how it behaves. Simulation is described in Chapter 6 and used in Chapters 9, 10 and 13.

The analysis of how a model works or how well it works may require an advanced knowledge of mathematics. Fortunately the practical application of models to operational research problems does not usually need such knowledge and as far as we are concerned it is not important, within reason, how or why a model works but only that it does work. Operational research is in a more favourable position in this respect than subjects like civil engineering or electronics where even the routine application of a model can demand the use of higher mathematics.

## Monetary Values

Many of the variables occurring in models are amounts of money representing cash flow or the value of assets. Other types of 'costs' like labour and even time, are often measured in monetary terms. These quantities can be difficult to estimate, especially if the cost or benefit to the operation is going to occur in the future. There are also problems in assessing the value of intangibles like good-will, expected profits on new ventures, costs of emergencies, and so on.

References are given in the section on Further Reading at the end of this chapter which adopt the financial and management accounting points of view to costings. These are relevant when balance sheet values are needed but often depend on other estimates which have equally dubious degrees of accuracy. For example in costing the depreciation of a motor vehicle it may be necessary to estimate its lifetime in years, the residual value at the end of its life, or a monetary measure of the profit the vehicle earns in one year. Mathematically speaking this does not solve the valuation problem but simply moves it somewhere else.

The decision of how to measure the monetary value of a piece of equipment or activity depends on the context of the situation and we assume in this book that whenever such a variable appears it is being evaluated in an appropriate way. There are, however, one or two mathematical ideas which might be of help.

## Growth and Decay

There are two types of change which are frequently modelled and which correspond to the two basic operations of arithmetic, addition and multiplication. **Additive** growth occurs when a constant amount is added to a quantity at each period of time. Money earning simple interest grows in this way and, say, £100 invested at 6% per annum simple interest becomes £106 after 1 year, £112 after 2 years, £118 after 3 years and so on. The same amount, £6, is added at the end of each year.

A graph of the quantity concerned against time is a straight line for this type of growth and so it is also called **straight line** or **linear** growth. Accountants speak of straight line depreciation when they mean that the value of a piece of equipment is reduced by a fixed amount each year. We shall study straight line graphs later in this chapter.

The second type of growth, **multiplicative,** occurs when a quantity is multiplied by some constant at each time period. Money earning compound interest grows like this and, say, £100 invested at 6% per annum compound interest becomes £106 at the end of 1 year, £112.36 at the end of 2 years, £119.1016 at the end of 3 years and so on. Each amount is 106% of, or 1.06 times, the previous figure.

Projecting the growth forward for $t$ years involves multiplying the original amount by the same constant $t$ times. For instance, compound growth of £200 at 5% for 7 years results in £200 × (1.05)[7], the 7 being an **index** denoting $1.05 \times 1.05 \times 1.05 \times \ldots \times 1.05$ (7 terms).

Similarly depreciation or decline at a constant percentage rate can be expressed as multiplication by 1 minus the appropriate rate. For example suppose a motor vehicle depreciates at the rate of 20% per year. Each year it is valued at 80% of its previous value and so, after say 4 years, it is worth (0.8)[4], which is 0.4096 or 40.96%, of its original value.

As the time over which the growth or decay occurs appears as an index, this type of growth is also called **exponential.** Now logarithms are indices and so exponential growth or decay can be detected by seeing whether the logarithms of the growing quantity behave like time and increase linearly. This technique is used in the Population Example on growth in Chapter 12.

## Discounted Cash Flow

When an operation extends over several years, it is necessary to compare costs and benefits with each other even though they relate to different times. Clearly, £100 received today, which can be invested to grow in value, is worth more than £100 which will be received in, say, 3 years' time. A common method of comparing such amounts is to **discount** them both to some convenient time, usually the start of the operation. Hence a receipt of £100 in 3 years can be thought of as being equivalent to a smaller income today which will grow to £100 if it is invested for 3 years. Suppose that the appropriate return is 6% compound interest per year, then the equivalent amount is £100/(1.06)[3], or £83.96. In other words multiplying £83.96 by (1.06)[3] to calculate its value in 3 years gives the result £100. Here is a worked example to show how a complete project can be assessed by discounting all the cash flows into present-day terms.

### The Assurance Example
An assurance policy has the following revenues and expenditures associated with it:

| Year | 1 | 2 | 3 | 4 |
|---|---|---|---|---|
| Premium (£) payable at the start of the year | 10 000 | 2000 | 0 | 0 |
| Income (£) received at the end of the year | 0 | 1000 | 2000 | 16 700 |

Many policies of this nature have an insurance element to them in that the death or injury of the assured person results in the payment of a sum of money by the insurance company. As such risks can be covered separately by other policies, we assume that it is possible to estimate the insurance part of the premiums involved and appraise the remainder as a sequence of expenditures made for purely investment purposes. It is then reasonable to compare the resulting cash flow with that which would be obtained from investing all monies in some alternative scheme.

In this example we assume that the above premiums do not contain an insurance element and we decide whether the policy represents a good investment if money can earn 15% per year compound interest elsewhere.

*Solution*   Ignoring the fact that the various costs and benefits occur in different years and so are not directly comparable, the total cost of the policy is £12 000 while the total benefit is £19 700. The apparent profit is therefore £7700 and as it is spread over 4 years this can be divided by 4 to give £1925 per year. This represents a percentage rate of return on the £12 000 capital sum employed of $(1925/12\,000) \times 100$, or 16.04%. Hence a superficial non-discounting analysis indicates that the policy is indeed preferable to the alternative investment quoted in the question at 15%.

A proper analysis can be performed in two ways. The first way is to trace the balance of an imaginary bank account which yields the alternative rate of interest and has the same cash flow. It is important that the dates on which the cash is paid or received are exactly the same in the analysis as they are in the original project. If this is not so then we are not comparing like with like. The working for the present example is given in Table 1.1.

**Table 1.1**

| Year | Balance brought forward | Added at start of year | Balance | Add interest at 15% for year | Balance | Subtract at end of year | Balance carried forward |
|---|---|---|---|---|---|---|---|
| 1 | 0 | 10 000 | 10 000.00 | 1500.00 | 11 500.00 | 0 | 11 500.00 |
| 2 | 11 500.00 | 2000 | 13 500.00 | 2025.00 | 15 525.00 | 1000 | 14 525.00 |
| 3 | 14 525.00 | 0 | 14 525.00 | 2178.75 | 16 703.75 | 2000 | 14 703.75 |
| 4 | 14 703.75 | 0 | 14 703.75 | 2205.56 | 16 909.31 | 16 700 | 209.31 |

The amounts added and subtracted from the 'bank' balance are the premiums and benefits given in the question and they occur in the alternative cash flow at precisely the same times as they do in the project being evaluated. As this alternative leaves a positive balance of £209.31 at the end of 4 years, we conclude that it is preferable to the assurance policy, which leaves a residual balance of zero, although the superficial analysis indicated otherwise.

A second, equivalent, way of appraising a project is to relate all monetary values in present-day terms. Each amount corresponds to a sum of money which, if invested today at 15% compound interest, would become worth that amount at the appropriate time it appears in the cash flow. For instance, the income of £2000 given by the policy at the end of year 3 is worth £1315 today as that is the amount of money which has to be invested at 15% per annum compound interest now to become £2000 in 3 years' time. The interest value of 15% is called the **discount rate** and Table 1.2 shows all the cash flow figures discounted back into **net present value** terms.

**Table 1.2**

| Year | Expenditure at start of year | Income at end of year | Net present value at 15% | Total net present value |
|---|---|---|---|---|
| 1 | 10 000 | 0 | −10 000 | −10 000 |
| 2 | 2000 | 1000 | −982.99 | −10 982.99 |
| 3 | 0 | 2000 | +1315.03 | −9667.96 |
| 4 | 0 | 16 700 | +9548.28 | −119.68 |

The analysis shows that the overall net present value of the cash flow profile using a discount rate of 15% is negative. **This means that the project has a net present cost rather than a net present benefit and is therefore not preferable to an investment giving 15% per annum compound interest.**

The two methods we have used give the same conclusion and the resulting values obtained for the project can be reconciled. The residual bank balance of £209.31 which is accumulated in Table 1.1 is a sum of money receivable at the end of the fourth year. Its net present value in terms of today's money is £209.31/(1.15)$^4$ which is £119.67 and, to within the limits of numerical accuracy, this is the same as the net present value of the whole project as calculated in Table 1.2. In fact either of the two methods can be used although it is easier to compare the net present values of two projects which extend over different time periods than their residual balances as the latter relate to different times.

The discount rate which gives a project the net present value of zero is the equivalent compound interest rate that the project represents. The appropriate value for the assurance policy described above can be found by repeating the last analysis for several different discount rates. The computer program at the end of this chapter is particularly useful for this task and the results, which can also be obtained using a pocket calculator, are given in Table 1.3.

**Table 1.3**

| Discount rate (%) | 14.0 | 14.5 | 14.6 | 14.7 | 15.0 |
|---|---|---|---|---|---|
| Net present value (£) of policy | 252.77 | 64.53 | 27.37 | − 9.63 | −119.68 |

This shows that the 'breakeven' discount rate is between 14.6% and 14.7% and gives an indication of the investment value of the policy. Credit companies operating in certain countries have to quote the value of this breakeven rate in their advertising in order to comply with the law. It is often called the **annual percentage rate** and abbreviated to **APR.** For a loan it is the discount rate for which the net present values of all the repayments equals the value of the loan. In other words, the overall net present value of the cash flow consisting of the loan and the repayments is zero. The **APR** for interest charged monthly can be found from the amount by which a debt is multiplied over a complete year. For instance a credit card company charging 2% per month multiplies an outstanding amount by (1.02)$^{12}$, or 1.2682, in a complete year. Hence the Annual Percentage Rate is 26.8%.

## Sensitivity and Accuracy

Table 1.3 is a form of **sensitivity analysis** as it displays the results of repeating the calculations for several values of one of the variables. It therefore describes the sensitivity of the model to changes in the value of that variable. A sensitivity analysis can be performed whenever there is a doubt about the accuracy of the data being used in a model. In the Assurance Example, it tells us that if the interest rate on the investment which is the alternative to the policy is not 15% but 14.5%, then the previous decision to adopt the alternative would be reversed. Our conclusion is thus seen to be sensitive to the alternative interest rate, to the extent of 0.5%.

The concept of the sensitivity of a model is linked with ideas of numerical accuracy. Again using Table 1.3 as an illustration, suppose that the net present value of the policy is required only to the nearest hundred pounds. The discount rates 14.6% and 14.7% both give the same answer now and either of them can be taken as the equivalent compound interest rate for the policy.

It is important to be aware of sensitivity and accuracy when using a computer or calculator. For example, suppose that a data value is quoted as being 8.2 correct to one decimal place. This means that the actual value can be anything between 8.15 and 8.25. If the square of this number is required, then we would obtain 67.24 as the square of 8.2 but the range of possible values is from $(8.15)^2$ to $(8.25)^2$ which is from 66.4225 to 68.0625. Hence quoting the answer to be 67.24 with the implied claim of two decimal place accuracy is clearly wrong when the whole number part could possibly be 66 or 68! It seems more sensible to give the answer as 67 and acknowledge that it may be in error by plus or minus 1.

In the Population Example of Chapter 12 the above argument of **numerical sensitivity** is used to decide how many decimal places to work with when taking logarithms. One of the data values concerned is 1194 and by quoting it without decimal places the question implies that it is correct only to the nearest whole number. This means that the true value could be any number between 1193.5 and 1194.5 with its logarithm being between $\log(1193.5)$ and $\log(1194.5)$, that is between 3.07682 and 3.07719. As these results agree to only 3 decimal places, it is incorrect to claim a higher degree of accuracy than this for $\log(1194)$.

It is a good idea to keep an extra **guard digit** in addition to the number decided upon for reasons of numerical sensitivity. This minimises the risk of rounding errors when performing arithmetic. For example the calculation 8.61−7.36 has the exact solution 1.25. If the numbers are rounded off to 1 decimal place, the subtraction becomes 8.6−7.4, which is 1.2. This is *not* the 1 decimal place equivalent of the exact result, 1.25. It is always advisable to maintain as much accuracy as is feasible during the course of a calculation for intermediate answers and so on, and round off the final answer to the appropriate number of decimal places before quoting it. The very minimum degree of accuracy to keep to during the calculation is that of the guard digit in addition to the accuracy required in the final answer.

## Straight Line Graphs

We end this chapter with a description of a type of model which is very commonly used. It arises from the simplest form of mathematical relationship that two variables can have with each other, that one of them is equal to a multiple of the other, plus or minus a constant. A graph of one of the quantities against the other is then a straight line and the relationship is said to be **linear** for this reason. We study straight line graphs in the following worked example.

### The Pencils Example

A factory has fixed overheads of £2000 per week and manufactures pencils which it sells for 50p each. If the raw materials and labour necessary to make a pencil are estimated to cost 30p, how many of them should the company sell each week in order to break even?

*Solution*  As the answer required is the number of pencils sold each week, we introduce the symbol $x$ to stand for this quantity. The revenue and expenditure resulting from making and selling $x$ pencils per week can be expressed in terms of $x$ using the information in the question to give the model:

$$\left.\begin{array}{l} \text{Revenue} = 0.5\,x \\ \text{Expenditure} = 0.3\,x + 2000 \end{array}\right\} \tag{1.1}$$

These equations simply state that the weekly revenue, in pounds, is 0.5 for every pencil sold, making a total of $0.5\,x$. The expenditure is 0.3 for every pencil sold plus the fixed overheads of 2000.

Although the model (1.1) can be analysed algebraically, mathematicians like to draw graphs as pictures of the way variables depend on each other. Graphs give an overall indication of the behaviour of the quantities of interest which no single calculation can provide on its own.

Points on a graph are specified by quoting their **coordinates.** These are distances along the $x$ and $y$ **axes** and are written as a pair of numbers inside brackets, separated by a comma. For example the point (3,5) is 3 units along the $x$ axis and 5 units along the $y$ axis. A curve is a set of points whose $x$ and $y$ coordinates bear some mathematical relationship to each other.

Now the simplest relationship that two variables can have is that one of them is some multiple of the other one plus, or minus, a constant. These are the relationships in our model (1.1). It so happens that all points $(x,y)$ whose coordinates have such a linear relationship with each other lie on a straight line. Hence the simplest type of equation in algebra corresponds to the simplest type of curve in geometry, the straight line. This fortuitous correspondence makes the 'marriage' between algebra and geometry, called **coordinate geometry,** a very fruitful one as it enables each subject to be studied using ideas borrowed from the other one.

As both of the expressions in the model (1.1) are linear functions of $x$ their graphs are straight lines. These can be plotted on graph paper very easily as it is necessary to plot only 2 points for each line and then join them together with a pencil and ruler. The points plotted could be (0,0) and (20 000,10 000) for $y = 0.5\,x$ and (0,2000) and (20 000,8000) for $y = 0.3\,x + 2000$.

The graphs are shown in Fig. 1.1 and give a picture of the model formed by the equations (1.1). The financial consequences of any level of sales, $x$, can be read and in particular the **breakeven point** can be found. This represents the minimum level of sales for which the business remains viable in that revenue covers expenditure. **In this example, as can be seen from Fig. 1.1, it is 10 000 pencils, and that is the solution to the question.**

The graph also gives an idea of the sensitivity of the model to changes in the costings or the value of $x$. Broadly speaking, the smaller the angle at which the lines cross, the more sensitive the position of the breakeven point is to changes in their slopes. As we shall see below, these slopes are the multipliers of $x$ in the equations, in this case the unit costs.

Other readings can be taken from the graph. For instance, the level of sales which results in a profit of, say, £1000 can be found by looking for the $x$ value for which the expenditure line is 1000 units on the $y$ axis below the revenue line. Alternatively, the line $y = 0.3\,x + 3000$ can be plotted. This is the old expenditure function plus £1000 profit

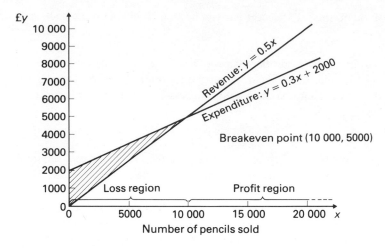

**Fig. 1.1**    Breakeven analysis for the Pencils Example

which is treated as an additional 'overhead'. When plotted, it shows a new breakeven point at $x$ equal to 15 000.

Sometimes, instead of starting with an equation and drawing a graph, we start with a straight line graph and need to deduce the mathematical relationship between the variables. This is the case in the Cosmetics Example of Chapter 12 where the points on the graph represent various observed data values. We begin by measuring the **slope** or **gradient** of the line. This is the rate of change of $y$ with respect to $x$, in other words the height measured along the $y$ axis corresponding to 1 unit along the $x$ axis. This height, and therefore the slope itself, will be negative if the line slopes downwards as it does in the Glue Factory Example of Chapter 2.

The slope is measured by drawing a right-angled triangle on the graph with the line as one of the sides, as shown in Fig. 1.2. The lengths $a$ and $b$ are measured in the units of the $y$ and $x$ axes respectively and the slope of the line is the ratio $(a/b)$, denoted by the letter $m$. It is the appropriate multiple in the relationship between $x$ and $y$ and readers

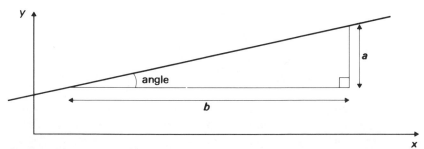

**Fig. 1.2**    Measurement of the slope of a straight line graph

familiar with trigonometry will also recognise it as the tangent of the angle marked in Fig. 1.2.

The specification of the linear relationship corresponding to a given straight line graph is completed by calculating the value of the additive constant. This is found by reading off the coordinates of any point lying on the line, call it $(f,g)$, and the equation is:

$$y = mx + c \text{ where } c = g - mf \tag{1.2}$$

The constant term in the equation is called the **intercept** of the line. It is the $y$ value for which $x$ is zero and hence the point where the line intercepts the $y$ axis, assuming that the $x$ axis begins with $x$ equal to zero.

There is a further discussion of straight line graphs in the section on Correlation and Regression in Chapter 12, in particular the desirability of plotting an 'average' point when fitting a straight line through a collection of points which represent observed data values.

## Computer Program

The following program performs a discounted cash flow analysis on given revenues and expenditures over a period of at most 20 years. In fact this upper time limit can be extended if necessary by altering line 1Ø of the program accordingly. As in the Assurance Example, income is assumed to accrue at the end of the period to which it applies while any expenditure is assumed to be due at the beginning. Naturally the time period does not have to be measured in years although the program has been written using the word 'year'.

```
1Ø  DIM R(2Ø),E(2Ø)
2Ø  PRINT "DISCOUNTED CASH FLOW PROGRAM"
3Ø  PRINT "---------------------------"
4Ø  PRINT
5Ø  PRINT "DISCOUNT RATE (AS A DECIMAL) ";
6Ø  INPUT D
7Ø  PRINT "ENTER INCOME AND EXPENDITURE"
8Ø  PRINT "FOR EACH YEAR, ENDING WITH -1"
9Ø  N=Ø
1ØØ N=N+1
11Ø PRINT "YEAR ";N
12Ø INPUT R(N),E(N)
13Ø IF R(N)<>-1 THEN 1ØØ
14Ø N=N-1
15Ø T=Ø
16Ø M=1
17Ø PRINT "YEAR INCOME EXPENDITURE NET PRESENT   TOTAL NET"
18Ø PRINT "                          VALUE    PRESENT VALUE"
19Ø FOR Y=1 TO N
2ØØ M=M/(1+D)
21Ø V=(R(Y)-(1+D)*E(Y))*M
22Ø T=T+V
23Ø PRINT Y;R(Y),E(Y),V,T
24Ø NEXT Y
25Ø END
```

**Specimen Run**

```
DISCOUNTED CASH FLOW PROGRAM
----------------------------

DISCOUNT RATE (AS A DECIMAL)   ?0.14
ENTER INCOME AND EXPENDITURE
FOR EACH YEAR, ENDING WITH -1
YEAR   1
 ?0,5000
YEAR   2
 ?500,2000
YEAR   3
 ?3000,0
YEAR   4
 ?4000,0
YEAR   5
 ?-1,-1
YEAR   INCOME   EXPENDITURE   NET   PRESENT   TOTAL   NET
                              VALUE       PRESENT   VALUE
   1   0          5000        -5000           -5000
   2   500        2000        -1369.65        -6369.65
   3   3000       0            2024.91        -4344.74
   4   4000       0            2368.32        -1976.42
```

**Program Notes**

**1**   Lines 10 to 60 open arrays to store the revenues and expenditures, print a heading and read the value of the discount rate, D, from the user.

**2**   Lines 70 to 130 read values for the yearly revenues and expenditures from the user. A counter, N, is initialised to 0 in line 90 in order to count the number of years of data. Every time revenue and expenditure values R(N) and E(N) are read in line 120, the IF instruction in line 130 tests R(N) to see whether it is equal to $-1$. If it is not, then control is sent back to line 100 where the counter N is increased by 1 and another year's data read. When the user has finished entering all the cash flows and types $-1$ for each of them, line 130 sends control to line 140 which adjusts the value of the counter N back to the correct number of years. This is necessary so that the remainder of the program ignores the artificial values of $-1$ which are taken as signals from the user.

**3**   Lines 150 and 160 initialise the variables T, the total net present value of the project, and M, the **discount factor.** This is the amount by which a sum of money must be multiplied to find its net present value. At the end of the $n$th year it is $1/(1+D)^n$.

**4**   Lines 170 and 180 print headings and lines 190 to 240 work through the project year by year. The discount factor is updated in line 200 and used to generate the value of V, the net present value of the cash flow for that particular year, in line 210. There is an adjustment of $(1+D)$ to the expenditure for the year as it falls due at the beginning of the year, unlike the revenue which accrues at the end of the year. Line 220 adds V to the running total of net present values, T, and line 230 prints out the year number, revenue and expenditure for the year, the net present value and the total net present value to date. Control is then passed back to line 190 by line 240 until all the years of the project have been dealt with.

## Summary

**1**  Operational research is the science of planning and executing an operation to make the most economical use of the resources available. Many of its techniques were developed during the Second World War and were subsequently adopted by large companies for peace-time use.

**2**  Mathematical models are equations, formulae or procedures for obtaining a numerical description of how a system behaves. It is important to identify the variables of interest in the system when building a model. The use of worked examples throughout the book should help the reader to locate a suitable model for a specific problem. Models are to be regarded only as management tools. They depend for their accuracy on the validity of the assumptions upon which they are based and may or may not reflect a degree of causality between the variables they contain.

**3**  Models are analysed by a variety of methods including the use of formulae, algorithms, which are step-by-step procedures, and simulation, which is a 'playing through' of the real system on paper or in a computer.

**4**  Care should be taken with variables measured by means of monetary values. There are several ways of defining costs but whichever one is used the principle of discounting can relate them to present-day terms.

**5**  Geometric or exponential growth occurs when a quantity is multiplied by some constant over a period of time, like money earning compound interest. The net present value of an amount of money to be received or spent in the future is the amount which would have to be invested now at compound interest to become worth the same at that time in the future. The rate of interest used is called the discount rate. Whole projects can be appraised by comparing their net present values with each other or with an investment yielding a fixed yearly rate of interest.

**6**  Linear or straight line growth occurs when a quantity has a constant added to it over each period of time. Such quantities have straight line graphs and in general two variables $x$ and $y$ have a linear relationship with each other if $y = mx + c$ for some constants $m$ and $c$. The value of $m$ is called the slope of the line while the value of $c$ is called the intercept.

## Further Reading

Many Operational Research textbooks begin like this one with a brief history of the development of the subject. The interested reader will also discover in those books listed under the heading 'General Operational Research' in the Bibliography that different authors have slightly different conceptions of what the subject actually is. The remainder of this book can be thought of as further reading on mathematical modelling and the ideas are reviewed in Chapter 13 which deals with its computing aspects.

The sections of the present chapter on growth, monetary values and discounted cash flow are elaborated on in accountancy books such as (15) and (16). The work on straight line graphs can be found in books like (2) as well as in more formal mathematics textbooks.

## Exercises

**1**   Discuss which should come first in a scientific investigation, the model or the data.

**2**   A farmer was told that his donkey could survive on a tenth of the food he gave him each day. Henceforth the farmer halved the donkey's daily rations whenever business was bad and continued to feed it at the new reduced level. After the next bad day the donkey would therefore receive half his original food and after the second bad day a quarter of it. Explain why the donkey should become worried after the farmer has had three bad days of trading.

**3**   A company sets aside £7000 at the start of each year as a reserve fund. If the money is invested at 11.2% compound interest how much is the fund worth at the end of 5 years?

**4**   The population of a country is 2% greater at the end of each year than it is at the beginning. How many years will it take for the population to double in size?

**5**   How many complete years must £300 be invested at 13% to become worth more than £4000 when interest is (i) simple, (ii) compound?

**6**   An antique vase is on sale for £2032 and an impartial expert believes that it will be worth £5000 in 3 years' time. What equivalent annual percentage rate of compound interest does this investment represent?

**7**   A credit card company charges 3% compound interest per month on any outstanding balance. By considering an outstanding balance of, say, £1000, calculate the equivalent rate of interest per year.

**8**   A piece of machinery costs £11 400 and will give a profit of £4000 at the end of every subsequent year. (i) If money is worth 15% per year, in how many years would you consider the machine to have paid for itself? (ii) How sensitive to the discount rate is your answer to part (i)?

**9**   A piece of equipment costs £10 000 and is guaranteed for two years, so maintenance costs for those years are zero. The costs at the beginning of years 3, 4 and 5 are estimated to be £500, £800 and £950 respectively. If money is worth 14% per year, calculate the net present cost of buying and maintaining the equipment over the 5-year period. By how much is your answer reduced if the machine can be sold for £3000 at the end of the fifth year?

**10**   A factory has fixed overheads of £600 per week and produces packets of sweets at a cost of 60p each which are then sold for 75p. Plot graphs of total revenue and total expenditure on the same axes for numbers of packets of sweets ranging from 0 to 6000 per week. From your graphs estimate: (i) the number of packets the factory must produce to break even with revenue equal to expenditure, (ii) the number of packets which results in a net profit of £210 per week, and (iii) the number of packets which results in a net loss of £300 per week.

# Part 1   Deterministic Models

# 2  Linear Programming

Many management decisions involve maximising the amount of profit whilst keeping the level of usage of labour and raw materials within certain limits. Finding a combination of different types of activities which fully exploits the available resources is called **programming.** Often the restrictions on the use of resources have a particularly simple algebraic form, which we shall study soon, and the programming is **linear.**

In the example which follows we decide how much of each type of a certain product should be manufactured in order to maximise profit. There are simple, linear, constraints on the amount of labour and raw materials available but as we shall see in a later example the same method can deal with more than two constraints on the company's activities.

### The Glue Factory Example

A glue factory can produce either 'Infa-glue' or 'Supa-glue'. They need 7 litres of acid and 5 manhours to make 1 kilogram of the first type and 13 litres of acid and 3 manhours to make 1 kilogram of the second, superior type. Each kilogram of Infa-glue gives them £4 profit while the corresponding amount for Supa-glue is £7. If on each day there are 182 litres of acid and 60 manhours of labour available, find the quantities of each type of glue they should manufacture in order to maximise their total profit.

*Solution*   The reader should not be overwhelmed by the amount of information contained in this problem. The answer we are seeking is simply a pair of numbers, the number of kilograms of Infa-glue and the number of kilograms of Supa-glue. In true mathematical tradition, we assign letters to these unknown quantities and examine the consequences.

Suppose the factory produces $x$ kg of Infa-glue and $y$ kg of Supa-glue every day. Each possible combination of $x$ and $y$ values can be represented as a point on a graph (Fig. 2.1).

Not all points on the graph correspond to a feasible way of operating the factory. Clearly it is impossible to make negative amounts of glue and so $x$ and $y$ must both be positive or zero. This restricts the representative point to the top right of the diagram bounded by the axes. However, there are more subtle restrictions on the $x$ and $y$ values due to the availability of acid and labour. Consider first the amount of acid needed to produce $x$ kg of Infa-glue and $y$ kg of Supa-glue. One kilogram of Infa-glue needs 7 litres and so $x$ kg needs 7 times $x$, or $7x$, litres. Similarly $y$ kg of Supa-glue needs $13y$ litres of acid and hence the total amount of acid required is $(7x + 13y)$ litres. This must not exceed the amount available which is 182 litres and we can write this **constraint** algebraically:

$$7x + 13y \leqslant 182 \qquad (2.1)$$

The symbol '$\leqslant$' should be read 'less than or equal to'.

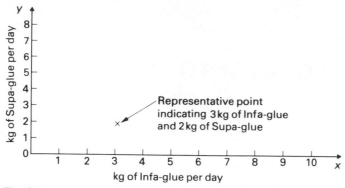

**Fig. 2.1**

Turning now to the labour involved in the operation, $5x$ manhours are needed to make $x$ kg of Infa-glue, that is 5 manhours per kilogram for $x$ kilograms, and $3y$ for $y$ kg of Supa-glue. This gives the labour constraint:

$$5x + 3y \leqslant 60 \qquad (2.2)$$

as there are only 60 manhours of labour available each day.

The constraints can now be incorporated on the graph to see how they restrict the possible positions of the representative point. To do this, imagine the point wandering about on the diagram. Obviously $x$ equal to 0 and $y$ equal to 0 is a way of operating the factory within the constraints. If $x$ and $y$ now increase, the point will move until the company is using all its supply of acid, which from equation (2.1) means that $7x + 13y$ is equal to 182. When this happens, neither $x$ nor $y$ can be increased any further because that would increase the value of $7x + 13y$ and there would not be enough acid to support the manufacturing process. The set of all points for which $7x + 13y = 182$ is in fact a straight line (Fig. 2.2).

It is fortuitous that the vast majority of constraints in practical problems are like $7x + 13y \leqslant 182$ and give rise to straight line 'thresholds'. This is the reason that the topic is called LINEar programming and all the non-mathematical reader need know is that any equation of the form $ax + by = c$, where $a$, $b$ and $c$ are constants, results in a straight

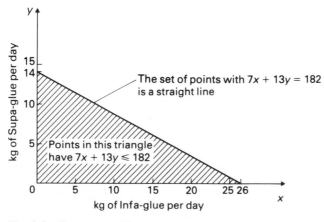

**Fig. 2.2**   The acid constraint in the Glue Factory Example

line. To draw such a line on graph paper we merely calculate where it crosses the axes and join those points together using a ruler. For example, to draw Fig. 2.2, we see from the equation $7x + 13y = 182$ that when $x$ is 0, $y$ is $182/13$ which is 14. We can therefore plot the point $x = 0$, $y = 14$ as the point where the line crosses the $y$ axis. We then put $y$ equal to 0 in the equation, giving $x = 182/7$ which is 26, and plot that point. It is then a simple matter to join the points together with a straight line.

Processing the labour constraint $5x + 3y \leqslant 60$ in the same manner gives the complete diagram (Fig. 2.3). This represents the effects of the acid and labour constraints on the

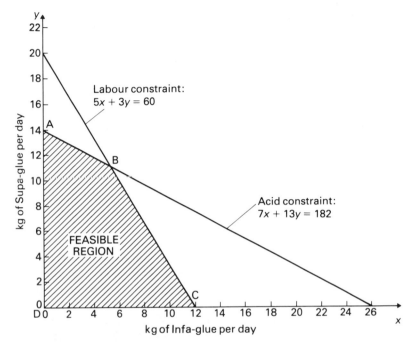

**Fig. 2.3**   The feasible region in the Glue Factory Example

way in which the factory can be programmed. It has the advantage that it turns the information given in the problem into pictorial form with the lines being thresholds of operational feasibility. Any combination of $x$ kg of Infa-glue and $y$ kg of Supa-glue must result in a point on the graph which is below both of the lines. Hence the area on the diagram satisfying these conditions is called the **feasible region** and the point representing the factory's operation is confined to it. We now have to determine which of all these viable points yields the most profit.

It is intuitively obvious that the maximum profit will be obtained by manufacturing as much glue as possible within the two resource constraints. In other words, the profit arising from an interior point of the feasible region can be increased by moving the point to an edge, and the profit at an edge can be increased further by moving to a vertex. This argument can be generalised to all problems of this type and means that we need only consider the vertices A, B, C and D of the feasible region as possible ways of operating the factory. We list these points with their respective profits in Table 2.1.

The $x$ and $y$ values of vertex B have been read from the graph to one decimal place. The more mathematical reader could have calculated them exactly by solving the

**Table 2.1**

| Vertex | $x$ (kg of Infa-glue) | $y$ (kg of Supa-glue) | Profit $(4x+7y)$ |
|--------|------------------------|------------------------|-------------------|
| A | 0 | 14 | 98 |
| B | 5.3 | 11.1 | 98.9 |
| C | 12 | 0 | 48 |
| D | 0 | 0 | 0 |

simultaneous equations $5x+3y=60$ and $7x+13y=182$. In a simple problem such an algebraic approach is useful. However, when there are several constraints, as in the next example, the graphical method is preferable as it shows which of the many different intersections of lines are in fact vertices.

By inspecting this table we see that the maximum profit is £98.90 and occurs when $x$ is 5.3 and $y$ is 11.1. **The conclusion of our analysis is that the factory should produce 5.3 kg of Infa-glue each day with 11.1 kg of Supa-glue in order to maximise the total profit.**

There are one or two features of the method we have used which are worthy of discussion. Firstly there were four constraints in our problem, $x$ being non-negative, $y$ being non-negative, the total acid requirement being less than or equal to 182 litres, and the total labour needed being less than or equal to 60 manhours. Each constraint gave rise to a straight line, or linear, boundary to the feasible region in Fig. 2.3. There could have been more constraints on the running of the factory and they would have resulted in more straight lines on the graph. We shall work through an example with more than four constraints shortly.

Another feature of the problem just considered was that we were trying to *maximise* something, more precisely the profit, $4x+7y$, which is called the **objective function.** Yet the procedure would have been exactly the same if we had wanted to *minimise* the objective function. Our answer in that case would have been $x$ equal to 0 and $y$ equal to 0 corresponding to vertex D in Table 2.1 because the profit at that vertex is smaller than at all the others. We shall use the word **optimise** for whichever of 'minimise' or 'maximise' is appropriate in a given situation and note that the method of examining the vertices of the feasible region applies to all optimisation problems. Incidentally, it is the nature of the objective function which determines the vertex where the solution occurs. Suppose that the profit resulting from making $x$ kg of Infa-glue and $y$ kg of Supa-glue is $(2x+y)$ instead of $(4x+7y)$ as in the example. The most profitable vertex then would be C and not B while if the profit is $(x+2y)$ then the optimal one is A. Finally, notice how easy it is to take an overview of the factory's operation using the graph (Fig. 2.3). Even if we are not able to optimise anything such diagrams are valuable as a way of seeing how near our operations bring us to violating a constraint. For example, if the glue factory produces 8 kg of Infa-glue per day and 4 kg of Supa-glue then because the point representing this is nearer to the labour constraint line than the acid constraint line we conclude that the operation is more sensitive to changes in the labour supply than in the acid supply. Put another way, if the labour supply were cut by 9 manhours then the labour constraint line would move and reduce the size of the feasible region to exclude this point $x$ equals 8 and $y$ equals 4. However the acid supply could be cut by more than 70 litres before that point would be affected. Furthermore, as the objective function is not brought into the analysis until the end, we can cope with changes in its form without redrawing the graph. The constraints on an operation are usually of a permanent nature reflecting availability of labour, materials, machinery and space. The diagram of the feasible region is therefore fairly constant in time. On the other hand the profitability of the different operating modes will vary depending on costs, product markets etc. and so the profit function will change. This will affect only the analysis of the vertices and not the diagram itself.

## Integer Programming

The last example was intended as an introduction to graphical linear programming. Amongst the assumptions made for the sake of simplicity was that the factory can produce fractions of a kilogram of glue. In many operations it is possible only to implement solutions which are whole numbers, like the number of aircraft an airline can fly, as in the next example.

### The Airline Example

An airline has 26 aircraft with 20 passenger seats and 13 aircraft with 30 passenger seats. Each 20-seater aircraft needs a pilot and 2 cabin crew members while a 30-seater aeroplane needs a pilot and 5 cabin crew members. The airline wants to carry at least 420 passengers on a certain route and has 60 cabin crew available. What is the minimum number of pilots it has to employ?

*Solution* As in the last example, it is important to identify the nature of the decision to be taken and give letters to the appropriate unknowns. In this case the airline must decide how many of each type of aircraft to fly so let us suppose it uses $x$ 20-seater ones and $y$ 30-seater ones. The various constraints on the values of $x$ and $y$ implied by the information given in the problem are shown in Table 2.2.

**Table 2.2**

| Constraint | Meaning |
|---|---|
| $x \geqslant 0$ <br> $y \geqslant 0$ <br> where the symbol '$\geqslant$' stands for 'greater than or equal to' | Common sense. The airline cannot fly negative numbers of aircraft. |
| $20x + 30y \geqslant 420$ | The total number of passengers carried by $x$ 20-seater aircraft, $20x$, and $y$ 30-seater aircraft, $30y$ must be greater than or equal to 420. |
| $2x + 5y \leqslant 60$ | The total number of cabin crew needed by $x$ planes with 2 members each and $y$ planes with 5 each must be less than or equal to 60. |
| $x \leqslant 26$ | The number of 20-seater aircraft cannot be greater than 26 as there are only that number available. |
| $y \leqslant 13$ | The number of 30-seater aircraft cannot exceed 13 as there are no more available. |

Adopting the same procedure as in the Glue Factory Example, we consider pairs of values of $x$ and $y$ as coordinates of points on a graph. Each constraint then has a 'threshold', which is a straight line, marking the boundary between points which are possible and points which are impossible as far as that particular constraint is concerned. The first two constraints in the above table, that $x$ and $y$ are not negative, are dealt with by using axes which begin at zero. We therefore never consider points on the graph with negative coordinates. The third constraint, that the total number of passengers carried should be at least 420, is about to be violated when the value of $20x + 30y$ is exactly equal to 420. Any decrease in $x$ or $y$ would then result in the constraint being broken. We therefore plot the line $20x + 30y = 420$ as the threshold between points which satisfy the restriction and points which do not (Fig. 2.4).

Notice that because we want $20x + 30y$ to be *greater than or equal to* 420 the set of possible points is *above* the line representing the threshold as these are points with $x$ and $y$ values bigger than those on the borderline. This diagram should be compared with Fig. 2.2 where the inequality sign in the constraint was the reverse way round and the set of feasible points was below the threshold. Incidentally, an easy method of identifying which side of the straight line is possible and which side is not is to consider the point where $x$ and $y$ both equal 0. This is the point where the axes cross each other on the graph and is called the **origin.** In the Glue Factory Example the origin is clearly a feasible point. Making 0 kg of Infa-glue and 0 kg of Supa-glue requires no acid or labour and so does

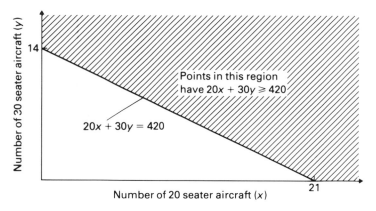

**Fig. 2.4**    The passenger constraint in the Airline Example

not exceed any limits on their availability. On the other hand, inactivity, with no aeroplanes being flown, is not possible in the present example because of the passenger constraint. We therefore conclude that the origin is not feasible and points on the other side of the line to the origin are feasible. We thus obtain Fig. 2.4 by this argument.

The cabin crew constraint $2x + 5y \leqslant 60$ is similar to those in the Glue Factory Example while the last two constraints $x \leqslant 26$ and $y \leqslant 13$ mean that we cannot allow points to the right of the line of points with $x$ equal to 26 or above the line of points with $y$ equal to 13. The lines representing these restrictions are all drawn on the graph, resulting in Fig. 2.5.

As argued earlier, the feasible region is the area above the passenger constraint, below the cabin crew constraint, and to the left and below the aircraft numbers constraints. Notice that the constraints $x \geqslant 0$ and $y \leqslant 13$ are **redundant** in the sense that they do not affect the shape of the feasible region at all. In fact the other constraints have proved to be more stringent restrictions on the airline's operations than these two are and so define a feasible region which automatically satisfies them as well.

Having identified the feasible region, we proceed as we did in the Glue Factory Example and examine the value of the objective function at each vertex of that region. The airline wants to minimise the number of pilots it employs and every aircraft needs a pilot. Hence

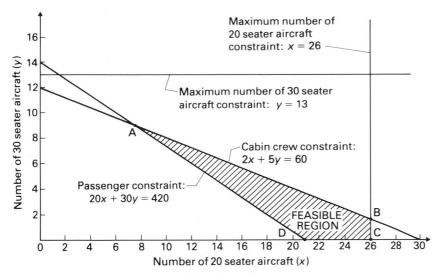

**Fig. 2.5** The feasible region in the Airline Example

if it flies $x$ 20-seater aeroplanes and $y$ 30-seater ones it needs $x+y$ pilots and this is the objective function. We tabulate its value at each vertex of the feasible region.

**Table 2.3**

| Vertex of feasible region | Number of 20-seater aircraft $(x)$ | Number of 30-seater aircraft $(y)$ | Objective function: number of pilots $x+y$ |
|---|---|---|---|
| A | 7.5 | 9.0 | 16.5 |
| B | 26.0 | 1.6 | 27.6 |
| C | 26.0 | 0.0 | 26.0 |
| D | 21.0 | 0.0 | 21.0 |

We see from this table that the minimum number of pilots needed is 16.5 and the airline should fly 7.5 20-seater aircraft and 9 30-seater ones! Clearly such a solution is impossible to implement in practice as, unlike in the Glue Factory Example, realistic values of $x$ and $y$ must be whole numbers. In fact the feasible region of the graph in the present example is not an area of points but a lattice of points with whole number coordinates (Fig. 2.6).

The general theorem that optimal values of the objective function occur at vertices of the feasible region still holds, so we list in Table 2.4 the vertices of this set which are ringed on Fig. 2.6.

**Table 2.4**

| Number of 20-seater aircraft $(x)$ | Number of 30-seater aircraft $(y)$ | Objective function: number of pilots $x+y$ |
|---|---|---|
| 9 | 8 | 17 |
| 10 | 8 | 18 |
| 25 | 2 | 27 |
| 26 | 1 | 27 |
| 26 | 0 | 26 |
| 21 | 0 | 21 |

Inspecting this list we see that **the minimum number of pilots needed is 17 and the airline should fly 9 20-seater aircraft and 8 30-seater planes.** Note that the requirement that $x$ and $y$ be whole numbers does not merely involve rounding off the original answers from Table 2.3 to the nearest suitable values. The set of feasible points with whole number coordinates often behaves differently from the original feasible region and should be analysed fully in any problem as we did by using the graph (Fig. 2.6) and the Table 2.4.

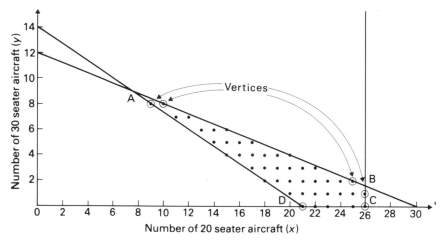

**Fig. 2.6**  Feasible ways of scheduling aircraft in the Airline Example

## The Simplex Method

The worked examples above have just two quantities, $x$ and $y$, which can be varied in order to optimise the objective function. In many operations there are more than two variables which the manager can control, for instance, the airline of the last problem might have 4 types of aircraft instead of 2 and then it could fly $u$ of one type, $v$ of another type, $w$ of the third type and $x$ of the last type. As each variable is represented by a separate axis on the graph, such situations give feasible regions in multidimensional spaces. We cannot construct diagrams in more than 3 dimensions and so graphical methods of solution are impossible. However there is an algebraic technique called the **Simplex** method which identifies, after a sequence of calculations, the vertex of the feasible region which optimises the objective function.

The non-mathematical reader who does not have a specific need to solve problems with more than 2 variables may wish to skip over the next example as all the important concepts of linear programming have now been covered in this chapter. The sole purpose of the example is to illustrate the Simplex method which is itself merely an algebraic procedure, or **algorithm,** for systematically examining the vertices of a feasible region in a multidimensional space. There are computer packages available to implement the algorithm; however, small problems like the following are readily solved manually.

### The Market Garden Example
A market gardener grows 4 kinds of crops, carrots, cabbages, onions and potatoes.

The cost and profit of each type are:

| Crop | Cost of fertiliser in kg per acre | Cost of pesticide in kg per acre | Profit in pounds per acre |
|---|---|---|---|
| Carrots | 4 | 2 | 50 |
| Cabbages | 2 | 9 | 40 |
| Onions | 5 | 2 | 10 |
| Potatoes | 0 | 3 | 20 |

The gardener has 400 kg of fertiliser available and 500 kg of pesticide. We shall find the number of acres of each crop he should plant in order to maximise his profit.

*Solution* If he allocates $w$ acres to carrots, $x$ to cabbages, $y$ to onions and $z$ to potatoes then the problem can be expressed algebraically:

Fertiliser constraint: $4w + 2x + 5y \leqslant 400$

Pesticide constraint: $2w + 9x + 2y + 3z \leqslant 500$

Objective function to be maximised: $50w + 40x + 10y + 20z$ (2.3)

Although the derivation and appearance of this algebraic system is similar to those for the Glue Factory and Airline Examples, it is impossible to represent these constraints graphically as we would need 4 axes, one each for $w$, $x$, $y$ and $z$. However, the maximum value of the objective function, $5w + 4x + y + 2z$, will still occur at a vertex of the feasible region which is now in 4-dimensional space.

In order to calculate the value of the objective function at these vertices, we convert the system into a standard form:

$$4w + 2x + 5y + s = 400$$
$$2w + 9x + 2y + 3z + t = 500$$
$$50w + 40x + 10y + 20z + C = 0 \qquad (2.4)$$

The variables $s$ and $t$ are called **slack** variables as they represent the amount by which the left hand side of a constraint inequality falls short of the upper limit on the right hand side. The variable $C$ in the last equation is to be made as large and negative as possible consistent with the constraint equations and all the variables being non-negative. It is customary to construct a table, or **tableau,** of these equations as in Table 2.5.

**Table 2.5**

| Line number | Basis | Value | Coefficient of | | | | | |
|---|---|---|---|---|---|---|---|---|
| | | | $w$ | $x$ | $y$ | $z$ | $s$ | $t$ |
| 1 | $s$ | 400 | 4 | 2 | 5 | 0 | 1 | 0 |
| 2 | $t$ | 500 | 2 | 9 | 2 | 3 | 0 | 1 |
| 3 | — | 0 | 50 | 40 | 10 | 20 | 0 | 0 |

Each line of the table corresponds to a constraint and the last line is the objective function. The table shows the state of affairs at a vertex of the feasible region and the initial tableau relates to the origin of coordinates with, in our case, $w$, $x$, $y$ and $z$ all equal to 0. The column headed 'Basis' contains the variables which are non-zero at the vertex under consideration and their values are in the adjacent column. The objective function, which is the last line, has the value 0 at the origin and is shown in that way.

Having set up the initial tableau we perform steps 1 to 6 below to obtain the tableau for a vertex where the value of the objective function is greatest.

*Step 1    Choose the variable with the largest positive coefficient in the last line of the tableau.* Increasing this variable from 0 will have more effect on the objective function than changing any other variable and we want to bring it into the basis. In our example this variable is *w*.

*Step 2    Choose the basis variable whose value divided by the coefficient of the new basis variable is the smallest while still being positive.* Of all the basis variables, this one is reduced to zero first when the new basis variable is increased gradually from 0. We shall take this variable out of the basis, or in other words put it equal to zero, and replace it with the variable from Step 1, 'arriving' at a new vertex of the feasible region. In our example, the ratios are 400/4 and 500/2 for lines 1 and 2. We therefore choose line 1 as 100 is less than 250. If the ratios happen to be equal then it does not matter which line is chosen.

*Step 3    Create a corresponding line in a new tableau by dividing the line chosen in Step 2 by the coefficient of the new basis variable. Insert the name of that variable in the column headed 'basis'.* The number in the column headed 'value' is now the value of the new basis variable we have substituted. In our example the top of the new tableau is this:

| Line number | Basis | Value | *w* | *x* | Coefficient of *y* | *z* | *s* | *t* |
|---|---|---|---|---|---|---|---|---|
| 4 | *w* | 100 | 1 | 0.5 | 1.25 | 0 | 0.25 | 0 |

*Step 4    Add or subtract multiples of the new line to each of the other lines to give zeros in the new basis variable column.* This reduces the tableau to standard form ready to begin again with Step 1 and proceed to the next feasible region vertex, if this is necessary. In our example we obtain the second tableau:

| Line number | Basis | Value | *w* | *x* | Coefficient of *y* | *z* | *s* | *t* |
|---|---|---|---|---|---|---|---|---|
| 4 | *w* | 100 | 1 | 0.5 | 1.25 | 0 | 0.25 | 0 |
| 5 | *t* | 300 | 0 | 8.0 | −0.5 | 3.0 | −0.5 | 1 |
| 6 | – | −5000 | 0 | 15 | −52.5 | 20 | −12.5 | 0 |

where line 5 is line 2 minus twice line 4 as this combination produces a zero in the *w* column. Similarly line 6 is line 3 minus 50 times line 4 as this gives a zero in the *w* column.

*Step 5    If any of the coefficients in the last line are positive, go back to Step 1. Otherwise go on to Step 6.* These coefficients indicate the effects of increasing non-basis variables from zero. If any of them is positive then the value of the objective function can be increased by increasing that particular variable, if not then the maximum has been reached. In our example we have some positive coefficients and working through Steps 1 to 4 gives:

| Line number | Basis | Value | *w* | *x* | Coefficient of *y* | *z* | *s* | *t* |
|---|---|---|---|---|---|---|---|---|
| 7 | *w* | 100 | 1 | 0.5 | 1.25 | 0 | 0.25 | 0 |
| 8 | *z* | 100 | 0 | 2.67 | −0.17 | 1 | −0.17 | 0.33 |
| 9 | – | −7000 | 0 | −38.4 | −49.1 | 0 | −9.1 | −6.6 |

where line 8 is written first in Step 3. Lines 7 and 9 follow from Step 4.

As none of the coefficients in the last line of this tableau is positive, the value of the objective function cannot be increased by changing the values of any of the variables. We therefore go on to Step 6.

*Step 6   Stop. The optimal solution is the set of values next to the basis variables. All other variables are equal to zero and the value of the objective function is the 'value' in the last line, ignoring the minus sign.* In our example, $w$ is equal to 100, $z$ is equal to 100 and the maximum profit is £7000. **Hence our advice to the market gardener is that he should plant 100 acres of carrots, no cabbages or onions, and 100 acres of potatoes.**

## Computer Program

The following program solves problems like the Glue Factory Example in which there are just two variables and two constraints of the 'less than or equal to' type. These constraints are supplied as data to the program as it is running, as is the objective function, and a redundant constraint is dealt with correctly, that is, ignored.

```
10  PRINT "LINEAR PROGRAMMING"
20  PRINT "------------------"
30  PRINT "IF FIRST CONSTRAINT IS AX + BY<=C, ENTER A,B,C";
40  INPUT A,B,C
50  PRINT "IF SECOND CONSTRAINT IS DX + EY <=F, ENTER D,E,F";
60  INPUT D,E,F
70  Y1=C/B
80  Z=F/E
90  IF Y1<Z THEN 110
100 Y1 = Z
110 X3=C/A
120 Z=F/D
130 IF X3<Z THEN 150
140 X3 = Z
150 V=4
160 R=A*E - B*D
170 IF R = 0 THEN 230
180 X4 = (C*E - B*F)/R
190 Y4 = (A*F - C*D)/R
200 IF X4 > 0 THEN 220
210 V=3
220 IF Y4 > 0 THEN 240
230 V = 3
240 PRINT "IF OBJECTIVE FUNCTION IS GX + HY, ENTER G,H";
250 INPUT G,H
260 PRINT
270 PRINT "X","Y","OBJECTIVE FUNCTION"
280 Z=H*Y1
290 PRINT "0",Y1,Z
300 PRINT "0","0","0"
310 Z=G*X3
320 PRINT X3,"0",Z
330 IF V = 3 THEN 360
340 Z=G*X4 + H*Y4
350 PRINT X4,Y4,Z
360 END
```

**Specimen Run**

```
LINEAR PROGRAMMING
-------------------
IF FIRST CONSTRAINT IS AX + BY<=C, ENTER A,B,C ?7,13,182
IF SECOND CONSTRAINT IS DX + EY <=F, ENTER D,E,F ?5,3,60
IF OBJECTIVE FUNCTION IS GX + HY, ENTER G,H ?4,7

X                 Y                  OBJECTIVE FUNCTION
0                   14                   98
0                    0                    0
 12                  0                   48
  5.31818           11.1364             99.2273
```

**Program Notes**

**1**   Lines 30 to 60 read the two constraints from the user.

**2**   Lines 70 to 100 calculate the $y$ coordinates of the points where the two constraint lines cross the $y$ axis. The point with the smaller $y$ coordinate is identified as a vertex of the feasible region and the variable Y1 is put equal to that coordinate.

**3**   Lines 110 to 140 calculate the $x$ coordinates of the points where the two constraint lines cross the $x$ axis. The variable X3 is put equal to the smaller of these two numbers as it is the $x$ coordinate of another vertex of the feasible region. So far the program has calculated the values shown in Fig. 2.7.

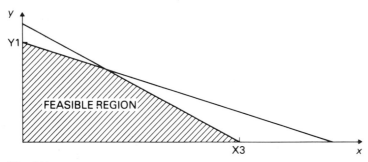

**Fig. 2.7**

**4**   Line 150 sets a variable V, which is the number of vertices of the feasible region, equal to 4, as it is in Fig. 2.7. It will be modified to 3 later on in the program if one of the constraints is redundant, as in that case the feasible region is a triangle.

**5**   Lines 160 to 190 calculate the coordinates of the point of intersection of the two constraint lines. Line 170 tests whether these lines are parallel and if they are it causes the program to jump to line 230 where the number of vertices, V, is modified to equal 3. Lines 200 and 220 of the program test the coordinates of the point of intersection. If either of them is negative then, again, the number of vertices of the feasible region is put equal to 3 and the program continues.

**6**   Finally, lines 240 to 350 read the details of the objective function from the user. Its value at each vertex of the feasible region is calculated and printed out together with the coordinates of that vertex. The intersection of the two constraint lines is included as a vertex if V equals 4 but excluded if it equals 3. The user then decides by inspection which vertex optimises the objective function.

## Summary

**1**   An operation has two variables, $x$ and $y$, associated with it whose values can be controlled. It is required to set them so as to optimise, that is maximise or minimise depending on the nature of the problem, the value of a given linear combination of $x$ and $y$ called the objective function. Often this is the profit arising from operating at production levels $x$ and $y$. There are also some constraints on the combinations of values of $x$ and $y$ which are possible due to the availability of manpower, raw materials, etc.

**2**   Each combination of an $x$ and a $y$ value is represented by a point on a graph with the coordinates $x$ and $y$. The threshold of each constraint is plotted as a straight line on the graph and is the boundary between those points which satisfy the constraint and those which do not. To determine which side of the line corresponds to points satisfying the constraint we test with a trial point, usually the origin of coordinates. If the trial point obeys the constraint then we conclude that *all* points on the same side of the line will also satisfy it. Alternatively, if it does not satisfy the constraint, then all points on the *other* side of the line will do so.

**3**   The feasible region is identified as the set of points which satisfy all the constraints. If by the nature of the problem $x$ and $y$ must be whole numbers then the feasible region is a lattice of points with integer coordinates, as in the Airline Example.

**4**   The value of the objective function is calculated at each vertex of the feasible region. The coordinates of the vertex where this function is optimal, that is either a maximum or a minimum depending on the problem concerned, are the solution to how the operation should be programmed.

**5**   Problems with more than 2 controllable variables can be solved by the Simplex Method. Slack variables are introduced into the constraint inequalities to turn them into equations and an initial tableau is drawn up. This displays a basis, which is a sub-set of the variables and specifies a vertex of the feasible region; all other variables are equal to zero. An algorithm is used to determine which non-basic variable would increase the value of the objective function the most, and to substitute it for an existing basic variable which is then put equal to zero. A new tableau results and the procedure is repeated until no further increase in the value of the objective function is possible. The optimal solution can be read from the final tableau together with the maximum value of the objective function.

## Further Reading

Linear programming is probably the most widely used technique in operational research. It therefore appears in almost all of the books listed in the 'General Operational Research' section of the Bibliography. References (1), (4), (12), (17) and (18) contain detailed mathematical treatments and (12) gives an account of post-optimal sensitivity. This is an analysis of the solution to a linear programming problem for its sensitivity to changes in the nature of the constraints. These books also cover the concept of duality which exploits a special relationship that can exist between two problems.

## Exercises

**1**   There are two types of water pipe which are equally suitable for a certain job. Their costs in labour and raw materials are:

| Type | Labour (manhours per metre) | Cost (£ per metre) |
|------|------------------------------|---------------------|
| A    | 2                            | 6                   |
| B    | 3                            | 5                   |

There are 66 manhours available per week and a budget for raw materials of £120. How many metres of each type should be laid each week in order to maximise the total length of piping used?

**2**   His hotel was burned down in a fire and the manager decided to sleep his guests in 4-person and 8-person tents. He needed to cope with at least 64 people but he had enough space for at most 13 tents. If each 4-person tent costs £15 per night and each 8-person tent costs £45 per night, how many of each type of tent minimises the overall nightly cost?

**3**   A popular music group is considering buying some amplifiers. There are two models available and their details are as follows:

| Model | Cost (£) | Space Needed on Stage (m²) | Power (watts) |
|-------|----------|-----------------------------|----------------|
| Little Big Horn | 50 | 0.7 | 55 |
| Big Big Horn | 120 | 0.8 | 90 |

The group can buy any number of each type but they have only £600 to spend and the total space available on stage is 5.6 square metres. (i) Determine the number of each type they should buy in order to maximise the total output power. (ii) Determine the number of each type they should buy in order to minimise the storage space needed but give a total power output of at least 200 watts.

**4**   A company manufactures three kinds of electrical appliances which require four different processes in their construction. The manpower requirements are:

| Product | Manhours spent on: | | | |
|---------|-----------|---------|------------|-----------|
|         | Metalwork | Fitting | Electrical | Finishing |
| Refrigerator    | 0.2 | 0.5 | 0.3 | 0.25 |
| Washing machine | 0.4 | 0.6 | 0.6 | 0.1  |
| Freezer         | 0.2 | 0.5 | 0.5 | 0.1  |

In any one day there are 56 manhours available in the metalwork shop, 120 manhours in the fitting section, 130 manhours in the electrical shop and 26 manhours in the finishing section. The profit is £18 on each refrigerator, £20 on each washing machine and £10 on each freezer. Use the Simplex Method to determine how many of each type of appliance the company should produce in order to maximise its profit.

# 3 Transportation

In this chapter and the next we consider operations whose costs are affected by the choice of which routes to use on a map or plan. We might want to reduce the cost of transporting goods between towns, minimise the total distance a salesman travels when visiting several places, or find the shortest length of electrical cable needed to wire together the rooms of a house. The reader who is not specifically concerned with the transportation problem may wish only to study other types of problems and proceed to the next chapter. In fact the work of that chapter does not assume a knowledge of any of the material treated here.

The shipment of cargoes from various supply points to different destinations forms a part of many companies' operations. As transportation costs can be considerable it is sensible to schedule deliveries in a way which minimises the overall expenditure. In some problems the cost is not measured directly in monetary terms and we optimise the total distance travelled or the overall time taken. We assume that each route can carry as many loads as we like and find the number each supply point should send to each destination in order to satisfy demand. This schedule may not be the only one incurring minimum cost but the method guarantees that there are no cheaper ones.

The first worked example concerns a commodity, milk, which is available for distribution at 3 farms, each having a different production capacity. Together the farms can meet the total requirements of 4 depots with each route between a farm and a depot

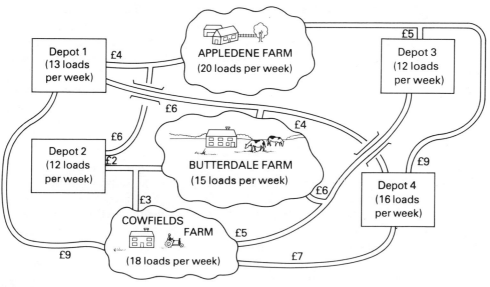

**Fig 3.1**

having a different cost per lorry load of milk. The second worked example is more complicated with supply exceeding demand, some routes which cannot be used, and has a solution which a mathematician would call 'degenerate'.

**The Dairy Farms Example**

A group of 3 farms owns 4 depots which store the milk they produce. The milk is transported by road and the cost per lorry load is given in the map (Fig. 3.1).

As can be seen on the map, the farms have various weekly production capacities and the depots have various requirements. We shall find an allocation of milk from the farms to the depots which minimises the total weekly transportation cost.

*Solution*    We begin by drawing Table 3.1, or **tableau** as it is called, which incorporates all the information in the problem:

**Table 3.1**

|  | Depot 1 | Depot 2 | Depot 3 | Depot 4 | Total farm output |
|---|---|---|---|---|---|
| Appledene Farm | 4 | 6 | 5 | 9 | 20 |
| Butterdale Farm | 6 | 2 | 6 | 4 | 15 |
| Cowfields Farm | 9 | 3 | 5 | 7 | 18 |
| Total depot requirement | 13 | 12 | 12 | 16 | 53 |

In this example, unlike the next one we consider, the total supply equals the total demand and this figure, 53, is found in the bottom right hand corner of the tableau. We shall see how to deal with problems where this is not the case later. Notice that each route between a farm and a depot is represented by a **cell,** or box, in the corresponding line and column of the tableau. Each cell contains the unit cost of the route and as the method of solution proceeds we shall include the numbers of lorry loads allocated along the route.

We begin the **algorithm,** or procedure, which solves the problem by finding a **feasible solution.** This is an initial allocation of lorries which we shall then modify, if necessary, to give a lower overall cost. By repeating this procedure until no further improvement is possible, we shall find a schedule which incurs the lowest transportation cost.

*Step 1    Obtain a feasible solution by the intuitively obvious strategy of using the lowest cost cells in the tableau first.* Looking at Table 3.1 we see that the route from Butterdale Farm to Depot 2 is the cheapest and we therefore allocate the maximum possible number of loads along this route. As Butterdale Farm produces 15 loads but Depot 2 can deal with only 12, we schedule 12 loads along that route. The figure 12 is written in the top left hand corner of the cell representing that particular route in the tableau.

We now look in Table 3.1 for the route with the next lowest unit cost. It is the one from Cowfields Farm to Depot 2, but Depot 2 has already been allocated to capacity so we cannot send any more loads along that route. The next cheapest ones are both £4 and go from Appledene Farm to Depot 1 and Butterdale Farm to Depot 4. We again consign the maximum amount of milk possible and write 13 in the cell for the route from Appledene to Depot 1 and 3 from Butterdale to Depot 4. This latter allocation is the most we can make as although 16 loads are needed by Depot 4, 12 of the 15 available from Butterdale Farm have already been used up. We can therefore send only the remaining 3 loads along that route.

By continuing this process of using the next lowest cost cell each time, we gradually obtain a feasible allocation of milk between farms and depots. If two or more cells have the same lowest cost at some stage of the exercise, it does not matter which one we use first and often, as above, we are able to use them both. After the feasible solution has been entered onto the tableau in the present example it looks like Table 3.2.

**Table 3.2**

|  | Depot 1 | Depot 2 | Depot 3 | Depot 4 | Total farm output |
|---|---|---|---|---|---|
| Appledene Farm | 13    4 |    6 | 7    5 |    9 | 20 |
| Butterdale Farm |    6 | 12    2 |    6 | 3    4 | 15 |
| Cowfields Farm |    9 |    3 | 5    5 | 13    7 | 18 |
| Total depot requirement | 13 | 12 | 12 | 16 | 53 |

We now try to alter this allocation in a way which lowers its cost. If such a change is not possible then the above tableau gives the optimum solution and the problem is solved. Now the cost of the present schedule could be calculated by multiplying the number of loads on each route by the cost of that route and adding the results together. However, to assess the effect of a change we need to compare the cost of the routes we are actually using with those of the routes we could be using. For example, in Table 3.2 we are not using the route from Butterdale Farm to Depot 3 and yet it costs less than the routes we actually use elsewhere.

The method of comparing individual route costs works in two stages. Firstly we calculate **shadow costs** for each supply point and destination which indicate the cost of a load leaving or arriving. The cost of a route in the present scheme is then considered as being the sum of two shadow costs as shown in Fig. 3.2.

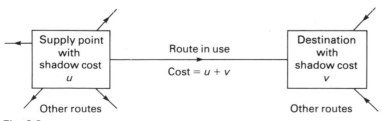

**Fig. 3.2**

The second stage compares the unit cost of an as yet unused route with the appropriate *u* and *v* total for its start supply point and its end destination (Fig. 3.3).

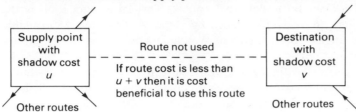

**Fig. 3.3**

To begin the determination of the shadow costs we can arbitrarily take one of them to be zero and measure all the others relative to it. After all, we only want to compare routes we could be using with those actually in use and so relative costings are adequate. Hence the second step of the transportation algorithm, or the first stage of the costing process, is:

*Step 2   Calculate the u and v values for supply points and destinations for those routes which are in use. Begin by giving the first supply point the u value zero.*

In our example we take the first supply point, Appledene Farm, as the 'base line' and assign it the *u* value zero. This is written in the 'total' column at the end of the top line of the tableau. Looking along that top row, we see that the route from Appledene Farm to Depot 1 is in use. As the route cost is £4 and this must equal *u* + *v*, the *v* value for Depot 1 must be 4. This is written in the 'total' row of its column in the tableau. Similarly the *v* value of Depot 3 must be 5 because the route cost is £5 and the *u* value for Appledene is 0.

Of the routes in use not yet processed, the one from Cowfields Farm to Depot 3 has a known *v* value and unknown *u* value. Its cost is £5 and so the *u* value for Cowfields Farm must be 0 giving 0 + 5 = 5. Knowing the *u* value for Cowfields Farm enables us to see that the *v* value for Depot 4 must be 7 to result in 0 + 7 = 7 for that route. Continuing in this way we find that as *v* is 7 for Depot 4 then *u* must be −3 for Butterdale Farm.

**Table 3.3**

|  | Depot 1 | Depot 2 | Depot 3 | Depot 4 | Total farm output |
|---|---|---|---|---|---|
| Appledene Farm | 13 <br> 4 | 6 | 7 <br> 5 | 9 | 20 <br> $u=0$ |
| Butterdale Farm | 6 | 12 <br> 2 | 6 | 3 <br> 4 | 15 <br> $u=-3$ |
| Cowfields Farm | 9 | 3 | 5 <br> 5 | 13 <br> 7 | 18 <br> $u=0$ |
| Total depot requirement | 13 <br> $v=4$ | 12 <br> $v=5$ | 12 <br> $v=5$ | 16 <br> $v=7$ | 53 |

Note that there is nothing surprising in negative $u$ or $v$ values as they are costs relative to that of Appledene Farm. Such negative shadow costs simply mean that this supply point is cheaper at emitting cargoes than the 'base line' supply point. This last $u$ value then implies that Depot 2 has a $v$ value of 5 to make $-3+5=2$ which is the route cost between Butterdale and that depot. We now have the tableau given in Table 3.3.

Having calculated the shadow costs we can use them to compare the costs of those routes we are not using with the present transportation schedule.

*Step 3 Calculate the potential benefit of each route which is not in use by subtracting the u and v values of its row and column from its unit cost. The result is written in the centre of the cell representing that route.* We saw above that for a route being used, $u$ and $v$ will add up to the unit cost of the route. If, then, a route is *not* in use and has a unit cost *less* than $u+v$, it should be advantageous to transfer loads onto that route. In other words, the cost of the route we are not using is less than the cost we are achieving by not using it! If, conversely, the unit cost of an unused route is greater than or equal to $u+v$, then there is no advantage in altering the schedule in order to bring it into use.

The value of (unit cost $-u-v$) for a potential route is thus a measure of its benefit to us for lowering the total transportation cost.

In our example we insert the difference between unit cost and $u+v$ for unused routes and obtain Table 3.4.

**Table 3.4**

|  | Depot 1 | Depot 2 | Depot 3 | Depot 4 | Total farm output |
|---|---|---|---|---|---|
| Appledene Farm | 13 — 4 | +1 — 6 | 7 — 5 | +2 — 9 | 20 $u=0$ |
| Butterdale Farm | +5 — 6 | 12 — 2 | +4 — 6 | 3 — 4 | 15 $u=-3$ |
| Cowfields Farm | +5 — 9 | -2 — 3 | 5 — 5 | 13 — 7 | 18 $u=0$ |
| Total depot requirement | 13 $v=4$ | 12 $v=5$ | 12 $v=5$ | 16 $v=7$ | 53 |

Notice that some of the subtractions of $u$ and $v$ from the unit costs involve a 'double negative'. For example in the second row, first column (unit cost $-u-v$) is $(6-(-3)-4)$ which is $(6+3-4)$, i.e. $+5$.

The next step of the algorithm chooses which as yet unused route to bring into the schedule.

*Step 4 Choose the cell with the most negative (unit cost $-u-v$) value. If none of them is negative then the present allocation has the least possible cost and the algorithm stops.* This chooses the route which would be most beneficial in reducing the transportation cost if we could alter the schedule and use it. In our example, the cell representing the route from Cowfields Farm to Depot 2 has a (unit cost $-u-v$) value of $-2$ which is the most negative one in the tableau.

*Step 5   Write the letter 'p' in the top left hand corner of the chosen cell and find a group of cells which are used in the present allocation and can be modified by the amount p to keep all the row and column totals unchanged.*

We have decided which route we want to introduce into the altered schedule and we consign $p$ loads to it. However this disturbs the route's row and column totals and we must adjust some of the other allocations in its row and column. This in turn will disturb their row and column totals and the chaos we are causing seems endless! Our only hope is to create a closed circuit of adjusted cells which balance each other out completely as in Table 3.5.

**Table 3.5**

|  | Depot 1 | Depot 2 | Depot 3 | Depot 4 | Total farm output |
|---|---|---|---|---|---|
| Appledene Farm | 13<br><br>4 | +1<br><br>6 | 7<br><br>5 | +2<br><br>9 | 20<br>$u=0$ |
| Butterdale Farm | +5<br><br>6 | $12-p$<br><br>2 | +4<br><br>6 | $3+p$<br><br>4 | 15<br>$u=-3$ |
| Cowfields Farm | +5<br><br>9 | $p$<br>$-2$<br>3 | 5<br><br>5 | $13-p$<br><br>7 | 18<br>$u=0$ |
| Total depot requirement | 13<br>$v=4$ | 12<br>$v=5$ | 12<br>$v=5$ | 16<br>$v=7$ | 53 |

These modifications can be made only to routes already in use as each change in the schedule should involve introducing just one route at a time.

**Table 3.6**

|  | Depot 1 | Depot 2 | Depot 3 | Depot 4 | Total farm output |
|---|---|---|---|---|---|
| Appledene Farm | 13<br><br>4 | <br><br>6 | 7<br><br>5 | <br><br>9 | 20 |
| Butterdale Farm | <br><br>6 | <br><br>2 | <br><br>6 | 15<br><br>4 | 15 |
| Cowfields Farm | <br><br>9 | 12<br><br>3 | 5<br><br>5 | 1<br><br>7 | 18 |
| Total depot requirement | 13 | 12 | 12 | 16 | 53 |

*Step 6    Set the value of p to be as large as possible consistent with non-negative amounts of goods. Redraw the resulting tableau and go to Step 2 in an attempt to lower its cost still further.* In our example, $p$ cannot be larger than 12 or the allocation from Butterdale Farm to Depot 2 will be negative. There will always be an upper limit like this on the value of $p$ which, if exceeded, will cause one or other of the consignments to become negative. Setting $p$ equal to 12 and redrawing the tableau without all the $u$ and $v$ values and (unit cost $-u-v$) values we obtain Table 3.6.

We now have a new schedule which is cheaper than the previous one. It may not, however, be the cheapest possible and so we go back to Step 2 of the algorithm and try to reduce its cost. Here is the tableau which results from repeating Steps 2 to 4.

**Table 3.7**

|  | Depot 1 | Depot 2 | Depot 3 | Depot 4 | Total farm output |
|---|---|---|---|---|---|
| Appledene Farm | 13    4 | +3    6 | 7    5 | +2    9 | 20 $u=0$ |
| Butterdale Farm | +5    6 | +2    2 | +4    6 | 15    4 | 15 $u=-3$ |
| Cowfields Farm | +5    9 | 12    3 | 5    5 | 1    7 | 18 $u=0$ |
| Total depot requirement | 13 $v=4$ | 12 $v=3$ | 12 $v=5$ | 16 $v=7$ | 53 |

The reader should check this as an exercise.

As none of the (unit cost $-u-v$) values in this tableau is negative, no further reduction in the overall transportation cost is possible at Step 4. The solution to the Dairy Farm Example is therefore as represented in Table 3.7.

**Appledene Farm sends 13 lorry loads to Depot 1 and 7 lorry loads to Depot 3. Butterdale Farm sends 15 lorry loads to Depot 4 and Cowfields Farm sends 12 loads to Depot 2, 5 to Depot 3 and 1 to Depot 4. The total cost of these deliveries is the sum of all the products of unit cost by allocation and is £215.**

The above example was intended as a straightforward illustration of the transportation algorithm. As this algorithm is used in so many different industries, we shall work through another example which contains some complicating features. The total supply capacity exceeds the amounts demanded, some of the routes cannot be used, and there is a form of degeneracy present.

**The Freezer Example**

A freezer manufacturer has factories at Bath, London and Oxford each capable of producing 200 freezers per week while the one at Leeds makes only 50 each week. Its 3 main customers in Cardiff, Norwich and York each want 100 freezers in any one week and the freezers are transported by a road haulage company at the following costs per freezer:

| Cost in Pounds | To: Cardiff | Norwich | York |
|---|---|---|---|
| From: | | | |
| Bath | 15 | 33 | 40 |
| Leeds | 21 | Route not available | 4 |
| London | 36 | 28 | 51 |
| Oxford | Route not available | 32 | 30 |

As usual in transportation problems we want an allocation of freezers from factories to customers which minimises the overall cost.

*Solution*   The first complication we encounter in this example is that when we add up the number of freezers available at the factories we find it is greater than the total demanded by the customers. The total factory capacity is $(200 + 200 + 200 + 50)$, which is 650, while the total demand is $(100 + 100 + 100)$, which is 300. Hence we have a spare production capability of 350 freezers per week, a far more common state of affairs than in the last example where supply and demand were exactly the same.

We deal with any mismatch in the total supply and demand by inventing a 'dummy' supply point or destination which supplies or demands the excess and so absorbs all of it. Any allocation we make from a dummy supply point must somehow be 'bought in' from outside our network while any allocation to a dummy destination need not be transported at all. In the latter case, which applies to our example, quantities shipped to dummy locations are often not even manufactured and the corresponding route unit costs are therefore zero. In short, these dummies are devices to enable us to 'balance the books' and make our totals for rows and columns the same. When we obtain the final solution any shipments from or to dummies are interpreted in the context of the problem in hand.

The second complication in this example is that two of its routes cannot be used. Possibly the haulage company does not serve these routes or there is a geographical, or political, barrier preventing their use. We take this phenomenon into account by giving such routes a very high unit cost. It is then unlikely that they will appear in the optimal solution but if they do then they should be given an even higher cost and the problem re-worked. In this example we take those routes to cost £500 each per freezer which is much higher than any other route costs in the problem.

With these extensions to the given data, we obtain the initial tableau and feasible solution using Step 1 of the previous example (Table 3.8).

Notice that in finding the feasible solution we start with the routes to the dummy customer as these have the lowest unit cost. We schedule as many freezers as we can onto those routes and only when all 350, which is dummy's requirement, have been allocated do we use other cells.

We see from Table 3.8 that the feasible solution uses a 'prohibited' route, that from Oxford to Cardiff. Although its unit cost is far higher than any other, we are forced to allocate freezers into its cell as, at the end of compiling the feasible solution, Oxford is the only factory left with spare capacity and Cardiff is the only customer with spare requirements. We shall see how the transportation algorithm will automatically remove that allocation from the schedule in the process of reducing the overall transportation cost.

The third and final complication of this example compared with the last one arises

**Table 3.8**

|        | Cardiff | Norwich | York  | Dummy | Total |
|--------|---------|---------|-------|-------|-------|
| Bath   | 15      | 33      | 40    | 200 / 0 | 200 |
| Leeds  | 21      | 500     | 4     | 50 / 0 | 50  |
| London | 36      | 100 / 28 | 51   | 100 / 0 | 200 |
| Oxford | 100 / 500 | 32    | 100 / 30 | 0   | 200 |
| Total  | 100     | 100     | 100   | 350   | 650 |

when we try to implement Step 2 of the algorithm and calculate the shadow costs, or $u$ and $v$ values, for the factories and customers. We begin by putting the top line $u$ value equal to 0. As $u+v$ equals the unit cost for routes in use, this implies that the dummy customer's $v$ value is 0 as well. This in turn implies that the $u$ values of Leeds and London are 0 but no more $u$ and $v$ calculations are possible except for Norwich. We have reached this impasse because the Oxford factory supplies all the needs of the Cardiff and York customers and hence all their shadow costs relate only to each other. They form a closed sub-system within the network and have no connection with the other towns. This form of degeneracy in the tableau occurs whenever the number of routes in use, in our case 6, is less than the number of supply points plus the number of destinations minus 1, which is 7 for this problem.

We break the deadlock caused by the network splitting into two disconnected sub-systems by allocating a minute quantity, $\varepsilon$, of freezers into the lowest unit cost cell. In the

**Table 3.9**

|        | Cardiff | Norwich | York | Dummy | Total |
|--------|---------|---------|------|-------|-------|
| Bath   | −485 / 15 | +5 / 33 | +10 / 40 | 200 / 0 | 200 $u=0$ |
| Leeds  | −479 / 21 | +472 / 500 | −26 / 4 | 50 / 0 | 50 $u=0$ |
| London | −464 / 36 | 100 / 28 | +21 / 51 | 100 / 0 | 200 $u=0$ |
| Oxford | 100 / 500 | +4 / 32 | 100 / 30 | $\varepsilon$ / 0 | 200+$\varepsilon$ $u=0$ |
| Total  | 100 $v=500$ | 100 $v=28$ | 100 $v=30$ | 350+$\varepsilon$ $v=0$ | 650+$\varepsilon$ |

tableau, the appropriate row and column totals are also increased by $\varepsilon$, as is the grand total in the bottom right hand corner, and this brings the number of routes in use up from 6 to 7. In other problems it may be necessary to introduce $\varepsilon$ into more than one cell in order to increase sufficiently the number of routes in use or to introduce it in a subsequent tableau when the number of such routes has fallen below the critical value.

In our example after Step 3 we obtain Table 3.9.

Proceeding with Steps 4 and 5 of the algorithm we allocate $p$ freezers along the route from Bath to Cardiff and subtract $p$ from those between Bath and Dummy and Oxford and Cardiff. In order to complete the process of returning the row and column totals to their original values, we add $p$ to the $\varepsilon$ freezers which go from Oxford to Dummy. Here is the new tableau.

**Table 3.10**

| | Cardiff | Norwich | York | Dummy | Total |
|---|---|---|---|---|---|
| Bath | $p$<br>$-485$<br>15 | $+5$<br>33 | $+10$<br>40 | $200-p$<br>0 | 200<br>$u=0$ |
| Leeds | $-479$<br>21 | $+472$<br>500 | $-26$<br>4 | 50<br>0 | 50<br>$u=0$ |
| London | $-464$<br>36 | 100<br>28 | $+21$<br>51 | 100<br>0 | 200<br>$u=0$ |
| Oxford | $100-p$<br>500 | $+4$<br>32 | 100<br>30 | $\varepsilon+p$<br>0 | $200+\varepsilon$<br>$u=0$ |
| Total | 100<br>$v=500$ | 100<br>$v=28$ | 100<br>$v=30$ | $350+\varepsilon$<br>$v=0$ | $650+\varepsilon$ |

Executing Step 6 of the algorithm results in $p$ being set equal to 100 and the next tableau, with its shadow costs, is given in Table 3.11.

**Table 3.11**

| | Cardiff | Norwich | York | Dummy | Total |
|---|---|---|---|---|---|
| Bath | 100<br>15 | $+5$<br>33 | $+10$<br>40 | 100<br>0 | 200<br>$u=0$ |
| Leeds | $+6$<br>21 | $+472$<br>500 | $-26$<br>4 | 50<br>0 | 50<br>$u=0$ |
| London | $+21$<br>36 | 100<br>28 | $+21$<br>51 | 100<br>0 | 200<br>$u=0$ |
| Oxford | $+485$<br>500 | $+4$<br>32 | 100<br>30 | $100+\varepsilon$<br>0 | $200+\varepsilon$<br>$u=0$ |
| Total | 100<br>$v=15$ | 100<br>$v=28$ | 100<br>$v=30$ | $350+\varepsilon$<br>$v=0$ | $650+\varepsilon$ |

Step 4 of the transportation algorithm consists of making an allocation in the cell with the most negative (unit cost $-u-v$) value. This is the route from Leeds to York and in completing steps 5 and 6 we notice that we can put the value of $\varepsilon$ to zero now as it no longer affects the number of cells with allocations in them. The small quantity $\varepsilon$ was introduced to break the deadlock of having too few occupied cells to calculate the shadow costs but as the algorithm proceeds we may find it becomes unnecessary, as in this case. Table 3.12 is now obtained.

**Table 3.12**

| | Cardiff | Norwich | York | Dummy | Total |
|---|---|---|---|---|---|
| Bath | 100 <br> 15 | +5 <br> 33 | +10 <br> 40 | 100 <br> 0 | 200 <br> $u=0$ |
| Leeds | +32 <br> 21 | +498 <br> 500 | 50 <br> 4 | +26 <br> 0 | 50 <br> $u=-26$ |
| London | +21 <br> 36 | 100 <br> 28 | +21 <br> 51 | 100 <br> 0 | 200 <br> $u=0$ |
| Oxford | +485 <br> 500 | +4 <br> 32 | 50 <br> 30 | 150 <br> 0 | 200 <br> $u=0$ |
| Total | 100 <br> $v=15$ | 100 <br> $v=28$ | 100 <br> $v=30$ | 350 <br> $v=0$ | 650 |

As all the (unit cost $-u-v$) values are positive in this table, there are no cells which, if used, would reduce the overall cost. We have therefore found an optimal allocation of freezers from the factories to the customers:

**100 freezers from Bath to Cardiff, 50 freezers from Leeds to York, 100 freezers from London to Norwich, 50 freezers from Oxford to York.**

Notice that allocations from factories to the dummy destination are not transported. In fact the company does not need to manufacture such freezers at all in order to supply the 3 customers specified in the problem.

Sometimes an optimal tableau will have one or more of the (unit cost $-u-v$) values equal to zero. This means that the overall transportation cost would be unchanged if those cells were used and is an indication that there is more than one optimal allocation of deliveries.

## Computer Program

The transportation algorithm is well suited to computerisation as, like all algorithms, it is a step-by-step procedure. The main problem for the computer is finding a closed loop of allocations with which to 'balance the books' in Step 5. A human is far better at spotting patterns of cells within a tableau but there are computer packages which do this and also deal with all the complications described in the Freezer Example. In particular, if the small quantity $\varepsilon$ is required then it can be taken as a hundredth of the minimum allocation to date, or something similar, and the results rounded off at the end of the calculation.

The brave reader who has struggled through the last example will not be surprised to learn that it is impractical to include here a fully fledged transportation computer program. Instead we give the listing of one which solves the problem when there are just two supply points and two destinations. This is the smallest possible transportation problem and the method of solution used by the program is not the one described in the chapter but a simple algebraic procedure applicable only to this tiny tableau. The reader might like to use the program to solve his or her own made-up problems and then check the solution by applying the method of this chapter. The program is also useful to anyone who just happens to have a two supply point and two destination transportation problem!

```
10  PRINT "TRANSPORTATION PROGRAM"
20  PRINT "----------------------"
30  PRINT "ENTER UNIT COSTS, ROW TOTALS AND COLUMN TOTALS"
40  INPUT C1,C2,R1,C3,C4,R2,K1,K2
50  S = R1 + R2
60  T = K1 + K2
70  IF S = T THEN 100
80  PRINT "TOTALS UNBALANCED"
90  GOTO 30
100  X1 = C1 + C4
110  X2 = C2 + C3
120  IF X1 > X2 THEN 180
130  A1 = R1
140  IF K1 > R1 THEN 160
150  A1 = K1
160  A2 = R1 - A1
170  GOTO 220
180  A2 = R1
190  IF K2 > R1 THEN 210
200  A2 = K2
210  A1 = R1 - A2
220  A3 = K1 - A1
230  A4 = K2 - A2
240  PRINT "LEAST COST SOLUTION"
250  PRINT
260  PRINT A1,A2
270  PRINT A3,A4
280  C=A1*C1 + A2*C2 + A3*C3 + A4*C4
290  PRINT TOTAL COST IS";C
300  END
```

**Specimen Run**

```
RUN
TRANSPORTATION PROGRAM
----------------------
ENTER UNIT COSTS, ROW TOTALS AND COLUMN TOTALS
?1,4,70,2,8,60,30,100
LEAST COST SOLUTION

      0              70
      30             30
TOTAL COST IS 580
```

**Program Notes**

**1** Lines 1Ø to 4Ø read the unit costs, row totals, and column totals. In the specimen run these are:

| | Destination 1 | Destination 2 | Total output |
|---|---|---|---|
| Supply point 1 | 1 | 4 | 70 |
| Supply point 2 | 2 | 8 | 60 |
| Total requirement | 30 | 100 | 130 |

**2** Lines 5Ø to 9Ø check that the total supply equals the total demand. If they are different then the message 'TOTALS UNBALANCED' is printed and control passed back to line 3Ø.

**3** Lines 1ØØ to 23Ø exploit the fact that in such a small problem all the allocations can be expressed in terms of A1, the amount that Supply Point 1 sends to Destination 1. Lines 12Ø, 14Ø, and 19Ø determine whether the total cost will be greatest for A1 being as large as possible or as small as possible or A2, the allocation from Supply Point 1 to Destination 2, being as large as possible or as small as possible. This complicated algebraic procedure enables the allocations to be made.

**4** Lines 24Ø to 3ØØ print out the results and end the execution of the program.

## Summary

**1** The transportation algorithm has the following steps.

*Step 1*  Determine a feasible solution using the lowest unit cost cells.

*Step 2*  Calculate the shadow costs for each row and each column.

*Step 3*  Calculate the (unit cost $-u-v$) values for as yet unused routes.

*Step 4*  Choose the cell with the most negative value of (unit cost $-u-v$). If none is negative then the solution is optimal and the algorithm stops.

*Step 5*  Make an allocation of $p$ units into the chosen cell and find a closed loop of occupied cells to 'balance the books' and keep all row and column totals correct.

*Step 6*  Set $p$ to the largest value possible consistent with having non-negative allocations in all the cells and go back to Step 2.

**2** The algorithm deals with routes between supply points and destinations which cannot be used for some reason by giving such routes a very high unit cost. The method automatically excludes them from the optimal allocation.

**3** In general the total supply available will not exactly equal the total demand. We add dummy supply points or dummy destinations in order to account for the discrepancy and interpret allocations to such dummies as meaning that either supplies have to be brought from outside the system or that some supply points have spare capacity which is not transported anywhere.

**4** It is sometimes necessary to increase the number of occupied cells in a tableau to the required value which is (number of supply points + number of destinations − 1). This is achieved by allocating a small consignment, $\varepsilon$, of goods into the lowest unit cost unoccupied cells. These quantities are set to zero at the earliest opportunity in the subsequent analysis.

## Further Reading

A transportation problem can be thought of as the minimisation of an overall cost subject to the constraints that total deliveries and collections to and from destinations and supply points do not exceed given values. The problem can therefore be formulated as a special case of linear programming and many textbooks treat it as such, for example references (6) and (7). In view of the importance of transportation, the topic appears in almost all the books listed in the 'General Operational Research' section of the Bibliography.

## Exercises

**1** A construction company has 3 supply points and 4 sites with the following transportation costs per lorry load between them, measured in pounds:

| Site<br>Supply point | Arkville | Brobdingnag | Erehwon | Oz |
|---|---|---|---|---|
| Nutwood | 3 | 4 | 3 | 2 |
| Toytown | 2 | 3 | 4 | 3 |
| Utopia | 1 | 3 | 2 | 4 |

The supply points' production capacities are 15, 60 and 25 lorry loads per week respectively while the sites require 30, 40, 20 and 10 lorry loads. Find the transportation schedule between the depots and sites which minimises the overall cost and calculate that cost.

**2** A company has 4 supply points and 3 destinations with the unit costs of transportation between them being as follows:

| Destination<br>Supply point | X | Y | Z |
|---|---|---|---|
| A | 8 | 6 | 3 |
| B | 9 | 11 | 8 |
| C | 6 | 5 | 7 |
| D | 3 | 10 | 9 |

The production capacities are 200, 200, 200 and 300 for A, B, C and D respectively and the requirements for X, Y, and Z are 200, 350 and 250 units respectively. Find *two* optimal allocations of units from supply points to destinations.

**3**   A company has 3 supply points A, B, and C and 3 destinations X, Y and Z. The costs of transporting unit loads of raw materials between them are as follows:

| Destination<br>Supply point | X | Y | Z |
|---|---|---|---|
| A | 2 | 10 | 4 |
| B | 5 | 3 | 5 |
| C | 2 | 3 | 5 |

The delivery capacities of A, B and C are 150, 200 and 200 units respectively while the needs of X, Y and Z are 300, 100 and 100 respectively. Find an optimal allocation of units from the supply points to the destinations.

# 4 Route Scheduling

The last chapter dealt exclusively with the problem of transporting goods from supply points to destinations at minimum cost. The map of routes between such places, or **nodes,** is called a **network** and in this chapter we consider three types of problems in which a distance through a network is to be minimised. It is natural to think of these distances as lengths although it is often more realistic to measure them as journey or activity times. For instance a salesman is not so much concerned with the geographical distance between two towns as with the time it takes him to travel from one to the other. In the next chapter we shall deal with networks of a more general nature where the activities occurring between the nodes are of interest.

Each example in this chapter is treated using an **algorithm** or step-by-step procedure. The reader who has a specific problem to solve may prefer to follow the numbered steps without having to study the explanations given in the text.

The first example is concerned with finding a routing diagram for laying cable or a pipeline to connect together all the nodes of a network in the most economical way. The diagram obtained is called a **minimal spanning tree.** The second example deals with tracing the shortest path through a network from one node to another while the last example,

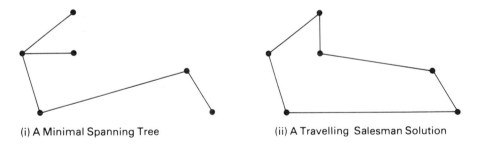

(i) A Minimal Spanning Tree          (ii) A Travelling Salesman Solution

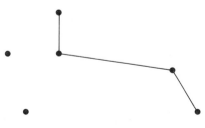

(iii) Shortest Path Solution

**Fig. 4.1**

appropriately called the Travelling Salesman Problem, requires a circular tour of all the nodes which minimises the total distance covered. The three types of problems can be illustrated for a simple network (Fig. 4.1).

Before we begin examining the formal approaches to these problems, it is worth mentioning a 'sledge-hammer' technique which, possibly with some computer help, can work for small networks. This is the simple method of direct enumeration. If a list of the possible routes can be drawn up together with their respective distances, then those with the shortest distance can be found by inspecting the list. Unfortunately the sheer number of possible routes on larger networks makes this method of solution impractical. For instance, the network shown in Fig. 4.1, with 6 nodes, has 120 possible travelling salesman routes; the corresponding number for a network with just 9 nodes is 40 320!

## Minimal Spanning Trees

### The Fairground Example

The owner of a fairground wants to lay electrical cable to supply power to all the sideshows on the ground. Figure 4.2 is a map showing the relevant distances. We find a wiring diagram which connects all the sideshows together using the least possible length of wire.

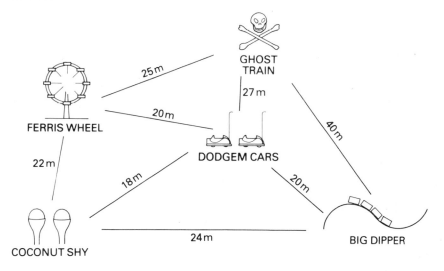

**Fig. 4.2**

*Solution*  There are two types of solution to minimum length wiring or pipeline problems. In the first type, cable or pipes can be laid anywhere and extra nodes can be created if they help in reducing the total length. For instance a junction box for telephone lines can be installed centrally between three houses with wires to them radiating from it. Such solutions are called **minimal Steiner trees** and can involve curved pathways as well as straight ones. There are no analytic methods of finding these trees but a computer can determine them by trial and error.

We assume here that the second type of solution is required in which cable can be laid only on the direct pathways between the nodes. The algorithm for finding it is quite straightforward.

*Step 1  Choose a node at random and join it to its nearest neighbouring node.* In our example we select the Ferris Wheel and join it to its closest neighbour, the Dodgem Cars.

*Step 2  Choose the unconnected node which is nearest to a connected node and join it to that node.* In our example, we join the Coconut Shy to the Dodgem Cars (Fig. 4.3).

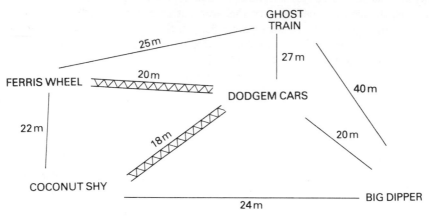

**Fig. 4.3**

*Step 3  If there are still any unconnected nodes, repeat Step 2. Otherwise stop.* In this example, repeating Step 2 for all the nodes remaining gives the solution shown in Fig. 4.4.

The reader might like to verify that the same solution is found when a node other than the Ferris Wheel is used to start the algorithm in Step 1.

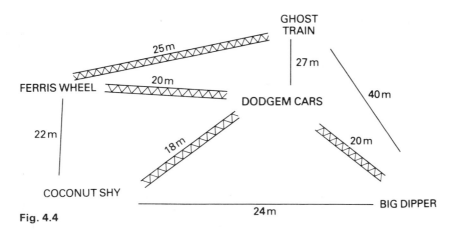

**Fig. 4.4**

## The Travelling Salesman Problem

The minimal spanning tree we have derived above cannot be travelled over without having to retrace a pathway. The tree suggests the tour Big Dipper, Dodgem Cars, Coconut Shy, Dodgem Cars again, Ferris Wheel, Ghost Train and back to Big Dipper as being one with minimum length. In fact its length is 141 metres whereas the circular tour

Big Dipper, Coconut Shy, Ferris Wheel, Ghost Train, Dodgem Cars and back to Big Dipper totals only 118 metres. This highlights the difference between a minimal spanning tree and a shortest circular tour, which is the solution to the Travelling Salesman Problem. The two types of solution are optimising different criteria, one the total length of connections and the other the total distance travelled in visiting each node just once.

Here is an example to illustrate the latter problem.

**The Tourist Example**

A tourist wants to visit London, Paris, Rome, Brussels and Bonn, spending as little time travelling as possible and staying at each city once only. The journey times are set out in Table 4.1.

**Table 4.1**

| Hours          To: | London | Paris | Rome | Brussels | Bonn |
| --- | --- | --- | --- | --- | --- |
| From: | | | | | |
| London | – | 1 | 4 | 2 | Impossible journey |
| Paris | 1 | – | 3 | 1 | 3 |
| Rome | 5 | 4 | – | 4 | 2 |
| Brussels | 2 | 1 | 5 | – | 1 |
| Bonn | 3 | 2 | 3 | 1 | – |

*Solution* As in many shortest path applications, distance is measured here in terms of a penalty or cost, which in this case is time. As a consequence of using a more meaningful measure of distance than the distance itself, we have an **asymmetric** table as although Paris, say, is as far from Rome as Rome is from Paris, the times of the two journeys are different.

The entries in the distance table are assumed to be the *shortest* distances between the nodes. In this example it may be that the quickest way of travelling from London to Rome is to change aircraft at Paris. The entry of 4 hours in the table for that route would then be the total journey time including the interchange. We would not count the transfer from one aircraft to another as a visit to Paris and we do not have to know the details of the individual journeys in order to solve the problem.

We could find the shortest tour in this example by direct enumeration of all possible tours. There are just 24 of these and we could compile a list of them together with their total times and choose the quickest. However the purpose of this example is to illustrate the use of an algorithm which can solve much larger problems. As was pointed out at the start of this chapter, a network with 9 nodes has 40 320 possible tours.

The algorithm which follows is an example of a **branch and bound** algorithm. It systematically examines each link in the network, for example 'Paris to Rome', and compares the lowest cost of tours which include that link with the lowest cost of tours which do not. The 'branch' with the lowest 'bound' is then followed and the set of all possible tours subdivided further until a single tour remains with the lowest cost.

Before we begin the algorithm we must complete the cost matrix given in the question by inserting costs for journeys from each city to itself and from London to Bonn. In this particular problem we do not want such journeys to be included in tours and so we take their cost to be infinite and write the symbol ∞ in the cost table. This ensures that they will not be part of a minimum cost tour. The reader should be aware of the flexibility that tampering with the costs can give us in setting up all sorts of network problems. For instance in the transportation problem we assigned a zero cost to dummy destinations in the Freezer Example when we intended no transportation along those routes to take place. In the Travelling Salesman Problem, infinite costs can be assigned to journeys which are impossible in just one stage.

Here then is the Travelling Salesman Algorithm:

*Step 1   Reduce each row and column of the cost matrix by its lowest entry. Any tour using only the zero entries will be optimal.*

In our example, somewhere on the trip the tourist will have to leave London, say. The 'cheapest' way of doing this is to go to Paris with a cost of 1 hour. Hence the lowest entry in a row is the minimum possible cost incurred at a certain point of the tour and can be written down as a necessary expense. If a different outward route is used then an even greater cost results and we must add to the cost already written down the route cost minus the row minimum. Forming the cost differences for each row of our cost matrix we obtain Table 4.2.

**Table 4.2.**   Partially Reduced 'All Routes' Matrix

| Hours         To:<br>From: | London | Paris | Rome | Brussels | Bonn | Reduction |
|---|---|---|---|---|---|---|
| London | ∞ | 0 | 3 | 1 | ∞ | 1 |
| Paris | 0 | ∞ | 2 | 0 | 2 | 1 |
| Rome | 3 | 2 | ∞ | 2 | 0 | 2 |
| Brussels | 1 | 0 | 4 | ∞ | 0 | 1 |
| Bonn | 2 | 1 | 2 | 0 | ∞ | 1 |

**Table 4.3.**   Reduced 'All Routes' Matrix

| Hours         To:<br>From: | London | Paris | Rome | Brussels | Bonn |
|---|---|---|---|---|---|
| London | ∞ | 0 | 1 | 1 | ∞ |
| Paris | 0 | ∞ | 0 | 0 | 2 |
| Rome | 3 | 2 | ∞ | 2 | 0 |
| Brussels | 1 | 0 | 2 | ∞ | 0 |
| Bonn | 2 | 1 | 0 | 0 | ∞ |
| Reduction | 0 | 0 | 2 | 0 | 0 |

We now use a similar argument on the columns of the last matrix. Each node has to be arrived at somewhere along the tour and so the minimum column entry represents the lowest cost of that part of the trip. Reducing all the columns by their minima gives Table 4.3.

The total reduction we have achieved in the cost matrix of all the rows and columns is 8 hours. Hence at this stage of the working we know that the tour cannot be undertaken with less than 8 hours' journey time. Furthermore, if we use any of the non-zero links in the table it will add to that time by the amount of the entry in the table. Now if we can spot any tours which use only zero cost cells in the table, then the problem is solved. For example we could try London to Paris, Paris to Rome, Rome to Bonn, and Bonn to Brussels but from Brussels to London costs more than 0 hours and there may be a quicker tour. As there are no such tours in Table 4.3 we proceed with the algorithm whose purpose is to reduce the cost matrix until such tours can be found.

*Step 2  Write the penalty for non-use against each zero entry in the table. This is the minimum of the other costs in its row and column added together.*

This process identifies which of the zero cost entries is most crucial, using as the criterion the penalty of ignoring the route in making a tour. For instance the link from London to Paris has zero cost in Table 4.3. If we do *not* use this route then the lowest cost of leaving London is 1, that is to Rome or Brussels and the lowest cost of arriving in Paris is 0, from Brussels. Hence the penalty for not using the London to Paris connection is $1+0$ and we write the answer, 1, to the top left of the zero in that position in the table. Processing all the other zero entries we obtain Table 4.4.

**Table 4.4**   Reduced 'All Routes' Matrix with Penalties

| Hours          To: | London | Paris | Rome | Brussels | Bonn |
| --- | --- | --- | --- | --- | --- |
| From: | | | | | |
| London | ∞ | 1 / 0 | 1 | 1 | ∞ |
| Paris | 1 / 0 | ∞ | 0 / 0 | 0 / 0 | 2 |
| Rome | 3 | 2 | ∞ | 2 | 2 / 0 |
| Brussels | 1 | 0 / 0 | 2 | ∞ | 0 / 0 |
| Bonn | 2 | 1 | 0 / 0 | 0 / 0 | ∞ |

*Step 3  Choose one of the zero entries with the largest penalty. Draw a new table which uses this route.*

In Table 4.4 we choose the route from Rome to Bonn as having the biggest penalty for non-use. To analyse all tours which use this route we copy the matrix, deleting the row for Rome and the column for Bonn as their entries are not needed in planning the rest of the trip. We also put the cost of the reverse journey, from Bonn to Rome, equal to infinity as going from Rome to Bonn automatically precludes its use. This gives us Table 4.5.

**Table 4.5**   'Rome–Bonn' Matrix

| Hours          To:  From: | London | Paris | Rome | Brussels |
|---|---|---|---|---|
| London | ∞ | 0 | 1 | 1 |
| Paris | 0 | ∞ | 0 | 0 |
| Brussels | 1 | 0 | 2 | ∞ |
| Bonn | 2 | 1 | ∞ | 0 |

*Step 4   Reduce the new table using Step 1. Summarise the working so far on a branch diagram.* As every row and column of Table 4.5 has a zero entry, no reduction is possible using the method described in Step 1. Furthermore there are no tours using only zero cost cells in matrix 4.5, for going from London to Paris precludes Brussels to Paris as Paris can be visited once only. However the zeroes representing these routes are the only zeroes in their respective rows. The current state of our working in this example can be represented on a diagram such as Fig. 4.5.

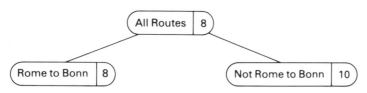

**Fig. 4.5**

The top of the diagram shows that the original matrix was reduced in Step 1 by a total of 8 hours. This means that all tours cost at least 8 hours and this is therefore a lower bound on 'All Routes'. In Step 3 we investigated tours which use the route from Rome to Bonn and found that the resulting matrix, Table 4.5, could not be reduced. Hence all trips using that particular link cost at least the original 8 hours plus the zero reduction, which gives the lower bound of 8 for such tours. On the other hand, all trips which do *not* include the connection from Rome to Bonn cost at least $8+2$ hours because the penalty in Table 4.4 for not using the Rome to Bonn route is 2 hours. We therefore write the figures 8 and 10 in the diagram as shown. In general, investigating whether to use a particular link or not involves two calculations. Firstly we reduce the cost matrix obtained by assuming it is used and add the total reduction to the previous total reduction. This is essentially Step 1 and gives the lower bound for all trips which include the link. Secondly the penalty for not using the route, found from the table generated by the previous Step 2, is added to the total reduction so far giving the lower bound for all tours which do not use the link. These values are then shown on a branch diagram such as Fig. 4.5. We now examine the branch diagram and investigate further an end-point with the lowest bound.

*Step 5   Choose a least cost possibility from the branch diagram and analyse its cost matrix from Step 1 onwards until all optimal tours have been found.* In our examples we have no choice at this point and we consider all routes which include going from Rome to Bonn.

The cost matrix is given by Table 4.5 and as it cannot be reduced using Step 1 we proceed to Step 2 and insert the penalties for not using the zero entries. This produces Table 4.6.

**Table 4.6**   'Rome–Bonn' Matrix with Penalties

| Hours          To:  From: | London | Paris | Rome | Brussels |
|---------------------------|--------|-------|------|----------|
| London | ∞ | 1<br>0• | 1 | 1 |
| Paris | 1<br>0 | ∞ | 1<br>0 | 0<br>0 |
| Brussels | 1 | 1<br>0 | 2 | ∞ |
| Bonn | 2 | 1 | ∞ | 1<br>0 |

In Step 3 we can choose to investigate the link from London to Paris. The new table with the London row and Paris column deleted and the Paris to London cost set infinitely high is:

**Table 4.7**   'Rome–Bonn' and 'London–Paris' Matrix

| Hours          To:  From: | London | Rome | Brussels |
|---------------------------|--------|------|----------|
| Paris | ∞ | 0 | 0 |
| Brussels | 1 | 2 | ∞ |
| Bonn | 2 | ∞ | 0 |

Step 4 involves reducing the rows and columns of this matrix using Step 1. This gives us Table 4.8.

**Table 4.8**   Reduced 'Rome–Bonn' and 'London–Paris' Matrix

| Hours          To:  From: | London | Rome | Brussels | Reduction |
|---------------------------|--------|------|----------|-----------|
| Paris | ∞ | 0 | 0 | 0 |
| Brussels | 0 | 1 | ∞ | 1 |
| Bonn | 2 | ∞ | 0 | 0 |

As there are no possible column reductions the total reduction is 1 hour. It means that tours using the Rome to Bonn and London to Paris connections cost at least $8+1$, or 9, hours. Conversely, we see from Table 4.6 that the penalty for not using the London to Paris link is 1 hour and so the least cost of tours which include Rome to Bonn but not London to Paris is $8+1$, or 9, hours. Figure 4.6 is the updated branch diagram.

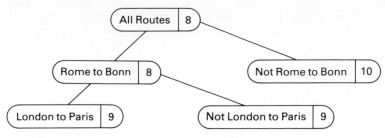

**Fig. 4.6**

We have now reached Step 5 of the algorithm for the second time so we choose a least cost possibility from the branch diagram. Suppose we take all tours containing the London to Paris link, itself a subset of those containing the Rome to Bonn link, and apply Step 1 to their cost matrix (Table 4.8). No reduction in the rows or columns is possible and we can find a combination of cells which give connections between the 5 cities involved (Table 4.9).

**Table 4.9**

| Hours          To: | London | Rome | Brussels |
| From: | | | |
| Paris | ∞ | $\boxed{0}$ | 0 |
| Brussels | $\boxed{0}$ | 1 | ∞ |
| Bonn | 2 | ∞ | $\boxed{0}$ |

This means that including the connections indicated in the above tables does not increase the cost we have written down so far as being a necessary lower bound. In other words the tour consisting of these links together with Rome to Bonn and London to Paris, as identified earlier in the branch diagram, costs just 9 hours of travelling. We can see also from Table 4.9 that the penalties for the non-use of each of these links are positive and so we have found the only optimal tour for this matrix.

The working so far can be displayed on a new branch diagram (Fig. 4.7).

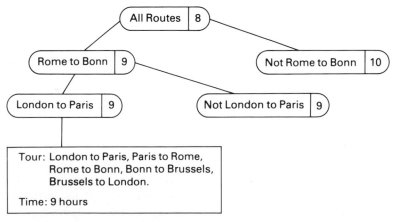

**Fig. 4.7**

Although we have found a least cost circular tour, we can investigate other branches of the diagram which hold out the possibility of similar trips. In this case we can examine all tours which include going from Rome to Bonn but exclude the link from London to Paris. According to the branch diagram, there is a possibility that such a tour could cost as little as 9 hours. It will also provide us with an opportunity to demonstrate how a cost matrix is constructed for tours which do *not* use a certain link.

Table 4.5 is the cost matrix for tours containing the Rome to Bonn connection. We can modify it so that a tour cannot go from London to Paris by setting the cost of that link to be infinitely high. This gives us Table 4.10.

**Table 4.10**   'Rome–Bonn' and 'Not London–Paris' Matrix

| Hours            To: | London | Paris | Rome | Brussels |
|----------------------|--------|-------|------|----------|
| From:                |        |       |      |          |
| London               | ∞      | ∞     | 1    | 1        |
| Paris                | 0      | ∞     | 0    | 0        |
| Brussels             | 1      | 0     | 2    | ∞        |
| Bonn                 | 2      | 1     | ∞    | 0        |

Applying Step 1 to this matrix we can reduce the first row by 1 hour to obtain Table 4.11.

**Table 4.11**   Reduced 'Rome–Bonn' and 'Not London–Paris' Matrix

| Hours            To: | London | Paris | Rome | Brussels |
|----------------------|--------|-------|------|----------|
| From:                |        |       |      |          |
| London               | ∞      | ∞     | 0    | 0        |
| Paris                | 0      | ∞     | 0    | 0        |
| Brussels             | 1      | 0     | 2    | ∞        |
| Bonn                 | 2      | 1     | ∞    | 0        |

Now the total reduction for Table 4.5, which represented all tours containing the Rome to Bonn connection, was 8 hours. We can see this from Fig. 4.5. Hence the further reduction of 1 hour we have made in obtaining Table 4.11 gives a total reduction of $8+1$, or 9, hours. If, therefore, we can find a way of linking the cities in Table 4.11 using only zero cost cells, then we will have found a tour costing just 9 hours.

We begin the search by noticing that the Brussels to Paris link must be used as it is the only zero cost cell in its row. Similarly the Bonn to Brussels connection has to be included. The route from Paris to London is likewise compulsory because it is the only zero cost way of arriving in London. Having thus eliminated 3 rows and columns from the table, we have no choice but to link London to Rome, again at zero cost. We have therefore found another tour which costs 9 hours and the complete analysis of this example can be displayed as a branch diagram (Fig. 4.8).

In this example we have found more than one tour with the same minimum cost and

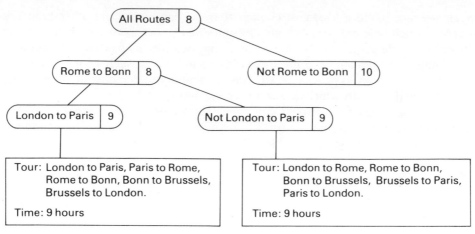

**Fig. 4.8**

this is not unusual when solving the Travelling Salesman Problem. In fact, for problems with a symmetric cost matrix where journeys in either direction between two nodes cost the same, we always expect answers to occur in pairs. For instance in the Fairground Example every circular tour, like Ferris Wheel, Ghost Train, Dodgem Cars, Big Dipper, Coconut Shy, Ferris Wheel has a corresponding reverse tour costing the same amount, in this case Ferris Wheel, Coconut Shy, Big Dipper, Dodgem Cars, Ghost Train, Ferris Wheel. Hence any optimal tour has a companion reverse tour which is also optimal and answers occur in pairs. Naturally the branch and bound algorithm we have described should yield both tours and the reader might like to verify that the above tours both arise when it is applied to the Fairground Example network.

In solving the Tourist Example we have examined perhaps the messiest algorithm in Operational Research. By their very nature, branch and bound methods involve keeping a record of previous working so that hitherto unexplored branches of the diagram can be revisited. We have therefore labelled each cost matrix carefully to make such references back to earlier working as easy as possible. The reader should also note how the cost matrices are derived and used in conjunction with the branch diagrams as an investigative tool, probing each subset of possible tours until just one remains which has the lowest cost.

## Shortest Route Problems

Having dealt with minimal spanning trees and travelling salesman tours, we now consider the problem of finding the shortest route from one node of a network through to another. The first example is about routing a wire over the surface of an electronic circuit board. Such problems arise in the computer-aided design of printed and integrated circuits. The second example is a navigational application where we want to find the shortest pathway across the delta of a river.

### The Electronic Circuit Example
The printed circuit board for a radio looks something like Fig. 4.9.

It is necessary to run a wire along the surface between the points A and B avoiding all the components mounted on the board. Insulated wire is needed in order to cross the

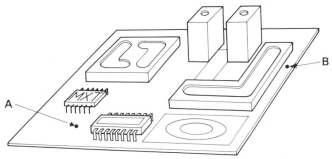

Fig. 4.9

metal sheeting on certain parts of the surface and this is twice as expensive as ordinary wire. We show how a drawing of the board can be used to determine the most economical routes.

*Solution* We assume in this example that the path of the wire is to be parallel with the sides of the circuit board and that only right angled bends are allowed in its route. The standard practice in electrical engineering and plumbing is not to take the geometrically shortest pathway between two points but to lay wires and pipes parallel to any existing boundaries. The method we use provides an accurate measure of all distances measured along the directions of the edges of the circuit board but not of those measured at an angle to them.

Firstly a plan of the board is converted into a network by drawing a lattice of squares over it. Each space in the lattice is then treated as a node and the cost of going from one node to an adjacent node is, say, 1 unit. Any engineering drawing, or even a map, can be treated like this.

Secondly the figure '1' is written in every square which can be reached in one step from the start of the journey, A. There are 4 such squares and they can be seen in Fig. 4.10. We next write a '2' in every square which can be reached in one step from a '1' square unless it has already been labelled, like the square A itself. There are 6 squares with a '2' label in Fig. 4.10.

The working continues in this manner with all the '3'-s being marked, then all the '4'-s and so on until each square on the diagram has been labelled with its shortest distance from A. The method allows for variations in the terrain of the surface by requiring more than one step per square over certain regions of the lattice. In this example we treat each square of metal sheeting in the plan as needing 2 steps to enter, move across or leave because the wire for such journeys is twice as expensive.

When all the squares have been labelled we find the shortest paths by backtracking from B. Starting from that point, each square is joined to an adjacent square with a smaller number in it until A is reached. In Fig. 4.11 we see that when this backtracking process arrives at a square with '15' written in it, there are two squares with the label '14' in adjacent positions. Both of these must be joined to it and all possible paths traced back to A. **Any route from A to B using the lines shown in Fig. 4.11 has a total length or cost of 29 units and is a solution to the problem.**

The method we have used, called the Moore Lee Algorithm, has the advantage that all routes are costed even if they are not optimal. In our example there may be some reason for wanting the wire to pass over the larger of the two pieces of metal sheeting. In that

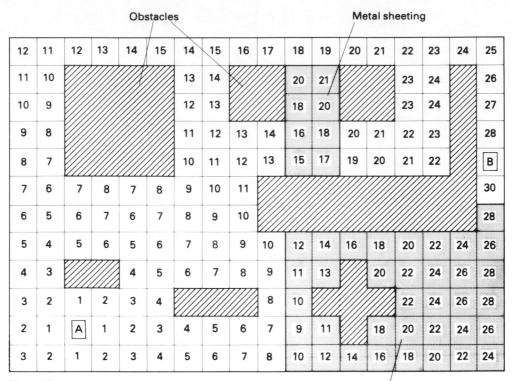

**Fig. 4.10** Electronic circuit plan with lattice

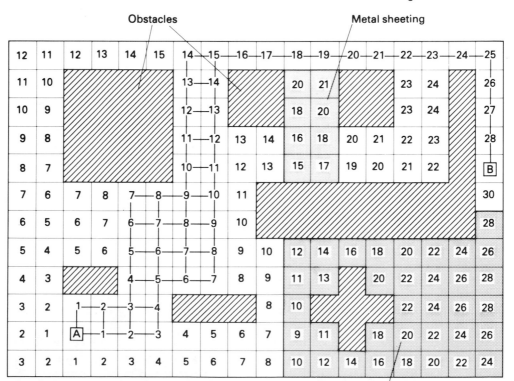

**Fig. 4.11** Electronic circuit with shortest paths

event we would not have to rework the problem as our diagram shows at a glance that this costs a minimum of 31 units. Another advantage of the algorithm is that its execution and the storage of the square lattice of numbers are ideally suited to computerisation.

We continue with an example of determining the shortest pathway through a network which is not in the regular form of being a lattice. Suppose we had been interested in finding the shortest route from the Ferris Wheel to the Big Dipper in the Fairground Example. We see from the map (Fig. 4.1) that this is the path via the Dodgem Cars and the problem is relatively simple. However, when costs are not measured as distances, as in the Electronic Circuit Example, an optimum route between two nodes may not be the one making the straightest line between them. In fact the network formed by the European cities in the Tourist Example has the property that the quickest way of going from Paris to Bonn is via Brussels! The next example illustrates a technique for finding all the optimal routes through any network.

### The River Crossing Example
A river flows to the sea through a delta as shown in the map (Fig. 4.12). Because of

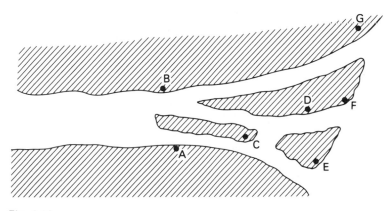

**Fig. 4.12**

the currents and other geographical hazards it is not realistic to take the distances between the points shown on the map as an indication of the time taken to travel from one to the other. When times measured in seconds are used instead of distances, the map is replaced by a network (Fig. 4.13).

We find the quickest route going from the point A to the point G.

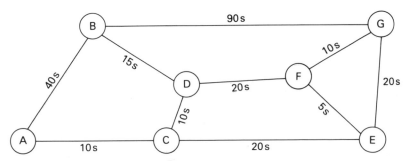

**Fig. 4.13**

*Solution*   The method used here has some similarity to that of the last example in that we work through the network from the start node taking one step at a time. Beginning at A, we see that there are 3 nodes which can be reached in one step. The other nodes are thus held to be infinitely far away at this stage and their distance written as ∞. After 2 steps through the network all the nodes except F can be reached and Table 4.12 can be constructed.

**Table 4.12**

| Node | Shortest distance from A after step 1 | 2 |
|------|------|------|
| A | 0 | 0 |
| B | 40 | 40 |
| C | 10 | 10 |
| D | ∞ | 20 |
| E | ∞ | 30 |
| F | ∞ | ∞ |
| G | ∞ | 130 |

The entry against node D of 20 seconds arises because, of the two routes from A to D which are possible in 2 steps, the one via node C taking 20 seconds is quicker.

Table 4.12 is extended to 3 steps by using the obvious fact that a node cannot be reached in 3 steps unless a neighbouring node was visited in 2 steps. For instance, the shortest path of 3 steps to node F must visit one of its neighbours after 2 steps. Now the distances of those nodes from A after 2 steps are the last column entries in Table 4.12, hence if we add to each of them the distance to node F we can choose the minimum by inspection. In our example, we can arrive at node F after 3 steps by

(a) being at D after 2 steps and travelling from D to F. The time taken would be 20 (from the table) plus 20 (from D to F), or 40 seconds.

(b) being at E after 2 steps and travelling from E to F. The time taken would be 30 plus 5 or 35 seconds.

(c) being at G after 2 steps and travelling on to F. The time taken would be 130 plus 10, or 140 seconds.

Of these 3 routes, which arise because F has 3 neighbouring nodes, (b) is the quickest and so the shortest distance from A to F in 3 steps is 35 seconds. Performing similar calculations for all the other nodes we obtain the extended Table 4.13.

**Table 4.13**

| Node | Shortest distance from A after step 1 | 2 | 3 |
|------|------|------|------|
| A | 0 | 0 | 0 |
| B | 40 | 40 | 35 |
| C | 10 | 10 | 10 |
| D | ∞ | 20 | 20 |
| E | ∞ | 30 | 30 |
| F | ∞ | ∞ | 35 |
| G | ∞ | 130 | 50 |

The method continues in this fashion until the last column of the table is a replica of the previous one. This should happen within the same number of columns as there are nodes although typically it occurs well before this upper limit is attained. The complete table for our example is given below.

**Table 4.14**

| Node | Shortest distance from A after step | | | | |
| | 1 | 2 | 3 | 4 | 5 |
|---|---|---|---|---|---|
| A | 0 | 0 | 0 | 0 | 0 |
| B | 40 | 40 | 35 | 35 | 35 |
| C | 10 | 10 | 10 | 10 | 10 |
| D | ∞ | 20 | 20 | 20 | 20 |
| E | ∞ | 30 | 30 | 30 | 30 |
| F | ∞ | ∞ | 35 | 35 | 35 |
| G | ∞ | 130 | 50 | 45 | 45 |

The last column of this table is now used to deduce the optimal routes from A to G. We see in that column that the quickest time to arrive at G from A is 45 seconds. Examining the nodes surrounding G in the network diagram it seems that we must arrive at E by 25 seconds or F by 35 seconds to avoid being late. This is because it takes 20 seconds to go from E to G and 10 seconds from F to G. Notice that we can rule out the route via B as it is not possible to make that journey in just 45 seconds because of the time from B to G. The choice, then, is between node E and node F but from the last column of Table 4.14 it is impossible to arrive at E in less than 30 seconds from A. We therefore conclude that the shortest route from A to G must be via F and sure enough, its shortest distance from A is 35 seconds according to the table, which agrees with the value we need by our backtracking method. Indeed, if there was not at least one node to which we could backtrack then our calculations so far must be in error.

Applying the same argument to node F we trace the path back to E and repeating once more **we obtain the entire route ACEFG.** As in the Electronic Circuit Example there may be more than one optimal pathway and they should all be followed back to A.

## Computer Program

Route scheduling techniques are used in computer-aided design packages. We list here a program which determines the minimal spanning tree for a network using the algorithm of this chapter. It illustrates how network data can be fed into a computer. The program sets all 'impossible' links between nodes to have a distance above the true maximum for the rest of the system. The algorithm therefore never selects those links in constructing the tree diagram. This is a similar device to that used in the Freezer Example on transportation where some of the routes were not to be included in the solution. The specimen run uses the data from the Fairground Example.

**Program Notes**

**1** Lines 1∅ to 9∅ print the heading, open arrays to store flags and the distances between the nodes, and initialise N, the number of vertices in the network and M, the maximum distance in the network.

**2** Lines 1∅∅ to 2∅∅ read the distances between the nodes as supplied by the user. The maximum distance, M, and the maximum node reference number, N, are updated if necessary as each distance is read.

```
10 PRINT "MINIMAL SPANNING TREE"
20 PRINT "---------------------"
30 DIM C(20,20),T(20),D(20,20)
40 PRINT "ENTER DISTANCES, ONE PER"
50 PRINT "LINE AS NODE A, NODE B,"
60 PRINT "DISTANCE.  GIVE 3 ZEROS"
70 PRINT "WHEN ALL THE DATA IS IN"
80 N=0
90 M=0
100 INPUT I,J,W
110 IF I=0 THEN 210
120 C(I,J)=W
130 C(J,I)=W
140 IF C(I,J)<M THEN 160
150 M=C(I,J)
160 IF I<N THEN 180
170 N=I
180 IF J<N THEN 200
190 N=J
200 GOTO 100
210 FOR A =1 TO N
220 T(A) = 0
230 FOR B=1 TO N
240 D(A,B)=0
250 IF C(A,B)<>0 THEN 270
260 C(A,B)=M+1
270 NEXT B
280 NEXT A
290 T(1)=1
300 V=1
310 L=M
320 FOR S=1 TO N
330 IF T(S)=0 THEN 410
340 FOR R=1 TO N
350 IF T(R)=1 THEN 400
360 IF C(S,R)>L THEN 400
370 S1=S
380 R1=R
390 L=C(S,R)
400 NEXT R
410 NEXT S
420 T(R1)=1
430 V=V+1
440 D(S1,R1)=1
450 IF V<N THEN 310
460 PRINT "MINIMAL SPANNING TREE"
470 PRINT "---------------------"
480 PRINT "NODE A","NODE B","DISTANCE"
490 FOR I=1 TO N
500 FOR J=1 TO N
510 IF D(I,J)=0 THEN 530
520 PRINT I,J,C(I,J)
530 NEXT J
540 NEXT I
550 END
```

**Specimen Run**

```
MINIMAL SPANNING TREE
---------------------
ENTER DISTANCES, ONE PER
LINE AS NODE A, NODE B,
DISTANCE.  GIVE 3 ZEROS
WHEN ALL THE DATA IS IN
 ?1,2,25
 ?1,3,20
 ?1,4,22
 ?2,3,27
 ?3,4,18
 ?2,5,40
 ?3,5,20
 ?4,5,24
 ?0,0,0
MINIMAL SPANNING TREE
---------------------
NODE A          NODE B          DISTANCE
 1               2               25
 1               3               20
 3               4               18
 3               5               20
```

**3**  Lines 210 to 280 set all the flags stored as the T and D arrays to be zero. Any distances, as stored in the C array, which are equal to zero are re-assigned to become (M + 1), which is a distance bigger than any given by the user. This ensures that such unconnected pairs of nodes are not connected by the subsequent algorithm.

**4**  Lines 290 and 300 begin the algorithm described earlier in the chapter by starting at node 1. The T flag is set equal to 1 to show that node 1 has been included in the minimal spanning tree. The counter V is set equal to 1 as it is the number of nodes included in the tree so far.

**5**  Lines 310 to 410 work through the network to find the as yet unconnected node which is nearest to the connected ones. Line 330 rejects node S if it has not yet been connected while line 350 rejects node R if it has been connected. Hence line 360 tests the distance between all connected nodes with all unconnected ones against the value of a variable called L. This is initially set to equal the maximum distance between the nodes but is updated whenever a smaller one is found. Therefore, when all possible links between connected and unconnected nodes have been examined, the value of L is the smallest of their distances apart. The variables S1 and R1 record the location of that distance when it is found.

**6**  Lines 420 to 440 incorporate node R1 into the minimal spanning tree. The T flag for R1 is set equal to 1 to show this, the vertex counter V is increased by 1, and the flag for the link between S1 and R1 is put equal to 1 to show that the link is used on the tree. Line 450 sends control back to line 310 if there are still more nodes to be processed.

**7**  Lines 460 to 540 print out the details of those links between nodes which have been included in the minimal spanning tree.

## Summary

**1**  Shortest path problems relate to a map, plan or engineering drawing which can be idealised as a network of routes joining nodes or vertices. Sometimes the network is called a graph or the routes are called arcs or links.

**2**  The first type of problem considered was the determination of a set of connections which link together all the nodes of a network and have the minimum possible total length. Such a linkage is called a Minimal Spanning Tree.

**3**  The Travelling Salesman Problem is concerned with finding a circular tour of all the nodes which has the minimum possible length. The method used is called a branch and bound technique because at each stage of the algorithm a branch of the diagram is chosen which represents a subset of tours with the least lower bound on their lengths.

**4**  The last two problems considered in the chapter were to find the shortest path between two given nodes of a network. In the Electronic Circuit Example a square lattice grid was superimposed onto an engineering drawing in order to convert the drawing into a network. In the River Crossing Example the 'distances' between the nodes of a network were measured as journey times because the real distances were irrelevant to the problem due to river currents and other geographical features. It is often preferable to measure distance in terms of journey time or even monetary cost.

## Further Reading

Network problems are an important part of deterministic operational research and most of the books named in the 'General Operational Research' section of the Bibliography contain work on them. Both the transportation problem of the last chapter and the coordinating and sequencing problems of the next chapter are particular types of network problems. Reference (14) deals with some specialised techniques and, like (52), shows how network algorithms can be computerised. Network analysis is used in computer-aided design and in subjects like ergonomics which attempt to optimise the layout of, for example, a factory or the controls in a motor car.

## Exercises

**1**  The distances between the telephone receivers in a suite of offices are shown in Fig. 4.14. Determine the minimal spanning tree for the network; this represents the method of connecting the telephones together using the shortest amount of cable.

**2**  Determine the shortest circular tour for visiting all the sideshows in the Fairground Example.

**3**  If a node can be visited more than once then the minimal spanning tree may give a shorter tour than the travelling salesman algorithm. Show that the minimal spanning tree for the network of Fig. 4.15 gives a shorter tour than the only circular trip possible.

**4**  The network diagram of Fig. 4.16 shows the numbers of stations between various junctions on the London underground railway system.

   (i)  Find a minimal spanning tree connecting the stations.

   (ii)  Use the travelling salesman algorithm to find a path which visits each station only once and covers the shortest possible distance.

**5**  Draw a diagram of a chess board and label the bottom left hand square with a zero.

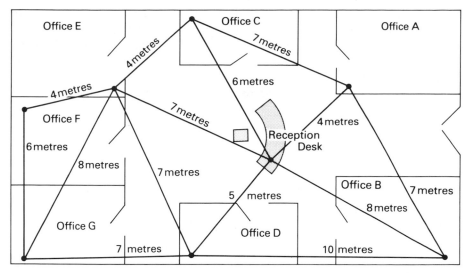

**Fig. 4.14**

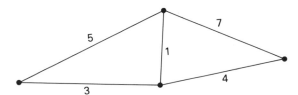

**Fig. 4.15**

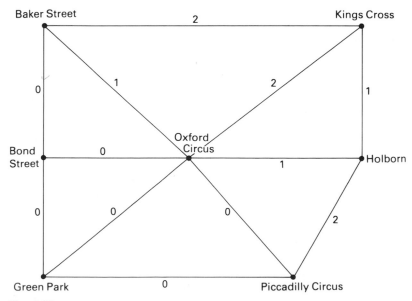

**Fig. 4.16**

Imagine a knight placed on that square and number the two other squares it can move to with '1'. Number all the squares it can move to from there with a '2' and continue in this way until every square on the board has a number. The diagram now shows the smallest number of knight's moves in which each square can be reached when the knight starts from a corner. Hence deduce that a knight can reach any square on the board in 6 moves wherever it starts. Trace out its shortest path from a corner to the diagonally opposite corner.

# 5 Coordinating and Sequencing

Industrial and commercial operations often consist of several activities performed sequentially or concurrently. A good example is a construction site where the coordination and scheduling of the various stages of the work is essential for the timely completion of the overall project. In this chapter we consider three techniques applicable to such operations in order to optimise their execution.

The first technique, Critical Path Analysis, displays the logistics of the operation as an activity network. It enables the identification of those tasks which are crucial to the total project time in that any delay in their performance causes the whole schedule to be delayed. We examine the derivation of Gantt charts from the analysis and the Project Evaluation and Review Technique, PERT.

Whereas critical path methods concentrate on coordinating interrelated activities, the second technique of the chapter is concerned with sequencing logistically unrelated jobs. We consider a production process where each item passes through two stages of manufacture and use the example of mixing and baking different cakes in a kitchen. Whilst the mixing and baking of each cake has to be done in strict sequence, the order in which the different cakes are processed is under the control of the production manager. Our objective in those operations is to sequence the various jobs in a way which minimises the total production time.

The last section of the chapter deals with projects in which all the activities can proceed simultaneously. Each task, however, has a different completion time or cost when assigned to different machines or people. We therefore determine the assignment of jobs to resources which minimises the overall cost.

## Critical Path Analysis

In an operation where some activities have to be completed before others can begin it is often difficult to forecast the effect of a delay in one of them. Sometimes the delay will increase the total project time and sometimes there will be enough flexibility in the timetable for the whole operation to remain on schedule. Critical Path Analysis uses a network diagram to display the interdependence of one job on another and then identifies those activities which are crucial for the timely completion of the project. The network itself helps the manager to take a meaningful overview of the operation and whilst in the first worked example the diagram is given we shall see how to develop one in the second example.

### The Coffee Making Example
The activities necessary to make a cup of coffee can be represented as an activity network diagram (Fig. 5.1).

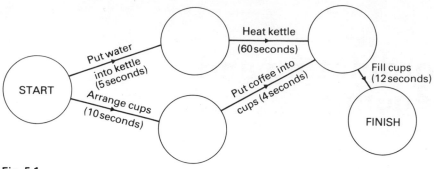

**Fig. 5.1**

We shall find the shortest time in which the coffee can be prepared and determine which activities within the network are crucial for this minimum project time to be achieved.

*Solution*    The network is redrawn numbering the time instants, called **events**, at the start and finish of each activity (Fig. 5.2). The one at the start of the activity is called its **tail**

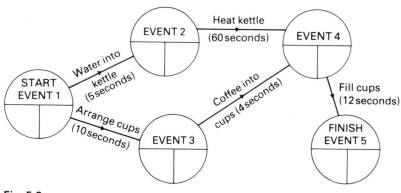

**Fig. 5.2**

**event** while the one at the finish is called the **head event**. These correspond to the head and tail of the arrow drawn on the line denoting the activity. Two spaces are left at each event in which to write the earliest and latest times that the event can occur.

Working through the network from the beginning we enter at each event the earliest time it can be reached. In our network, if event 1 occurs at time 0 then event 2 cannot occur before 5 seconds and event 3 before 10 seconds so we write those figures in the diagram. The result of this procedure is Fig. 5.3.

Notice that event 4 cannot happen until *both* the activities leading into it have been completed and although the coffee has been put into the cups by 14 seconds, which is 10 seconds to event 3 and 4 seconds to load the cups, the activity 'heat kettle' cannot be completed until 65 seconds from the start. Hence the earliest time event 4 can be reached and we are ready for the next activity is 65 seconds. In general the *earliest* time an event can happen is the *latest* time by which all the activities leading into it have occurred.

Figure 5.3 is completed by writing '77' as the earliest time event 5 can occur. This is simply 65 seconds, the earliest time for event 4, plus the duration of the activity from

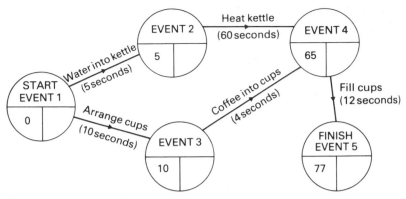

**Fig. 5.3**

event 4 to event 5, which is 12 seconds. **We now see that the whole project cannot be undertaken in less than 77 seconds.**

Critical Path Analysis proceeds by making this total project time the target for the operation. We write it as the latest time for the finish event and work backwards through the network entering the latest time each event must occur in order to achieve it. For example, event 4 must be reached by 65 seconds at the latest to ensure no delay in the total project time. This is because 77 minus 12 is 65. Figure. 5.4 is the final diagram with latest times as well as earliest times.

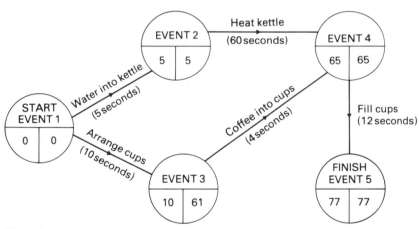

**Fig. 5.4**

Notice that for event 4 to occur by 65 seconds, event 2 must have occurred by time (65−60) seconds and event 3 by time (65−4) seconds. Eventually, if our logic and arithmetic are correct, we should arrive back at the start event and write its latest time as zero.

We can learn many things from the completed network diagram. It appears that **events 1, 2, 4 and 5 must occur at precise times for the project to stay on schedule** whilst event 3 can happen at any time between 10 and 61 seconds. This in turn means that the activities between these events are **critical** as any delay in their duration affects the specific event times. For example if it took 6 seconds instead of 5 to put water in the kettle then event 2 would not occur by its latest time and this would delay the whole project.

Any pathway through the network consisting entirely of critical activities is called a **critical path**. In our example the pathway joining events 1 to 2 to 4 to 5 is critical. As event 3 does not have to occur at a specified time the activities leading to it are not critical. We shall consider later how such 'floating' time can be utilised.

There may be more than one critical path through a network. In our example if it took 61 seconds to arrange the cups then every activity, and hence every path, would be critical. The golden rule is that an activity is critical if its duration time is equal to the latest time it can finish minus the earliest time it can start. There is thus no spare time available for its completion over and above its actual duration. As an example of the confusion that can arise in a large problem if the rule is not applied, consider the following network section in which only two of the three activities are critical (Fig. 5.5).

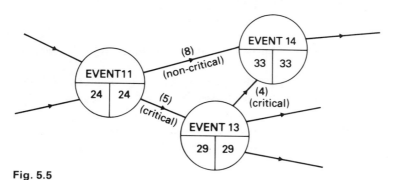

Fig. 5.5

Although all 3 events must occur at precise time instants for the project to remain on schedule, the activity between events 11 and 14 has a shorter duration than the difference in their times. There is therefore some spare time available for its execution. We now examine the 'free' time that such non-critical activities have.

## Float Times

In the Coffee Making Example, putting the coffee into the cups has a duration of 4 seconds. However, the latest time it can finish, 65 seconds, minus the earliest time it can start, 10 seconds, gives a time period of 55 seconds for its execution. We say that this

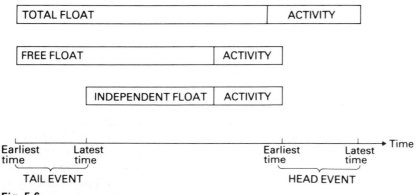

Fig. 5.6

activity has a **total float** of 51 seconds which can be used before, during or after its performance.

Utilising this extra time may, however, change the float times of other activities in the network. The **free float** is the amount of float time which can be used without affecting the timing of the head event and hence the rest of the project. It is the earliest time of the head event minus the earliest time of the tail event minus the activity duration. Finally the **independent float** is the amount of float time which can be used without affecting either the head or tail events. It is the earliest time of the head event minus the latest time of the tail event minus the activity duration.

All these float times can be represented graphically as in Fig. 5.6.

## Drawing Networks

For the critical path analysis to work it is important that not more than one activity joins any two events in the network. To achieve this, dummy activities of zero duration are used and, for example, instead of Fig. 5.7 we must draw Fig. 5.8.

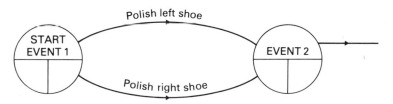

**Fig. 5.7**

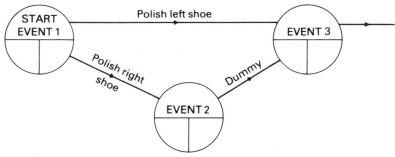

**Fig. 5.8**

Sometimes dummies are used to ensure that activities occur in the correct sequence. For example, the network of Fig. 5.9 shows that while each shoe can be put on immediately after it has been polished, the shoe polish cannot be put away until *both* shoes are finished.

The last two examples highlight another consideration to have in mind when drawing a network. This is that the total resources available, measured in manpower, equipment or materials, may be insufficient to allow the network to operate. In the first shoe polishing example it is assumed that both shoes can be polished simultaneously while in the last example it may be necessary for both shoes to be put on at the same time as the shoe polish is being stored away. This requires at least three people! Such constraints involving

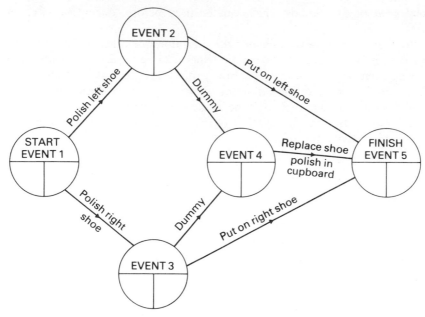

**Fig. 5.9**

resources can radically alter the structure of the network as activities which could other-wise proceed concurrently have to be done consecutively.

In practice, then, the shape of the activity network is imposed on the project manager by the logistics of the operation concerned and the limitations of the available resources. Theoretically two project managers given the same operation should draw almost identical networks. In contrast, the estimated duration times placed on the activities will often be different when assessed by different people. Unfortunately the analysis can be sensitive to the values of the activity times and it can indicate a false critical path. For instance, if it was estimated that arranging the cups in the Coffee Making Example would take 62 seconds then a different critical path would emerge. One attempt to overcome this weak-ness of the method is the Project Evaluation and Review Technique.

## Project Evaluation and Review Technique (PERT)

Acknowledging that it is difficult to estimate the exact duration times of future activities, in PERT we employ a probabilistic approach to them. For each task, the project manager specifies a most likely value, $m$, an optimistic value, $a$, and a pessimistic value, $b$. The actual duration time is assumed to have a probability distribution called the beta distri-bution but the details of this, need not concern us here. The only results we use are that the expected duration time is $(4m + a + b)/6$ and its variance is $(b - a)^2/36$.

### The House Building Example

Critical Path Analysis is used a lot in the construction industry but real applications give rise to large networks. As a simplified example to illustrate PERT we consider the acti-vities necessary to construct a house. The times are measured in weeks (Table 5.1).

**Table 5.1**

| Number | Activity | Must be preceded by activities | Optimistic duration (*a*) | Pessimistic duration (*b*) | Most likely duration (*m*) |
|--------|----------|-------------------------------|-----------------------------|------------------------------|-------------------------------|
| 1 | Lay foundations | – | 3.0 | 6.0 | 4.0 |
| 2 | Excavate for drains | – | 1.5 | 2.0 | 1.7 |
| 3 | Lay drains | 2 | 1.5 | 2.1 | 2.0 |
| 4 | Brickwork | 1, 2, 3 | 13.0 | 17.0 | 15.0 |
| 5 | Plastering | 4 | 4.0 | 6.0 | 4.8 |
| 6 | Carpentry | 4 | 7.2 | 9.3 | 8.4 |
| 7 | Roofing | 6 | 9.0 | 11.0 | 10.0 |

We identify the critical paths and activities and calculate the probability of each event being behind a given schedule.

*Solution*  We begin by drawing the network diagram. This was given in the Coffee Making Example but would usually have to be drawn up by the analyst from data such as that in the above table. Firstly all activities which have no prerequisite tasks are drawn with the start event as their tail event. In this example we draw activities 1 and 2 from event 1. We can then incorporate, one at a time, those tasks whose prerequisites have already been included in the network, in this case number 3, then 4, then 5 and 6, and finally 7.

The duration times of the activities for the diagram are expectations and are calculated along with the variances, correct to two decimal places, using the formulae shown in Table 5.2.

**Table 5.2**

| Activity | Expected duration $\left(\dfrac{4m+a+b}{6}\right)$ | Variance $\left(\dfrac{(b-a)^2}{36}\right)$ |
|----------|-----------------------------------------------------|----------------------------------------------|
| Lay foundations | 4.17 | 0.25 |
| Excavate for drains | 1.72 | 0.01 |
| Lay drains | 1.93 | 0.01 |
| Brickwork | 15.00 | 0.44 |
| Plastering | 4.87 | 0.11 |
| Carpentry | 8.35 | 0.12 |
| Roofing | 10.00 | 0.11 |

The complete network diagram (Fig. 5.10) is analysed in the same way as the Coffee Making Example.

Remembering that an activity is critical if its duration is equal to the latest time of its head event minus the earliest time of its tail event, we see that **laying the foundations, the brickwork, the carpentry and the roofing are all critical.** We could now calculate the float times for each non-critical activity but PERT enables us to investigate the critical path itself in more detail.

The technique assumes that the earliest times the events can occur are normally distributed. Readers unfamiliar with the normal probability distribution might wish to read Chapter 8 at this point or continue here as the calculations are not over-complicated. To apply that distribution to the earliest event times we need their expected values and their

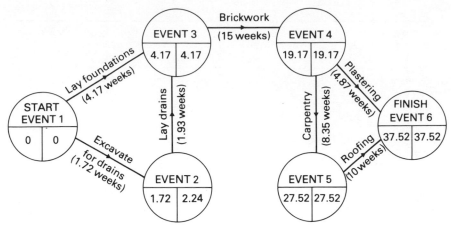

**Fig. 5.10**

variances. Now each earliest time is a sum of activity times and so we add the appropriate expected durations and variances. The results for each event are given in Table 5.3.

**Table 5.3**

| Event | Expected earliest time (from network) | Variance of earliest time (sum of activity variances) |
|-------|------------------|---------------------|
| 1 | 0.00 | 0.00 |
| 2 | 1.72 | 0.01 |
| 3 | 4.17 | 0.25 |
| 4 | 19.17 | 0.69 |
| 5 | 27.52 | 0.81 |
| 6 | 37.52 | 0.92 |

For instance, the variance of event 4 is the sum of the variances of laying the foundations and brickwork from Table 5.2. These are the activities whose durations make up the earliest time of that event.

Armed with Table 5.3 we can calculate any probability of interest regarding the earliest event times. We conclude the example by tabulating the probabilities that each event is late according to a given timetable for the project (Table 5.4).

**Table 5.4**

| Event | Scheduled time (s) | Network earliest time (t) | Normal z-value $\dfrac{s-t}{\sqrt{\text{variance}}}$ | Probability of earliest time being greater than scheduled time from normal tables |
|-------|-----------|---------|---------|------------------|
| 1 | 0 | 0.00 | – | 0.0000 |
| 2 | 2 | 1.72 | 2.80 | 0.0026 |
| 3 | 5 | 4.17 | 1.66 | 0.0485 |
| 4 | 18 | 19.17 | −1.41 | 0.9207 |
| 5 | 26 | 27.52 | −1.69 | 0.9545 |
| 6 | 37 | 37.52 | −0.54 | 0.7054 |

Looking at the results it seems that there is a high probability of events from 4 onwards being behind schedule. Hopefully some remedial action could be taken to prevent this, or the project manager might decide that the proposed timetable is unrealistic.

## Crashing

We have not yet considered the financial implication of delays. Whilst PERT enables us to calculate probabilities for the project as if we were bystanders, there are often ways the manager can intervene and influence activity duration times directly as the work progresses. For example, suppose in the Coffee Making Example we are offered an electric kettle which reduces the time taken to boil the water from 60 seconds to 55 seconds but the extra cost is 5p on the total project cost. As boiling the water is an activity on the network's critical path the overall project time will be reduced by spending this money and a decision can be made on that basis. On the other hand, **crashing** a non-critical activity, like arranging the cups, will not affect the total project time and so money spent on that is not as cost beneficial. Sometimes crashing an activity, that is running it on a crash programme, alters the nature of the network and the critical path analysis has to be done again. Deciding which activities to crash is thus vital to the success of the project and crashing an inappropriate one is a bit like rearranging the deck-chairs on the 'Titanic'.

## Gantt Charts

Whether the activities of a project are scheduled using a standard critical path analysis or PERT, it is often desirable to display the timetable graphically. For the House Building Example we could draw a **bar chart** or **Gantt chart** using the earliest event times (Fig. 5.11).

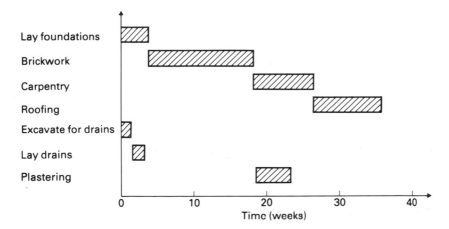

**Fig. 5.11**   Bar chart of the house building solution

By examining the jobs in progress at any one time the total requirements in labour, raw materials, plant etc. for the whole project can be found. For example, from time 19.17 to 24.04 there are two activities in progress, while from 3.65 to 19.17 there is only one. We can therefore build up a profile of the number of gangs of workmen employed on the project (Fig. 5.12).

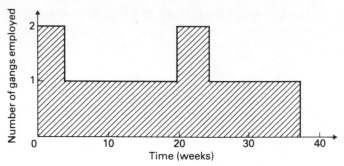

**Fig. 5.12**  Labour requirements of the house building solution

Graphs like this show how the needs of the project for labour, raw materials, equipment or even cash, will vary in time. They are extremely useful in project appraisal and planning.

## Production Sequencing

The analysis of the critical pathways through a network helps in coordinating the activities concerned in order to minimise the total project time. The logistics of which task can precede which tends to dominate such an analysis and the level of resources needed by the project as it progresses is of only secondary importance. In this section we consider the scheduling of jobs all needing the same piece of machinery or the same labour force. These resources therefore form a bottleneck in the production process and we want to reduce the delay caused. It is assumed that production items can be processed in any order and that the only logistic constraints are the finite handling capacity of the various manufacturing stages.

Our worked example is set in a domestic kitchen, a factory familiar to most of us. Each production item passes through a manual stage where the ingredients are prepared and a cooking stage where a machine, the oven, is used. The example corresponds to any factory where there are two production phases and a number of jobs with different duration times in each phase. The method described gives the sequence of jobs which minimises the overall production time.

### The Cookery Example

A housewife wants to make 5 cakes with the following preparation and baking times (Table 5.5).

**Table 5.5**

| Cake | Mixing time (minutes) | Baking time (minutes) |
|------|-----------------------|-----------------------|
| Flapjacks | 10 | 30 |
| Chocolate eclairs | 30 | 20 |
| Almond slices | 25 | 20 |
| Sponge cake | 5 | 20 |
| Jam tarts | 30 | 15 |

She has only enough room in the oven for one cake at a time but naturally the activities of mixing one recipe and baking another can proceed simultaneously. We find in which sequence cakes should be baked to minimise the total production time.

*Solution* As in the previous sections, we can represent the project as a network of activities (Fig. 5.13). In this case we need to insert dummy activities to prevent the events having more than one task joining them together.

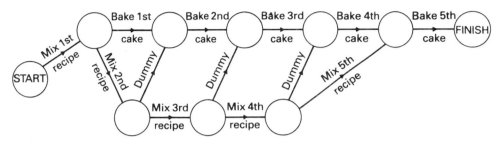

Fig. 5.13

Unfortunately there are 120 different sequences in which the 5 cakes can be prepared and baked. Each one gives rise to a network diagram like the one above but with different durations for '1st recipe', '2nd recipe' and so on depending on which cakes they represent. In order to use these diagrams we have to calculate the total project time of each of them and select the sequence of recipes giving the smallest one.

Investigating the consequences of scheduling the jobs in every possible way is feasible when there are not many of them. Here, however, we examine other methods of solution beginning with graphical techniques. The housewife in our example who is in search of the optimum timetable could cut out pieces of paper or card with lengths proportional to the production times of the cakes. She could then try to arrange them on a sheet of graph paper to form the shortest sequence. The 'working' at some stage might look like Fig. 5.14.

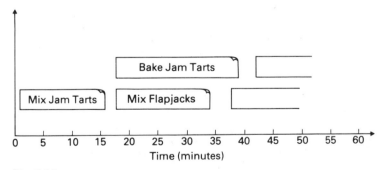

Fig. 5.14

Although useful for gaining a 'feel' for the problem, such methods are not reliable and, bearing in mind that there are 120 possible sequences, can be time consuming and unprofitable.

We therefore turn our attention to a method which utilises a particular feature of the network diagram (Fig. 5.13). We see there that baking cannot begin at all until the first recipe is mixed and so it is sensible to choose that recipe to be the one with the shortest mixing time. Similarly, all the mixing must be completed before the last recipe can be baked, so we choose the final recipe to have the shortest baking time. This type of argument gives us the reasoning behind the first step of the general method.

*Step 1   Find the smallest entry in the table. If it is in the left hand column, schedule that job as near to the start of the project as possible. If it is in the right hand column schedule it as near to the end as possible. If there are two or more equal values in the same column, choose the one with the smallest entry in the other column.*

In our example, we place 'Sponge cake' to be the first recipe in the sequence for mixing. Clearly, once the ingredients have been prepared, that cake will also be first in the oven for baking.

*Step 2   Cross the job just allocated off the list and if there are any remaining jobs repeat Step 1.*

Applying the two steps 5 times, we obtain the sequence **Sponge Cake, Flapjacks, Chocolate Eclairs, Almond Slices and Jam Tarts.** At the 4th execution of Step 1 there is a tie between Chocolate Eclairs and Almond Slices which both have the lowest entry of 20. As Almond Slices has the smaller mixing time of the two recipes it takes priority and is scheduled later than Chocolate Eclairs.

## The Assignment Problem

As our final topic in this chapter we examine projects consisting of many activities which can proceed simultaneously. The optimal planning of such operations is to assign available resources to the different tasks in a way which minimises the overall project time. In the worked example we assign manpower to jobs in an optimal way but the assignment problem in general applies to machinery or treatments assigned to different tasks.

### The Zoo Example

A small zoo has 5 animal cages and 5 keepers. The time each keeper takes to feed each animal is given in Table 5.6.

**Table 5.6**

| Feeding time in minutes | Lions | Bears | Giraffes | Monkeys | Birds |
|---|---|---|---|---|---|
| Alf | 30 | 21 | 10 | 19 | 13 |
| Bob | 25 | 15 | 15 | 25 | 13 |
| Cathy | 30 | 22 | 15 | 20 | 16 |
| Doris | — | 20 | 10 | 22 | 20 |
| Eric | 25 | 25 | 12 | 23 | 18 |

Notice that Doris is frightened of the lions and cannot be assigned to feed them. The zoo manager wants to allocate each type of animal to a specific keeper in a way which minimises the total feeding time.

*Solution*   The activity network diagram for an assignment problem has a special form as shown in Fig. 5.15.

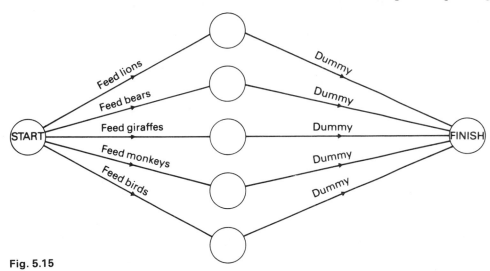

**Fig. 5.15**

Unfortunately we do not know the activity duration times to write on the network until an assignment of keepers is made. This is a similar dilemma to that of the Cookery Example and again we have 120 possible networks to consider. The use of a computer to do this is discussed in the chapter on Computer Modelling but we continue here with the description of an algorithm for finding the optimal assignment. We deal with the constraint that Doris cannot feed the lions by giving that activity a very large cost relative to the others, in this case, say, 100 minutes. This ensures that the activity will not appear in a lowest cost assignment.

*Step 1    Reduce each row and column of the cost matrix by its lowest entry. Any assignment using only the zero entries will be optimal.*

Consider the first keeper on the list, Alf. The least time he takes to feed any animal is 10 minutes and he has to be used somehow in the operation. This minimum of 10 minutes can thus be 'written off' as a necessary expenditure of time. Subtracting it from all the entries in Alf's row gives the 'penalties' over and above this cost for assigning him to the various jobs. Using the same argument for all the keepers we obtain the new cost matrix.

**Table 5.7**

| Minutes | Lions | Bears | Giraffes | Monkeys | Birds | Reduction |
|---------|-------|-------|----------|---------|-------|-----------|
| Alf     | 20    | 11    | 0        | 9       | 3     | 10        |
| Bob     | 12    | 2     | 2        | 12      | 0     | 13        |
| Cathy   | 15    | 7     | 0        | 5       | 1     | 15        |
| Doris   | 90    | 10    | 0        | 12      | 10    | 10        |
| Eric    | 13    | 13    | 0        | 11      | 6     | 12        |

We now examine the columns of Table 5.7 and see that feeding the lions, for example, incurs a penalty cost of at least 12 minutes. Someone has to feed the lions and so this column minimum is a necessary expenditure of time. We can extend this argument to all the animals and subtract each column minimum from all the entries in the column to find the penalties from non-optimal assignments. This gives us Table 5.8.

The cost matrix reduction performed above is similar to that of the Tourist Example in Chapter 4. As in that example, we can add all the row and column reductions to give

**Table 5.8**

| Minutes | Lions | Bears | Giraffes | Monkeys | Birds |
|---------|-------|-------|----------|---------|-------|
| Alf | 8 | 9 | 0 | 4 | 3 |
| Bob | 0 | 0 | 2 | 7 | 0 |
| Cathy | 3 | 5 | 0 | 0 | 1 |
| Doris | 78 | 8 | 0 | 7 | 10 |
| Eric | 1 | 11 | 0 | 6 | 6 |
| Reduction | 12 | 2 | 0 | 5 | 0 |

the minimum possible project time. In this case we obtain the value 79 minutes, but this will be attainable only if we can find an assignment of keepers to animals using the zero cost cells alone.

To investigate this possibility, we start with those rows and columns with just one zero in them. Such zeroes must be utilised for the minimum cost solution to be achieved. In this problem we see that whilst Alf must be assigned to feed the Giraffes, that allocation precludes Doris from doing so but there is no other zero in Doris' row. Hence there cannot be an assignment using only zero cost cells and we proceed to the next step of the algorithm.

*Step 2    Draw lines through the least number of rows and columns to delete all the zero entries. Subtract the lowest uncovered entry from all the uncovered entries. Add its value to any number covered by 2 lines.*

We want to reduce the matrix still further in order to introduce more zero cost cells with which to derive an optimal assignment. In order that the subtractions involved will not result in negative entries we must not apply them to any row or column containing a zero and these are therefore marked. In our example we cross through the Giraffes' column and Bob and Cathy's rows.

The manner in which the remainder of this step creates a zero in the table is quite cunning. In the discussion of Step 1 we saw that a constant can be subtracted from a row or a column without changing the values of the costs relative to each other. We now incur the least possible penalty by choosing the smallest uncovered entry to subtract from all the others. However, in order to avoid negative entries appearing we add back the same amount to covered cells thus preserving their original values. The only snag with this 'subtract everywhere but add back the same amount to covered cells' procedure is that entries with *two* lines through them have the subtraction compensated for twice and the net result is an increase in their value by the amount used. Hence the mechanics of the step are to subtract the minimum uncovered entry from all uncovered cells, thus creating a zero, leave once-covered cells unchanged and add the amount to twice-covered ones.

In our example we obtain the new cost matrix (Table 5.9).

**Table 5.9**

| Minutes | Lions | Bears | Giraffes | Monkeys | Birds |
|---------|-------|-------|----------|---------|-------|
| Alf | 7 | 8 | 0 | 3 | 2 |
| Bob | 0 | 0 | 3 | 7 | 0 |
| Cathy | 3 | 5 | 1 | 0 | 1 |
| Doris | 77 | 7 | 0 | 6 | 9 |
| Eric | 0 | 10 | 0 | 5 | 5 |

The next step is concerned with finding an assignment using the zero cost cells only. Such an allocation will be optimal.

*Step 3   If there are any assignments using only the zero cost cells then they are optimal. Otherwise go back to Step 2.*

The latest matrix represents the least reduction in the previous one which creates an extra zero entry. If that cell cannot help to solve the problem then the matrix must be further reduced, with correspondingly larger penalties, using Step 2.

In Table 5.9, starting with rows or columns with just one zero in them, we see that both Alf and Doris must be assigned to the Giraffes and that this is impossible. Hence we return to Step 2 and obtain a new matrix (Table 5.10).

**Table 5.10**

| Minutes | Lions | Bears | Giraffes | Monkeys | Birds |
|---------|-------|-------|----------|---------|-------|
| Alf     | 5     | 6     | 0        | 1       | 0     |
| Bob     | 0     | 0     | 5        | 7       | 0     |
| Cathy   | 3     | 5     | 3        | 0       | 1     |
| Doris   | 75    | 5     | 0        | 4       | 7     |
| Eric    | 0     | 10    | 2        | 5       | 5     |

We have now arrived at Step 3 for the second time. Examining the rows and columns with just one zero entry in them we see that Cathy, Doris and Eric must feed the Monkeys, Giraffes and Lions respectively. This leaves the Bears and the Birds unassigned but if Bob feeds the Bears and Alf feeds the Birds then only zero cost cells have been used.

Our answer to the problem is therefore: **Alf feeds the Birds, Bob feeds the Bears, Cathy feeds the Monkeys, Doris feeds the Giraffes and Eric feeds the Lions. The total feeding time of this assignment, found by adding the appropriate times together from the original data, is 83 minutes.**

## Computer Program

The following program accepts as input data the durations of the activities in a network. It performs a critical path analysis, prints out the earliest start and finish times for each activity and identifies those on a critical path. In running the program it is important that the head event of each activity has a larger event number than the tail event. For example, if an activity is given as being a line between events 3 and 4 on the network then the program will assume that the arrow on the activity goes *from* 3 *to* 4. The method used by the program is the one developed in the Coffee Making Example and an execution for that particular network follows the listing. Although the program can handle a network with at most 100 nodes, this restriction can be easily relaxed by altering line 3∅.

```
10 PRINT "CRITICAL PATH PROGRAM"
20 PRINT "----------------------"
30 DIM T(100,100),E(100),L(100)
40 FOR I=1 TO 50
50 E(I)=0
60 FOR J=1 TO 50
70 T(I,J)=-1
80 NEXT J
90 NEXT I
100 M=0
110 PRINT "ENTER ACTIVITIES AS TAIL EVENT, HEAD EVENT,"
120 PRINT "DURATION.  END INPUT WITH 3 ZEROS"
130 INPUT I,J,D
140 IF I=0 THEN 210
150 IF M>I THEN 170
160 M=I
170 IF M>J THEN 190
180 M=J
190 T(I,J)=D
200 GOTO 130
210 FOR I=1 TO M
220 FOR J=I+1 TO M
230 IF T(I,J)=-1 THEN 260
240 IF E(J)>E(I)+T(I,J) THEN 260
250 E(J)=E(I)+T(I,J)
260 NEXT J
270 NEXT I
280 PRINT "TOTAL PROJECT TIME IS ";E(M)
290 FOR K=1 TO M
300 L(K)=E(M)
310 NEXT K
320 FOR J1=1 TO M-1
330 J=M+1-J1
340 FOR I=1 TO J-1
350 IF T(I,J)=-1 THEN 380
360 IF L(I)<L(J)-T(I,J) THEN 380
370 L(I)=L(J)-T(I,J)
380 NEXT I
390 NEXT J1
400 FOR I=1 TO M
410 FOR J=I+1 TO M
420 IF T(I,J)=-1 THEN 540
430 PRINT
440 PRINT "ACTIVITY FROM EVENT ";I;" TO EVENT ";J
450 PRINT "------------------------------------"
460 IF T(I,J)<>L(J)-E(I) THEN 480
470 PRINT "*** CRITICAL ***"
480 PRINT
490 PRINT " DURATION          ";T(I,J)
500 PRINT " EARLIEST START    ";E(I)
510 PRINT " LATEST START      ";L(I)
520 PRINT " EARLIEST FINISH ";E(J)
530 PRINT " LATEST FINISH     ";L(J)
540 NEXT J
550 NEXT I
560 END
```

**Specimen Run**

```
CRITICAL PATH PROGRAM
---------------------
ENTER ACTIVITIES AS TAIL EVENT, HEAD EVENT,
DURATION.  END INPUT WITH 3 ZEROS
 ?1,2,5
 ?2,4,60
 ?1,3,10
 ?3,4,4
 ?4,5,12
 ?0,0,0
TOTAL PROJECT TIME IS 77

ACTIVITY FROM EVENT  1 TO EVENT  2
----------------------------------
*** CRITICAL ***

 DURATION          5
 EARLIEST START    0
 LATEST START      0
 EARLIEST FINISH   5
 LATEST FINISH     5

ACTIVITY FROM EVENT  1 TO EVENT  3
----------------------------------

 DURATION          10
 EARLIEST START    0
 LATEST START      0
 EARLIEST FINISH   10
 LATEST FINISH     61

ACTIVITY FROM EVENT  2 TO EVENT  4
----------------------------------
*** CRITICAL ***

 DURATION          60
 EARLIEST START    5
 LATEST START      5
 EARLIEST FINISH   65
 LATEST FINISH     65

ACTIVITY FROM EVENT  3 TO EVENT  4
----------------------------------

 DURATION          4
 EARLIEST START    10
 LATEST START      61
 EARLIEST FINISH   65
 LATEST FINISH     65

ACTIVITY FROM EVENT  4 TO EVENT  5
----------------------------------
```

```
*** CRITICAL ***

DURATION           12
EARLIEST START     65
LATEST START       65
EARLIEST FINISH    77
LATEST FINISH      77
```

**Program Notes**

**1**   Lines 1$\emptyset$ to 3$\emptyset$ print a heading and open arrays which will store the activity durations and the earliest start and latest finish times for the events.

**2**   Lines 4$\emptyset$ to 9$\emptyset$ initialise the earliest start times to zero and the activity times to $-1$. The latter is done to enable those connections between events which are not given as activities by the user to be identified later.

**3**   Lines 1$\emptyset\emptyset$ to 2$\emptyset\emptyset$ read the details of the activity durations from the user. The variable M, which is initially equal to $\emptyset$, is updated to a higher value if either of the event numbers read for a particular activity is larger than it. By the end of the input phase, it therefore records the largest event number which appeared in the data.

**4**   Lines 21$\emptyset$ to 27$\emptyset$ work through the events from 1 to M. Line 23$\emptyset$ rejects pairs of events which do not have an activity connecting them while lines 24$\emptyset$ and 25$\emptyset$ amend the earliest time of the head event of the activity if the earliest time of the tail event and the activity duration so dictate.

**5**   When all the activities have been processed, line 28$\emptyset$ prints the earliest start time of the final event as the total project time. Lines 29$\emptyset$ to 39$\emptyset$ work backwards through the network calculating the latest finish times. This is performed in accordance with the algorithm described earlier in the chapter.

**6**   The remainder of the program prints out all the activities and their details with line 46$\emptyset$ testing whether the activity is critical or not.

## Summary

**1**   Critical Path Analysis is a method for calculating the minimum time in which a project can be executed and for identifying those component activities of the project which are crucial to that time being realised. A sequence of such activities, all of which have to be completed on time, is called a critical path. Any activity not on a critical path has a float time within which it can be delayed without affecting the overall project time.

**2**   In the Project Evaluation and Review Technique, PERT, activity durations are not treated deterministically but are assumed to have the beta distribution of probability. The most likely duration, the optimistic value and the pessimistic value are specified for each activity and its expected duration calculated. A critical path analysis is performed and by assuming that the resulting event times are normally distributed various probabilities can be evaluated.

**3**   Crashing an activity involves spending more resources, usually money, in order to reduce its duration time. Gantt charts and bar charts are used to give a clear picture of the scheduling of the activities and the demand on the available resources as the project progresses.

**4**   When the resources available to carry out the activities of a project are limited, it is necessary to schedule the work in a way which optimises the usage of those resources.

This topic is called Production Scheduling and a simple case was considered in the Cookery Example.

**5** The Assignment Problem deals with projects in which all the activities can be performed together and there are adequate resources available for this to happen. It may then be possible to assign certain machines or people to certain tasks in a way which minimises the total project time.

## Further Reading

Critical Path Analysis is contained in most of the books listed in the 'General Operational Research' section of the Bibliography. References (19) and (20) are devoted entirely to it and as the method is widely used on construction and civil engineering projects the textbooks in those subjects often have relevant material.

Machine sequencing problems, in contrast to applications of critical path methods, are usually of a highly specialised nature. General techniques or analyses are therefore of limited value but a good treatment is given in reference (14). The complexity is aggravated by the need to optimise according to different criteria in different circumstances. For instance one production manager may want to minimise the total time one of his machines is running while another may wish to optimise the 'setting up' and 'tearing down' times involved in changing from one type of production run to another. Some sequencing problems can be formulated as jobs queuing for machines and the work of Chapter 10 on Queues may be of use, with its emphasis on simulation as a method of analysis.

The algorithm for solving the assignment problem is standard and can be found in many operational research textbooks. A more mathematical treatment than ours can be found in reference (1) which also illustrates its application to crew scheduling.

## Exercises

**1** The network diagram (Fig. 5.16) shows the relationship between the activities necessary to plan and stage a ballet. Determine the total project time, the critical path and the total, free and independent floats for all the activities.

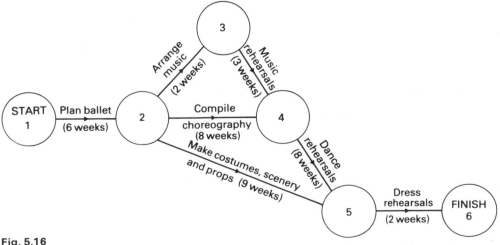

**Fig. 5.16**

**2**   The details of the activities involved in building a pyramid are given in Table 5.11.

**Table 5.11**

| Activity | Description | Must be preceded by | Optimistic duration (years) | Pessimistic duration (years) | Most likely duration (years) |
|---|---|---|---|---|---|
| A | Make plans | — | 1 | 3 | 2 |
| B | Round up slaves | — | 3 | 3 | 3 |
| C | Cut and transport rocks for statue and foundations | A, B | 7 | 11 | 8 |
| D | Train some slaves for statue carving | B | 2 | 4 | 3 |
| E | Carve statue of Pharaoh | C, D | 8 | 13 | 10 |
| F | Lay foundations | C | 5 | 15 | 10 |
| G | Move statue to base of pyramid | E, F | 3 | 7 | 5 |
| H | Lay rocks to form pyramid | G | 25 | 40 | 32 |

(i) Draw the network diagram and determine the expected total project time and the critical path.

(ii) Draw a Gantt chart for the activities.

(iii) Pharaoh's favourite wife has a baby boy as the project is begun. Use **PERT** to estimate the probability that the foundations of the pyramid will be laid by the boy's 21st birthday.

(iv) Use the normal distribution to estimate the probability that laying the foundations is delayed sufficiently to prolong the whole project.

**3**   A machine shop manager has several items to process and each one must pass through two stages with the times in each stage as follows:

| Item | A | B | C | D | E | F | G | H |
|---|---|---|---|---|---|---|---|---|
| Time in Stage 1 (hours) | 3 | 3 | 7 | 2 | 5 | 9 | 3 | 2 |
| Time in Stage 2 (hours) | 1 | 4 | 2 | 9 | 5 | 5 | 1 | 4 |

Find an order in which the items should be processed to minimise the total production time if only one item can be in each of the two stages at any one time.

**4**   A garage manager employs 5 mechanics and has 5 cars to allocate to them for repair. He believes that each mechanic will take a different time to attend to each vehicle in accordance with the following table:

| Time in hours Mechanic | Car | | | | |
|---|---|---|---|---|---|
| | A | B | C | D | E |
| Arthur | 11 | 11 | 4 | 7 | 16 |
| Bill | 10 | 13 | 5 | 9 | 14 |
| Charles | 9 | 9 | 3 | 6 | 17 |
| David | 12 | 11 | 4 | 8 | 16 |
| Eric | 13 | 12 | 5 | 10 | 16 |

(i) Determine an allocation of cars to mechanics which makes the overall time taken to repair the cars a minimum and give the value of that minimum time.

(ii) By how much would this optimum result be increased if, for some reason beyond the manager's control, Arthur is assigned to car E?

# Part 2   Stochastic Models

# 6 Probability, Expectation and Simulation

Chapters 2 to 5 were concerned with problems in which distances, times and other variables were almost always given precise numerical values. In many situations, however, there are quantities which are subject to random variation, like the weekly level of sales in a shop. Often the factors influencing the behaviour of these variables are so complicated that an exact analysis is either impossible or impractical. For example, we might be interested in whether a coin tossed into the air lands 'heads' or 'tails'. Now the laws of aerodynamics give a mathematical formulation of the way objects spin through the air and require a knowledge of, amongst other things, the launch velocity, mass distribution and axis of spin of the coin. The analysis itself is far from simple and would need the use of a computer if changes in the prevailing wind velocity were to be taken into account as well.

Fortunately it is not always necessary to have such a detailed **deterministic** model, in which, as the name implies, the system's precise status is determined as a set of accurate numerical quantities. We can choose to adopt a **stochastic** model, if appropriate, and describe the overall outcomes of the system's behaviour, like whether the coin lands 'heads' or 'tails', in statistical terms. To a certain extent this ignores the underlying factors which influence how those outcomes occur and indeed does not attempt to predict what will happen in any one operation of the system. Instead stochastic models give an average value over many operations, the probability of one outcome or another, or a trend line. This approach is particularly applicable in a subject like economics, where we know roughly which factors influence, say, the rate of inflation, but we cannot quantify that relationship in a deterministic way. There is then no alternative but to employ statistical methods of analysis.

**Statistics** itself is the science, some would say art, of converting the data gained from observing a system into useful information about that system. For instance, if one data item is that you are 5′ 10″ tall and another is that the river you have been thrown into with weights round your ankles is 6′ deep, then the information content is frighteningly clear. Of course it is not always quite so easy to extract relevant information from data and it has been said that statistical inference is like a bikini, what it reveals is interesting but what it conceals is vital.

In order to apply the optimisation philosophy of operational research to systems whose details we do not fully understand or cannot easily analyse, we borrow ideas from statistics and build stochastic models. In subsequent chapters we use averages, standard deviations and regression lines as statistical descriptions of system behaviour. In this chapter we develop the concept of probability and the associated topics of expectation and simulation.

## Probability

This is one of the main statistical tools used in operational research to gain information about a system. We try to compensate for our lack of knowledge of the detailed working of the system by making many observations of its outcomes. The relative frequency with which each one occurs is called its **probability** and the situation or experiment being observed is called a **trial**. For example, if the trial is 'tossing a coin' then the set of outcomes could be 'heads' and 'tails'. By tossing the coin many times we can estimate the probability of, say, 'heads' by dividing the number of times it occurs by the total number of tosses.

Note that there can be more than one set of outcomes relating to the same trial. In the coin tossing experiment, someone else might be interested in whether the coin falls down a drain or not. Our results on the number of 'heads' would be useless to such a person for the purpose of calculating probabilities. It is therefore necessary to specify the outcomes of interest as well as the nature of the trial in describing a probabilistic situation.

Clearly the number of repetitions of the trial should be as large as possible when measuring probabilities. This ensures that all the outcomes are represented in the sequence of results in the proportion with which they occur. The criterion for a scientific experiment to be valid is that other scientists can reproduce it if they wish. Therefore in a statistical experiment there should be sufficiently many trials for the values of the probabilities obtained to be approximately the same whenever the whole experiment is repeated.

So far we have discussed probabilities derived from observations of trials. These are called **a posteriori** probabilities as they are calculated after, 'post', the experiment has been performed. In practice, however, we often imagine what the results of such an experiment would be. For example, we expect the outcome 'heads' to occur for roughly half the number of times a fair coin is tossed and we can argue that the probability of 'heads' is therefore one half. Probabilities which have been deduced in this way are called **a priori** because they are estimated before, 'prior', any experiment has been performed, if indeed it is going to be performed at all. They are less reliable than a posteriori ones but are much less time consuming and expensive to evaluate. Of course, if the consequences of using them are unacceptable in that they give predictions for the real system which we observe to be false, then we must be prepared to revise them in the light of experimental data.

Before looking at some general properties of probabilities, we emphasise the importance of identifying correctly what the trial consists of and which are the outcomes of interest. For example, the probability that a person chosen at random has 14th July as his or her birthday can be argued to be 1/365. This ignores leap years and assumes that all of the 365 days of the year are equally likely as birthdays. Hence in every 365 trials where someone is chosen at random and asked for their birthday we expect one person to give the answer 14th July. So far so good and we have here a model example of the derivation of an a priori probability. We could even allow for leap years by arguing that on average there are $365\frac{1}{4}$ days in a year and so the probability is $1/365\frac{1}{4}$.

Suppose now that the trial is to ask two people chosen at random whether they have the same birthday as each other. What is the probability that they have? The trial here is in fact whether the second person says, 'Mine's the same' or, 'Mine's not the same' when told the first person's birthday. The first person's birthday is not itself an outcome of interest but merely replaces '14th July' in the previous problem. Therefore the probability of the second person agreeing with the first person is 1/365, and is the same answer as before.

We now investigate some of the general properties of probabilities. As they are relative frequencies their values are always between 0 and 1. The former value itself arises if the outcome concerned never occurs and is therefore considered to be impossible, while the latter value is a consequence of the outcome always occurring and being certain. Other values of probabilities represent varying degrees of likelihood between these two extremes.

In certain circumstances probabilities can be added together to give meaningful results. While the next example shows how this can be done, the multiplication of probabilities is illustrated in the next chapter.

### The Playing Card Example

A playing card is chosen at random from a pack of 52 cards. The 52 possible outcomes to this trial can be displayed as a diagram called the **outcome space** or **sample space** (Fig. 6.1). In set theory it is called a **Venn diagram.**

**Fig. 6.1**

|  | Ace | 2 | 3 | 4 | 5 | 6 | 7 | 8 | 9 | 10 | Jack | Queen | King |
|---|---|---|---|---|---|---|---|---|---|---|---|---|---|
| Hearts | . | . | . | . | . | . | . | . | . | . | . | . | . |
| Diamonds | . | . | . | . | . | . | . | . | . | . | . | . | . |
| Clubs | . | . | . | . | . | . | . | . | . | . | . | . | . |
| Spades | . | . | . | . | . | . | . | . | . | . | . | . | . |

*Question 1*   What is the probability of choosing the 2 of Clubs?

*Solution*   Using the a priori argument that for every 52 trials one of the cards will be the 2 of Clubs, we deduce that the probability of the 2 of Clubs, which we write as **$P$(2 of Clubs), is 1/52.** Note that in repeating a trial the conditions which existed originally must be restored. In this case, the card chosen is considered to be returned to the pack each time otherwise the trial is not an exact repetition of the previous one.

*Question 2*   What is the probability of choosing any 2?

*Solution*   On average 4 out of every 52 cards chosen will be a '2' as there are 4 '2's in the pack. Hence the answer is 4/52. We can also obtain this from the last solution as the fraction of trials resulting in 'any 2' is the sum of the fractions of times the 2 of Hearts, the 2 of Diamonds, the 2 of Clubs and the 2 of Spades occur. Hence

$$P(\text{any } 2) = \frac{1}{52} + \frac{1}{52} + \frac{1}{52} + \frac{1}{52} = \frac{4}{\mathbf{52}}, \text{ as before.} \tag{6.1}$$

*Question 3*   What is the probability of not getting a 2?

*Solution*   There are 48 cards which are not '2's, therefore $P$(not 2) is 48/52. Alternatively we can argue that on any trial the card chosen is either a '2' or it is not a '2'. Thus the fraction of trials on which a '2' occurs and the fraction on which a '2' does not occur must add up to 1. We can therefore calculate that

$$P(\textbf{not } 2) = 1 - P(\text{any } 2) = 1 - 4/52 = \mathbf{48/52,} \text{ as before.} \tag{6.2}$$

Using the letter A to stand for any event, we can generalise this idea:

$$P(\text{not A}) = 1 - P(\text{A}) \tag{6.3}$$

*Question 4*   What is the probability of choosing any 2 or any Club or both?

*Solution*   We see from Fig. 6.2 that there are 16 playing cards which are either a '2' or a Club or both.

**Fig. 6.2**

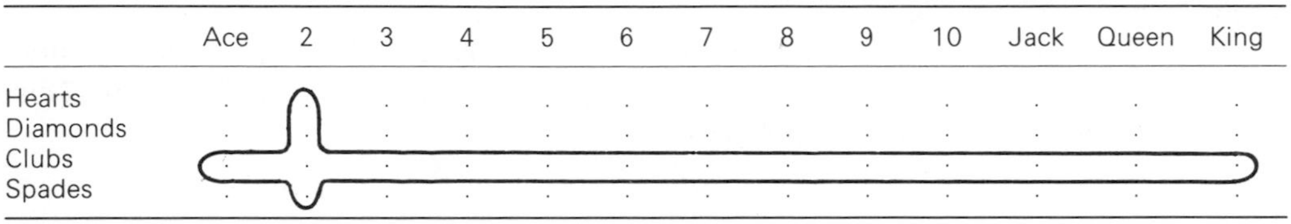

| | Ace | 2 | 3 | 4 | 5 | 6 | 7 | 8 | 9 | 10 | Jack | Queen | King |
|---|---|---|---|---|---|---|---|---|---|---|---|---|---|
| Hearts | · | · | · | · | · | · | · | · | · | · | · | · | · |
| Diamonds | · | · | · | · | · | · | · | · | · | · | · | · | · |
| Clubs | · | · | · | · | · | · | · | · | · | · | · | · | · |
| Spades | · | · | · | · | · | · | · | · | · | · | · | · | · |

Hence $P(2$ or Club or both$)$ is 16/52. The answer can be arrived at by calculation as well as by simply counting the dots in the diagram. The set 'any 2 or any Club or both' is the amalgamation or **union** of the sets 'any 2', which contains 4 cards, and 'any Club', which contains 13 cards. The number of cards in their union is the sum of these numbers minus the number of cards in the region where they overlap. Any points in this region, called the **intersection** of the two sets, have been counted twice, once in each set. Dividing all the numbers by 52 to turn them into probabilities, we see that

$$\textbf{P(any 2 or any Club or both)} = P(\text{any 2}) + P(\text{any Club}) - P(2 \text{ of Clubs})$$
$$= \frac{4}{52} + \frac{13}{52} - \frac{1}{52}$$
$$= \textbf{16/52,} \text{ as we found before.} \tag{6.4}$$

Using the letters A and B to stand for any two events, this equation can be generalised

$$P(\text{A or B or both}) = P(\text{A}) + P(\text{B}) - P(\text{A and B}) \tag{6.5}$$

*Question 5*   What is the probability of choosing any 2 or any 5?

*Solution*   The number of cards which are 'any 2 or any 5' is 8 and so the answer we want is 8/52. Alternatively, using the formula above with A corresponding to the event 'any 2' and B to the event 'any 5' we obtain

$$\textbf{P(any 2 or any 5 or both)} = P(\text{any 2}) + P(\text{any 5}) - P(\text{any 2 and any 5})$$
$$= \frac{4}{52} + \frac{4}{52} - \frac{0}{52}$$
$$= \frac{\textbf{8}}{\textbf{52}} \tag{6.6}$$

Notice that $P(\text{any 2 and any 5})$ is zero because a chosen card cannot be both a '2' and a '5'. Events which cannot occur together like this are called **mutually exclusive** and formula (6.5) reduces to a simple addition rule for their probabilities. An example of this can be seen in the solution to Question 2.

# Expectation

Many trials have a numerical value, called the **payoff**, associated with each of their outcomes. The expected value of the payoff enables us to take a long-term view of the way the trial behaves. This can help in making management decisions as it predicts the average cost or profit yielded by a large number of repetitions of the trial.

### The Gaming Example

Alf and Bob play a game whereby Alf gives Bob £6 if the result of throwing an unbiased die is '5' or '6' while Bob gives Alf £5 if the result is '1', '2' or '3'. Is the game fair to Alf?

*Solution*    The trial in this problem is the throwing of a die which produces one of the numbers 1, 2, 3, 4, 5, or 6. As money changes hands on the events '1, 2 or 3' and '5 or 6', we take these as the outcomes of interest for the trial. It is necessary to include the outcome '4' in the set to make it complete in the sense that we want to account for every possible number which can occur in the trial, including '4'. Table 6.1 gives the outcomes, their probabilities and the resulting payoffs to Alf.

**Table 6.1**

| Outcome | 1, 2 or 3 | 4 | 5 or 6 |
|---|---|---|---|
| Probability | 3/6 | 1/6 | 2/6 |
| Payoff to Alf (£) | +5 | 0 | −6 |

An assignment of probabilities across all the possible outcomes of a trial like this is called a **probability distribution**. The total probability of 1 is distributed over the outcomes and we can check that every possibility is incorporated by adding the probabilities together to make 1.

To decide whether the game is fair to Alf, we imagine 100 games being played and calculate the total expected payoff to him. Table 6.1 predicts that 3/6 of them will give Alf a payoff of $+5$, having a total cash value of $\frac{3}{6} \times 100 \times (+5)$. The table also implies that 1/6 of the 100 trials will give him 0 and 2/6 of them will result in $-6$. Adding the 3 totals we obtain

$$\text{Total payoff to Alf over 100 games} = \frac{3}{6} \times 100 \times (+5) + \frac{1}{6} \times 100 \times (0) + \frac{2}{6} \times 100 \times (-6) \quad (6.7)$$

The expected payoff to Alf *per game* is found by dividing this by the number of games, 100.

$$\textbf{Expected payoff to Alf per game} = \frac{3}{6} \times (+5) + \frac{1}{6} \times (0) + \frac{2}{6} \times (-6) = \textbf{+0.5} \quad (6.8)$$

There is nothing special about the number of games being 100 and any similar number would have cancelled out of equation (6.7) to give the same result (6.8). We therefore deduce the general formula for the **expectation** or expected payoff of a probability distribution to be

**Expectation = Sum over all possible outcomes of the probability times the payoff**    (6.9)

It is in fact an average of the various payoffs possible with each one weighted in proportion to its probability.

We now look at the use of expectations in helping to make decisions. Indeed, the result of the last example could influence Alf in deciding whether to play the game or not. The answer suggests that, provided he plays many such games rather than just one, and this is an important consideration, he will win on average. Bob, however, will receive the opposite advice as his expected payoff per game is $-0.5$. He may want to alter the values of the payoffs or charge Alf a 50p 'entrance fee' for the privilege of playing a game.

Strictly speaking, the expectation is a meaningful average only when many trials are performed. However, **games theory**, which is the study of probabilistic situations with payoffs to various players, is often applied when the trial occurs just once. It is used in military operations, for example, when the attack or battle will be fought once yet the strategy can be selected which gives the lowest expectation of casualties. There are also occasions in business when a company has an opportunity of running a venture having an element of financial risk associated with it. The next example illustrates the general problem.

### The Oil Company Example

An oil company thinks a particular site has a chance of containing oil. Drilling costs £100 000 and if oil is found it estimates that it will give a profit in present value terms of between £550 000 and £750 000.

*Question 1*   If it estimates the probability of oil being found to be 8%, does the expected payoff indicate that it would be profitable to drill?

*Solution*   The probability distribution for the trial 'drilling for oil' is given in Table 6.2.

**Table 6.2**

| Outcome | Oil | No Oil |
|---|---|---|
| Probability | 0.08 | 0.92 $(=1-0.08)$ |
| Payoff (£) | $+650\,000$ | $-100\,000$ |

Note the use of the mid-point, 650 000, of the given range of possible profit when oil is found. In the absence of more information it is the only estimate of this payoff we have.

Using formula (6.9), the expected profit is

$$0.08 \times (+650\,000) + 0.92 \times (-100\,000) = -40\,000 \qquad (6.10)$$

Comparing this expected loss of £40 000 with the zero payoff of not drilling at all, we see that our calculation indicates that **the company should not drill.**

Obviously decisions like whether to drill for oil are never made solely on the basis of the expected payoff, but, together with reports from geologists and others, such calculations can be of help. The reason for this, and the difference between using expectations and probabilities in this example and the Gaming Example, needs emphasising. When drilling for oil there can be only one trial whereas the concepts of probability and expectation are based on there being many many trials. Furthermore the probability of

8% quoted in the question cannot be measured directly as the trial has never yet taken place. The figure has been estimated presumably from the experiences of the company and its experts on other sites. In contrast, the inherent nature of the Gaming Example is the repetition of the trial. This allows the so-called 'Law of Averages', which incidentally statisticians call the Law of Large Numbers, to have an effect on the system's behaviour.

This objection to the use of probabilities and expectations in certain non-repeating stochastic situations sometimes prompts managers to turn to an 'optimistic', 'pessimistic' and 'most likely' approach similar to that of PERT in Chapter 5. The oil company could possibly gain £650 000 by drilling, a sum of money the manager might like the look of irrespective of its low probability. The optimistic decision is to drill as it gives a greater 'best payoff' than not drilling which gives the payoff of zero. On the other hand, the pessimistic decision is not to drill because the worst payoff of drilling is less than the payoff of not drilling. The 'most likely' outcome method suggests not drilling as the most likely outcome of drilling, with 92% probability, is to make a loss. Notice that to get a positive decision to do anything from a pessimistic approach the worst outcome has to be better than doing nothing while to refrain from action in the optimistic approach needs the best outcome to be worse than doing nothing. A compromise method is the 'most likely' criterion which suggests not drilling in this example, as the outcome with the highest probability, 92% in fact, results in a loss.

Those with statistical knowledge will appreciate the connection between the expectation of a probability distribution and the average of a sample, the 'optimistic' outcome with the maximum of a sample, the 'pessimistic' one with the minimum, and the 'most likely' with the mode. Each of these measures gives a different way of describing a probability distribution in an analogous way that the mean, maximum, minimum and mode are different descriptors of a statistical sample.

The intelligent manager will treat the expected payoff and other statistical measures as a management tool in the decision-making process alongside reports and opinions from accountants, lawyers and other experts. The quantitative work presented here is just part of the information necessary for such a decision.

The objection raised above to the use of a probability when the trial has never been performed and in any case will occur only once is overcome to a certain extent by the following analysis.

*Question 2*  Calculate the probability of oil being found which makes the company indifferent to drilling because the expected payoff is zero. How can this value help in the decision-making process?

*Solution*  We have now abandoned the company's estimate of 8% for the probability of oil in favour of a 'breakeven' analysis. This exposes the sensitivity of the expectation to the probability of finding oil. Calling this number $p$ the probability distribution for drilling is:

| Outcome | Oil | No oil |
|---|---|---|
| Probability | $p$ | $1 - p$ |
| Payoff (£) | $+650\,000$ | $-100\,000$ |

The expected payoff is

$$p \times (+650\,000) + (1-p) \times (-100\,000)$$
$$= 650\,000p - 100\,000 + 100\,000p$$
$$= 750\,000p - 100\,000 \qquad\qquad (6.11)$$

and we can tabulate or graph its value for different values of $p$.

From Fig. 6.3 we can read off the threshold value for $p$ between drilling being profitable and unprofitable. It is about 0.13, or 13%, and alternatively it can be calculated by solving the equation obtained by putting (6.11) equal to zero. If the company thinks there is a smaller chance than this of finding oil, then the expectation is negative and it should not drill. If on the other hand it estimates the probability to be greater then the expected payoff is positive and it should drill. If the probability of oil is thought to be exactly 13%, a very unlikely eventuality, then the expectation is zero and does not indicate whether to

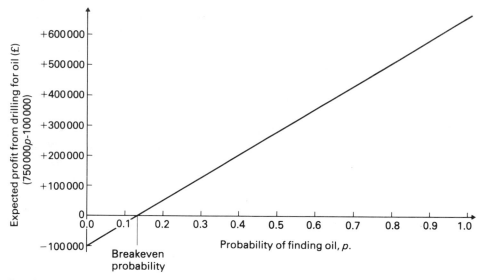

**Fig. 6.3**   Graph of the expected profit from drilling for the Oil Company example

drill or not. This **breakeven analysis** does not require the manager to provide an estimate of the probability of finding oil as in Question 1. Instead, the advice is **'Drill if you think there is a greater than 13% chance of finding oil'**. It is a more positive way of sounding out geologists and other experts and does not ask them to be mathematically precise about their professional opinion.

Figure 6.3 also gives a **sensitivity analysis** of the expected payoff on the probability of success. Sometimes it is considered that the probability in question is greater than the critical value but not by very much. The graph gives an idea of how sensitive the situation is to the exact probability and whether the expected payoffs for probabilities close to the breakeven one are sufficiently large to warrant drilling. For example, if $p$ is considered to be around 20% then the graph shows an expectation of £50 000, as indeed can be calculated from equation (6.11) with $p$ equal to 0.2. Management must then decide whether this level of profit is worth risking an outlay of £100 000 to drill.

Even when a decision is made to adopt a course of action giving a negative expected payoff, the expectation gives managers an idea of the size of the loss they should anticipate. In other words, when the choice is between the devil and the deep blue sea, expectations can quantify the wickedness of the devil and the depth of the sea!

## Simulation

A knowledge of the probabilities of the outcomes and the associated expected payoff is sometimes insufficient to answer all our questions about the trial. In the next example we simulate the results of many trials using random numbers in order to study the long-term behaviour of a system.

### The Chef Example
The number of customers at a restaurant each evening is distributed as shown below.

| Number of customers | Lots | Average | Very few |
|---|---|---|---|
| Probability | 0.2 | 0.4 | 0.4 |

The chef refuses to work on an evening when there are very few customers and walks out. He will not return to work until an evening when there are lots of customers although he always comes in on Fridays because he gets paid then. We are interested in the fraction of evenings that the chef is at the restaurant.

*Solution*   The trial in this example is whether the number of customers is 'lots', 'average' or 'very few' and it is repeated for each evening that the restaurant is open. Whether the chef is 'in' or 'out' depends not only on the outcome of this trial but also on his whereabouts the previous evening and whether it is a Friday or not. As we shall see in the chapters on Stock Control and Queues, simulation problems are typified by having one or more trials whose outcomes have to be combined with various rules before they tell us how the system is behaving.

The method of simulation is to 'play through' many time periods of the system's operations on paper or on a computer in order to analyse its progress. We do this by interpreting the outcomes of some readily repeatable trials, like throwing a die or choosing a number at random, as if they were the outcomes of the trials in the real system. For example, if it was equally likely to be 'raining' or 'sunny' each day, we could simulate the weather by tossing a coin. 'Heads' could stand for 'raining' and 'tails' for 'sunny'. The sequence of outcomes generated then forms a simulated record of the system's history. Any long-term averages, maxima or minima etc. required can be calculated from this record.

In the present example we simulate the level of attendance at the restaurant on each evening. The rules governing the chef's behaviour given in the question are then used to determine whether he is 'in' or 'out' on that particular evening. The sequence of 'in's and 'out's forms a simulated history of the system and enables us to calculate the fraction of evenings for which the chef is 'in'.

Our first task, then, is to simulate the number of customers each evening. One way is to use random digits and the given distribution as follows (Table 6.3).

**Table 6.3**

| Number of customers | Lots | Average | Very few |
|---|---|---|---|
| Probability | 0.2 | 0.4 | 0.4 |
| Digits | 0,1 | 2, 3, 4, 5 | 6, 7, 8, 9 |

The attendance on a specific evening is simulated by choosing a digit, from 0 to 9 inclusive, at random. Using the table above we can interpret the digit as a state of the restaurant and because of the number of digits allocated to each one, the outcomes in the simulation will have the same probability of occurrence as those in the real system. Clearly this is important if the simulation is to be an accurate enactment of that system.

Having generated an attendance level in this way, we can determine whether the chef works or not by the rules given in the question. Table 6.4 is a specimen run of the simulation.

**Table 6.4**

| Day | Day of the week | Random digit | Number of customers | Chef | Number of days 'in' to date | Fraction of days 'in' to date |
|---|---|---|---|---|---|---|
| 1 | Monday | 3 | Average | In | 1 | 1.00 |
| 2 | Tuesday | 5 | Average | In | 2 | 1.00 |
| 3 | Wednesday | 1 | Lots | In | 3 | 1.00 |
| 4 | Thursday | 8 | Very few | Out | 3 | 0.75 |
| 5 | Friday | 6 | Very few | In | 4 | 0.80 |
| 6 | Saturday | 6 | Very few | Out | 4 | 0.67 |
| 7 | Sunday | 4 | Average | Out | 4 | 0.57 |
| 8 | Monday | 4 | Average | Out | 4 | 0.50 |
| 9 | Tuesday | 0 | Lots | In | 5 | 0.56 |
| 10 | Wednesday ... | | | | | |

The random digits should not be 'dreamed up' as the human mind tends to be biased towards, or away from, certain digits. Most published books of statistical tables, like (30), contain random numbers and many computers and calculators have the facility to generate them. The tables are used by choosing a digit within the table at random and taking further digits from along the same row or column or again choosing one at random. It is also possible to generate random numbers by throwing dice, tossing coins, etc.

The specimen run (Table 6.4) was started with a 'Monday' and with the chef being 'In'. Bearing in mind that we are trying to reproduce the long-term behaviour of the restaurant the initial conditions of the simulation will not affect the results we obtain. Computer simulations are often carried out over hundreds if not thousands of simulated time periods, hence any contribution made by numerical values from the first few time periods to the long-term averages is negligible.

As far as measuring any average effects is concerned, the more time periods simulated the better. In practice, however, we need a criterion for deciding when the simulation should stop. In the specimen run we could continue until the fraction at the end of each line does not change very much. When this happens there is no point in going on and we have the answer we want. In our example, it tends to 0.49 and **the chef is 'in' for 49% of all days.** Another criterion for stopping the simulation is to use the sequence of random digits employed in it to solve a problem with a known solution. When this known solution is achieved we assume that the simulation has proceeded sufficiently far. In the Chef Example we could calculate, for each evening, the average of all the random numbers used to date. When this average becomes close to its expectation, 4.5, and stays close over several evenings, we can assume that the simulation can be stopped. Alternatively the probability distribution given in the question could be the 'known solution' and we could count the fraction of evenings simulated with 'lots', 'average' and 'very few' customers. When these experimental probabilities are close to 0.2, 0.4, and 0.4 respectively then the distribution observed in the simulation is the same as that in the real system. The simulation is then exhibiting the same long-term properties as the real system and can be ended.

The methods described above for deciding when to stop are applicable to all computer or manual simulations. However, the advent of interactive computing has enhanced the value of simulation just as it has changed the way we use computers in other applications. With the computer user present at a terminal during the running of the simulation, the program can pause to ask for the user's decisions or give regular progress reports. In particular, the user can decide, as the simulation proceeds, how many time periods it should go on for and whether enough information has emerged to make further running pointless. This is the approach used in the computing example at the end of Chapter 9 on Stock Control. That example contains a more complicated probability distribution than the Chef Example, as do the Bank and Filling Station Examples of Chapter 10 on Queues. The reader is referred to those examples for further reading on simulation as well as to Chapter 13, while the computer program section at the end of this chapter contains a report on a longer simulation of the Chef Example than the specimen one above.

We finish this section by discussing a feature of simulation which is extremely useful to managers. By repeating the entire run with different governing rules we can see how changing those rules would affect the real system. This 'What If?' facility is demonstrated in the Stock Control Bakery Example of Chapter 9 where the re-order level, a parameter of the system, can be varied by the program user between simulations in order to find the value which results in the lowest cost.

An extension of this idea is incorporated in flight simulators for training pilots. A computer monitors the student's handling of the controls in a simulated aeroplane flight deck. The instruments are then operated by the computer to give the same readings that they would in a real flight. An instructor can intervene with 'catastrophes' like an engine failure or a bad storm and a television camera is moved over a model of some countryside to give the trainee visual feedback of how the aircraft is behaving.

The combination of computing and simulation has also resulted in the production of TV games. Players interrupt the way a computer program moves various images around the screen from a keyboard or hand-held controller. The computer incorporates their responses into these movements in accordance with the rules of the particular game. Incidentally such programs make extensive use of random numbers to determine the angle of deflection of tennis balls, the positioning of hostile space ships, etc.

In fact the idea of simulating real systems for entertainment purposes is not new. The game of chess is a non-probabilistic simulation of a battle between the white and black armies. The game of snakes and ladders was originally intended to simulate the moral progress of the players who moved up ladders when they were 'good' and fell down snakes, representing temptation, when they were 'bad'. As in many other board games, dice are used as random number generators.

## Computer Program

The examples of computer simulations contained in Chapters 9 and 10 were mentioned above. Computers are suited to performing simulations which for humans are tedious and time-consuming and most of them have a built-in capability to generate random numbers. Here is a BASIC program to carry out a simulation of the Chef Example.

```
1Ø PRINT "RESTAURANT SIMULATION"
2Ø PRINT "--------------------"
3Ø C=Ø
4Ø P=1
5Ø PRINT "HOW MANY WEEKS ARE TO"
6Ø PRINT "BE SIMULATED";
7Ø INPUT N
8Ø FOR I=1 TO N
9Ø FOR J=1 TO 6
1ØØ K=INT(1Ø*RND)
11Ø IF K>1 THEN 14Ø
12Ø P=1
13Ø GOTO 16Ø
14Ø IF K<6 THEN 16Ø
15Ø P=Ø
16Ø C=C+P
17Ø NEXT J
18Ø P=1
19Ø C=C+1
2ØØ NEXT I
21Ø F=C/(7*N)
22Ø PRINT
23Ø PRINT "FRACTION OF EVENINGS"
24Ø PRINT "CHEF IS IN ";F
25Ø END
```

### Specimen Run

```
RESTAURANT SIMULATION
--------------------
HOW MANY WEEKS ARE TO
BE SIMULATED ?1ØØØ

FRACTION OF EVENINGS
CHEF IS IN  Ø.5Ø1
```

### Program Notes

**1**   Line 3Ø sets C, the number of days the chef is 'in' to date (column 6 of the specimen simulation), to zero. Line 4Ø sets P, an indicator variable which is Ø if the chef is 'out' and 1 if he is 'in' (column 5 of the specimen simulation), to 1. Thus the run begins with the chef being 'in'.

**2**   Lines 5Ø, 6Ø and 7Ø ask the user how many weeks are to be simulated and store the answer as the variable N.

**3**   Line 8Ø starts a FOR loop to count N weeks and line 9Ø starts another to count 6 evenings within each week. Because the chef is always 'in' on Fridays, that particular evening in each week is dealt with separately after this 'day-count' loop has ended.

**4**  Line 10Ø creates a random digit, K, by multiplying the computer-generated decimal RND by 1Ø and taking the whole number part of it. Some computers will provide a random digit without this extra programming and the precise way the system is instructed to do this varies from machine to machine.

**5**  Lines 11Ø and 12Ø set P equal to 1 if the random digit K is Ø or 1. In other words, if the restaurant has 'lots' of customers according to Table 6.3 then the chef is 'in'.

**6**  Lines 14Ø and 15Ø set P equal to Ø if the random digit K is 6, 7, 8 or 9. In other words, if the restaurant has 'very few' customers according to Table 6.3 then the chef is 'out'.

**7**  Line 16Ø increases C, the number of days the chef is 'in' by the value of P. From whichever part of the program the computer has come, P will be Ø if the chef is 'out' and 1 if he is 'in'.

**8**  Lines 18Ø and 19Ø simulate each Friday of each week by putting P equal to 1 and increasing the value of C by 1. This is done because the chef always comes in on Fridays, as described in the question.

**9**  Lines 21Ø to 24Ø calculate and print out the fraction of evenings, F, in the simulation of the $(7 * N)$ evenings for which the chef is 'in'.

## Summary

**1**  $P(\text{event A}) = \left( \dfrac{\text{Number of times A occurs}}{\text{Number of trials performed}} \right)$

measured over a large number of trials.

**2**  $P(\text{not A}) = 1 - P(\text{A})$

**3**  $P(\text{A or B or both}) = P(\text{A}) + P(\text{B}) - P(\text{A and B})$

**4**  If A and B are mutually exclusive, which means that they cannot both occur at the same trial, then $P(\text{A and B})$ is zero and
$$P(\text{A or B}) = P(\text{A}) + P(\text{B})$$

**5**  The expectation of the payoff resulting from a trial with numerical outcomes is the sum of probability times payoff for every outcome. If the outcomes are ranges of numerical values then, in the absence of further information, the payoffs are taken to be the mid-points of the ranges.

**6**  Simulation identifies the outcomes of readily repeatable trials like choosing random digits or throwing a die with the outcomes which occur in a real system. This enables the system to be 'played through' on paper or in a computer in order to analyse its long-term behaviour.

## Further Reading

The concepts of probability theory considered in this chapter are fundamental to both statistics and operational research. Most of the books listed in the 'Statistics' section of the Bibliography include this material. References (25) and (27) are more mathematical with reference (24) being a good statistics book for non-mathematicians and mathematicians alike. Reference (28) contains many worked and unworked examples and (31) is devoted to the theory of games which was given a superficial treatment in the Gaming Example of this chapter.

Discussions of expectation and simulation are more often found in operational research books, for example reference (5), than statistics texts. Indeed, the remainder of this book makes almost constant use of these concepts. The computing aspects of simulation can be found in books such as (46), (47) and (49) which contain details of computer languages especially developed to facilitate the writing of simulation programs. Subsequent uses of simulation in this book, together with Chapter 13 on Computer Modelling, also form further reading on this topic.

## Exercises

**1**   A mysterious illness affects 337 out of every million people in the population. What is the probability that a person chosen at random suffers with this illness? How many would you expect to have the illness in a sample of 10 000 people chosen at random?

**2**   Four people sit in random order around a circular table. By considering all possible arrangements, calculate the probability that two given people are sitting next to each other.

**3**   Out of a hundred animals, 84 have long hair, 72 are dogs, and 13 of the dogs have short hair. Copy and complete this table which illustrates this information:

|              | Dog | Not dog | Total |
|--------------|-----|---------|-------|
| Long hair    |     |         | 84    |
| Not long hair| 13  |         |       |
| Total        | 72  |         | 100   |

(i) What is the probability of an animal chosen at random being a long-haired dog?

(ii) If the animal chosen is not a dog, so the outcome space is the second column of the table only, what is the probability of it being not long-haired? (Such tables are called **contingency** tables. Probabilities calculated in the light of partial information about the outcome of a trial are called **conditional** probabilities.)

**4**   In roulette, every number from 0 to 36 inclusive has an equal probability of occurring at each game. A gambler bets £1 that an odd number will result. If it does then the casino pays the gambler £2 while if the number is not odd the casino keeps his stake money. Calculate his expected loss per game.

**5**   A company estimates the profit of a new product it is considering marketing to have the following probability distribution:

| Profit (£)  | −15 000 to −5000 | −5000 to +5000 | +5000 to +20 000 |
|-------------|------------------|----------------|-------------------|
| Probability | 0.2              | 0.3            | 0.5               |

(i) Replace each profit range by its mid-point and calculate the company's expected profit. Does its value indicate that it should accept an offer of £5000 for all rights to the new product?

(ii) A second new product available to the company has the profit distribution:

| Profit (£) | − 5000 to 0 | 0 to + 5000 | + 5000 to + 9000 | + 9000 to + 15 000 |
|---|---|---|---|---|
| Probability | 0.1 | 0.1 | 0.3 | 0.5 |

Which product should it market to maximise its expected profit?

(iii) Which product should it market to maximise the maximum possible profit? This is the decision criterion of the optimist.

(iv) Which product should it market to minimise the maximum possible loss? This is the decision criterion of the pessimist.

**6** A die is thrown and the value of the outcome squared. Draw up an 'outcome, probability, payoff' table and calculate the expectation of the result. Notice that it is not the same as the square of the expected value of the dice throw.

**7** You are the captain of a nuclear submarine with just one guided missile left. There are two enemy aircraft within range and each carries 9 missiles. You have 0.5 probability of hitting the first aircraft but it will be able to fire one of its missiles before it is destroyed. The second aircraft can despatch two missiles before destruction and your missile has a higher probability of hitting it, namely 0.6. Both aircraft will fire all their missiles at you if they can. Which aircraft should you aim for in order to minimise the expected number of missiles fired back?

**8** A tower crane contains a part which costs either £100 if bought as a spare together with the crane, or £500 if bought at a later date. From experience a construction company finds that the number of these parts needed during the lifetime of a crane has the following probability distribution:

| Number of parts needed | 0 | 1 | 2 | 3 |
|---|---|---|---|---|
| Probability | 0.70 | 0.25 | 0.03 | 0.02 |

Calculate the expected cost of spares if the company does not buy any with the crane. Repeat the calculation if it buys 1 spare with the crane, then 2 spares with it and finally 3 spares with it. Hence advise it on how many spares to buy initially so that the expected cost of spares is a minimum.

**9** An airline passenger is afraid that the aeroplane he is due to travel in will be blown up by a bomb. He discovers that although many single bombs are found on aircraft, it is extremely rare for two or more bombs to be found on the same flight. He therefore decides to take a bomb with him. Comment.

**10** A car-hire company has 4 limousines which are hired out by the week. The demand for cars is observed to be as follows:

| Number of cars required per week | 0 | 1 | 2 | 3 | 4 |
|---|---|---|---|---|---|
| Percentage of weeks | 8 | 18 | 19 | 30 | 25 |

(i) A car in use needs two drivers. Calculate the expected number of drivers required per week.

(ii) The company is considering a maintenance scheme whereby a car is taken out of service for a week and overhauled if it has been used for 5 weeks. Use two-digit random numbers to simulate the demand for cars and draw up a time plot showing whether each of the 4 cars is in use, idle or being overhauled for every week. Extend the simulation for 25 weeks and explain how a longer one could be used to estimate the fraction of weeks the maintenance scheme would result in the company not being able to meet the demand for cars.

# 7 Compound Trials and the Binomial Distribution

In the last chapter we defined the probability of an outcome to be the fraction of trials for which that outcome occurs. The trials considered there are simple in the sense that they have only one incidence of randomness in them. As an example of a more complicated, or **compound,** trial consider observing the weather on two consecutive days. If each day is classified as being either 'wet' or 'dry' then the possible outcomes for two consecutive days are 'wet and wet', 'wet and dry', 'dry and wet' and 'dry and dry'. The compound trial of observing the weather on two days has two incidences of randomness, the weather on each day, and consists of two simple trials, one following the other.

Compound trials occur in applications of probability to statistical quality control, reliability theory and stochastic processes like queues. Here is an example on the reliability of a system to illustrate the method of analysing such trials. Although the example concerns a simple system with just two components, the method is readily applicable to more complicated systems having many constituent parts.

**The Firework Example**
A firework consists of a single fuse which lights two rockets. One of the rockets burns with a red colour and has probability 0.6 of firing successfully while the other burns with a blue flame and has corresponding probability 0.8. We analyse the compound trial of igniting the complete firework to find a measure of the overall system reliability, which should ideally involve both rockets firing successfully.

*Solution* An attempt to use the firework can be represented by a **probability tree** (Fig. 7.1). This shows the way in which the individual simple trials make up the compound trial.

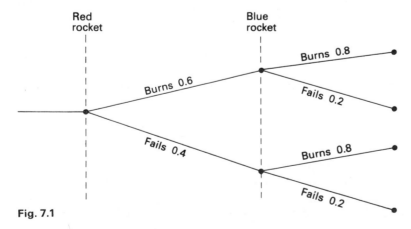

Fig. 7.1

The numbers near each section, or **branch,** of the tree are probabilities. It is possible to label each branch using the information given because at every branch point the probabilities must add up to 1. For example, given the probability of the red rocket firing to be 0.6, then the probability of it not firing is $1 - 0.6$ which is 0.4.

Every route through the tree from left to right is a sequence of outcomes of the simple trials of whether the individual rockets burn successfully or not. Each *route* is therefore an outcome of the *compound* trial of lighting the whole firework and the set of all four routes constitutes the outcome space for that trial.

We calculate the probability of a route using the probabilities of the branches making up that route. For instance, as the probability of the red rocket firing is 0.6, we know that 0.6 of all attempts to light the whole firework will result in the red rocket burning. Of *those* firings, the blue rocket will work 0.8 of the time and hence for 0.8 of 0.6 of all trials *both* rockets will fire. This gives a probability of $0.8 \times 0.6$, which is 0.48, for both rockets to work and hence for the whole system to function correctly. The probabilities of all the routes through the tree can be found by similar arguments.

As the four routes through the tree diagram (Fig. 7.2) represent all the possible out-

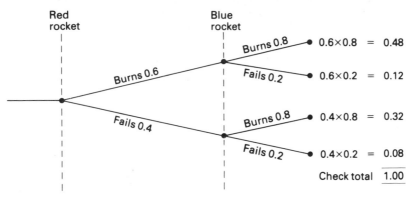

**Fig. 7.2**

comes for the trial of lighting the firework, their probabilities should add up to 1 and this check total is included in the diagram.

The analysis gives us a description of all aspects of the system's reliability. We see, for example, that the probability of neither rocket firing, the lowest of the four routes in the diagram, is 0.08. We might also be interested in the probability of only one rocket firing irrespective of its colour. This is $0.12 + 0.32$, or 0.44, because 0.12 of all trials result in only the red rocket working while 0.32 of all trials have only the blue rocket firing. Hence the overall fraction of trials for which just one rocket works is the sum of those two fractions. **We conclude that the probabilities of 0, 1 or 2 rockets firing are, respectively, 0.08, 0.44 and 0.48.**

## Statistical Independence

In the firework example we could have drawn the tree diagram differently by considering the firing of the blue rocket as the first trial and the red rocket as the second one.

The multiplications of the probabilities in Fig. 7.3 give the same answers as the corresponding multiplications in Fig. 7.2 and any reliability probabilities derived are the same.

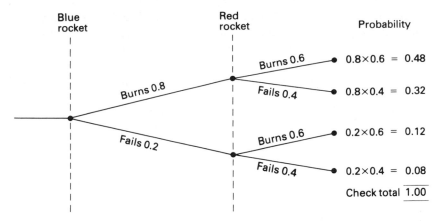

**Fig. 7.3**

Whenever the outcome of one trial does not affect the probabilities of the outcomes of the other trial, the trials are said to be **statistically independent.**

Here is an example of trials which are dependent on each other. The example also shows the use of probability trees in statistical quality control.

**The Light Bulb Example**
A batch of 40 light bulbs contains 6 defectives. If 2 bulbs are chosen at random and tested, without replacing them in the batch, calculate the probability that at least one of them is defective.

*Solution* The tree diagram for the two simple trials of choosing a bulb is given in Fig. 7.4.

The probabilities for the first bulb are obtained from the information given in the

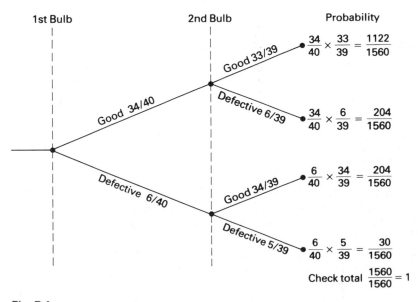

**Fig. 7.4**

question. The probabilities for the second bulb depend on whether the first bulb was defective or not, for if it was 'good' then there are still 6 defectives amongst the remaining 39 bulbs. On the other hand, if it was defective then there are only 5 defectives left when the second bulb is chosen. Hence if the first bulb was 'good', the probability of the second bulb being defective is 6/39 but if the first bulb was defective then the probability of the second bulb being defective is 5/39.

Completing the probabilities in the diagram using arguments like these we see that although the trial 'choose and test a second light bulb' is the same at two branch points, the probabilities of the outcomes are different depending on whereabouts in the tree the branch point is. The choice of the second bulb is therefore not statistically independent of the choice of the first bulb.

The calculations in the column headed 'probability' of Fig. 7.4 use the general rule developed earlier that the probability of a route through the tree is the product of the probabilities of its branches. The results of these calculations enable us to solve the problem and find the probability of at least one defective bulb. The routes through the tree corresponding to at least one defective are the bottom three of the list. Hence the probability of any one of them occurring is $(204/1560) + (204/1560) + (30/1560)$ which is $(438/1560)$, or **0.2808.**

## The Expectation of a Compound Trial

In the last chapter we used the concept of expectation to measure the average payoff of a trial with numerical outcomes. The next example applies the same idea to a compound trial.

### The New Town Example

A company is considering running a sales campaign in a town which has a 35% chance of being designated a 'new town' by the government. If it is so designated, then the company expects to make a profit of £50 000 from the campaign with probability 0.8 and a loss of £2000 with probability 0.2. Alternatively, if the town is not so designated, then the estimated profitability is £20 000 with probability 0.7 and £3000 with probability 0.3. In order to give themselves enough time to plan the campaign, the company must decide on whether to run it before they know whether the town will be designated a new town or not. If all the cash amounts are in present value terms and are therefore directly comparable with each other, calculate the expected profit the company should make from the campaign.

*Solution*   The tree diagram is shown in Fig. 7.5.

One way of calculating the expected profit would be to work out the probability of each route, multiply it by the payoff of that route and add the results together. This corresponds to forming the sum of probability × payoff, a formula developed in Chapter 6. We shall adopt a different procedure and reduce the diagram by replacing the final trial by its expectation, giving Fig. 7.6. The calculations on the right hand side are the expectations of the right hand trials in Fig. 7.5.

This reduction process can be repeated several times until a single trial diagram is obtained. In our example this has already happened as there were only two trials to begin with. The expectation of the remaining trial is $(0.35 \times 39\,600) + (0.65 \times 14\,900)$ which is **£23 545 and is the answer we want.** As we discussed in the Oil Company Example in

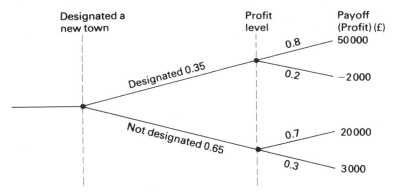

**Fig. 7.5**

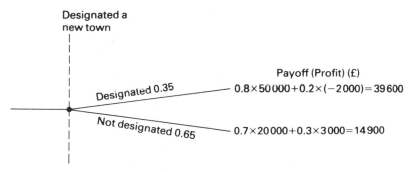

**Fig. 7.6**

Chapter 6, the concept of expectation does not really apply to 'one off' trials. The analysis should be interpreted as a management tool along with accountants' reports, publicity managers' reports etc.

An advantage of the reduction method used above is that intermediate expectations are found. Suppose that in our example the company found out earlier than expected whether the town was to be designated 'new' or not. We could use Fig. 7.6 to give a revised expectation in the light of the additional information, for if we know for a fact that the new town will be approved then the expected profit is £39 600 while if we know for a fact that it will not be approved then it is £14 900.

## The Binomial Distribution

We have studied three examples of compound trials, one in which the probability of the second trial is independent of the outcome of the first trial and two in which it is not. The next example develops the former case where the component trials are identical and independent of each other. Many applications involve a compound trial which is the repetition of the same trial several times. We are often interested only in the *number* of 'successes' and 'failures' amongst the component trials and not so much in the specific sequence with which those outcomes occurred. We shall see how the binomial distribution of probability can be used to describe such situations and how it enables us to obtain an analysis without drawing the tree diagram. This is useful in cases where the compound trial consists of many simple trials and the diagram would be very large.

**The Aircraft Engines Example**

An aircraft has 3 engines which each have probability 0.95 of responding correctly when tested. We want to know the probabilities of 0, 1, 2 and 3 engines working correctly when the aircraft is tested. Each of these outcomes represents a different level of reliability and when the aircraft is in flight would have different consequences in terms of its safety.

*Solution*    As the question is concerned with the number of engines working correctly, we keep a record of that number for each route through the tree (Fig. 7.7).

We shall now derive a formula which summarises Fig. 7.7 and other similar tree diagrams. The reader who is not interested in the derivation might wish to continue reading from the formula itself, equation (7.1), where its application to the present problem is given.

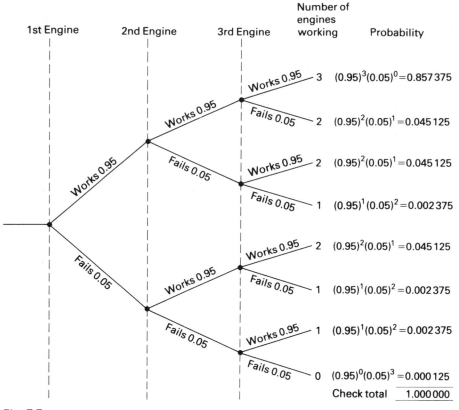

**Fig. 7.7**

We begin by spotting a pattern in the calculation of the probabilities in the tree diagram (Fig. 7.7). If a route consists of $r$ working engines and therefore $(3-r)$ engines which fail, the probability of that route is $(0.95)^r (0.05)^{3-r}$. This is because the product of the probabilities along the route contains $r$ of value 0.95, corresponding to the $r$ engines which work, and $(3-r)$ of value 0.05 representing the $(3-r)$ failures. The formula holds good for $r$ equal to 0 or 3 because any non-zero number raised to the power zero is equal to 1.

The results of the tree diagram analysis can be summarised in Table 7.1.

**Table 7.1**

| Number of engines working ($r$) | 0 | 1 | 2 | 3 |
|---|---|---|---|---|
| Number of routes | 1 | 3 | 3 | 1 |
| Probability of each route | $(0.95)^0 (0.05)^3$ | $(0.95)^1 (0.05)^2$ | $(0.95)^2 (0.05)^1$ | $(0.95)^3 (0.05)^0$ |
| Probability | 0.000 125 | 0.007 125 | 0.135 375 | 0.857 375 |

The first three lines of the table are obtained from the tree diagram where we see that each route giving rise to the same number of engines working has the same probability. This means that although, for example, there are 3 routes for which 1 engine works, they all have the same probability which is then written in the third line of the table. The last line of the table is the overall fraction of trials for which the appropriate number of engines work. For instance, there are 3 routes representing 2 engines working, and as we have just pointed out, each of these routes has the same probability. Hence the combined probability of the 3 routes is $3 \times (0.95)^2 (0.05)^1$, which is the number in the fourth line of the table. The complete set of probabilities in the fourth line forms a probability distribution over the outcomes 0, 1, 2 and 3 engines working and answers the question. As with any probability distribution the total probability is 1, a fact discussed in Chapter 6, and this provides a check on our arithmetic.

We now generalise the above derivation and imagine that there are $n$ trials each with individual probability of success $p$. In our example, $n$ is 3 and $p$ is 0.95. In the general case, the probability of a route through the tree diagram which contains $r$ successes and hence $(n-r)$ failures is $p^r(1-p)^{n-r}$ and this compares with the third line of Table 7.1. It remains to multiply this by the number of such routes to find the probability of $r$ successes out of the $n$ trials. The number of routes is the number of ways of choosing $r$ of the $n$ trials to be successful and mathematical combinatorics tells us that this is $^nC_r$. We thus obtain the formula

$$P(r \text{ successes out of } n \text{ trials}) = \frac{n!}{(n-r)!\, r!} p^r(1-p)^{n-r} \qquad (7.1)$$

The factorial sign, !, after a number means the product of all the whole numbers from 1 up to that number, for example, 4! is 24. Most scientific calculators have a special key which gives this product.

Formula (7.1) is called the **binomial distribution** and it gives us the probability of $r$ successes out of $n$ repeated trials when the probability of success on each individual trial is $p$. The distribution takes its name from the fact that the right hand side of equation (7.1) is the term involving $p^r$ in the expansion of $(p+(1-p))^n$ using the binomial theorem, but that need not concern us here. We shall verify that it gives the same answers as above for the Aircraft Engines Example and then look at its use in quality control.

The trial of testing an aircraft engine was performed 3 times and so the value of $n$ we use in the formula is 3. The probability of success at each individual trial, $p$, is 0.95 and hence we obtain

$$P(0 \text{ successes}) = \frac{3!}{(3-0)!\, 0!}(0.95)^0(1-0.95)^{3-0} = \textbf{0.000 125}$$

$$P(1 \text{ success}) = \frac{3!}{(3-1)!\,1!}(0.95)^1(1-0.95)^{3-1} = \mathbf{0.007\,125}$$

$$P(2 \text{ successes}) = \frac{3!}{(3-2)!\,2!}(0.95)^2(1-0.95)^{3-2} = \mathbf{0.135\,375}$$

$$P(3 \text{ successes}) = \frac{3!}{(3-3)!\,3!}(0.95)^3(1-0.95)^{3-3} = \mathbf{0.857\,375}$$

Notice that the factorial definition does not apply to 0! which is taken to be equal to 1 by convention. We have also used the fact that any non-zero number raised to the power zero is equal to 1.

Although it is not a pretty formula, the binomial distribution is used in applications of probability in areas ranging from genetics to statistical testing. In the next chapter, on the Poisson and normal distributions, we see how the formula can be dispensed with for large values of $n$ and small values of $p$. Whilst the problems at the end of the chapter reflect the wide range of applicability of the binomial distribution, here is another worked example showing its use in quality control.

### The Crying Doll Example

A toy factory produces dolls which are supposed to make the sound 'mama' when they are tilted forward. It is found from experience that 32% of all the dolls manufactured do not function properly.

*Question 1*    What is the probability that in a batch of 20 dolls, exactly 3 do not work?

*Solution*    The testing of the batch is a compound trial involving 20 individual trials. Each of these trials has probability 0.32 of 'success' where 'success' means 'doll does not work'. Note the technical use of the word 'success' here. The doll manufacturer would not call 'doll does not work' a 'success' but we are interested in the probability of 3 such dolls being in the batch and the outcome of interest in the binomial distribution is called 'success'.

As the trials of testing a sequence of dolls are statistically independent we use the binomial distribution formula (7.1) with $n$ equal to 20 and $p$ equal to 0.32.

$$\begin{aligned}
\mathbf{P\,(3 \text{ do not work out of } 20)} &= P\,(3 \text{ successes})\\
&= \frac{20!}{(20-3)!\,3!}(0.32)^3(1-0.32)^{20-3}\\
&= \frac{20 \times 19 \times 18}{3 \times 2 \times 1}(0.32)^3(0.68)^{17}\\
&= \mathbf{0.0531}
\end{aligned}$$

The calculation is simplified in the third line by cancelling 17! on the top and bottom of the fraction. Such cancellations always occur when using the binomial formula and improve the accuracy of the answer. Furthermore, factorials are often very large numbers and if they are not simplified in the formula they can cause a calculator or computer to overflow.

*Question 2*    What is the probability that in a batch of 12 dolls less than 2 do not work?

*Solution*    **P (less than 2 successes out of 12)** $= P$ (0 or 1 successes out of 12)

$$= P \text{ (0 successes out of 12)} + P \text{ (1 success out of 12)}$$

$$= \frac{12!}{(12-0)!\,0!}(0.32)^0(1-0.32)^{12-0} + \frac{12!}{(12-1)!\,1!}(0.32)^1(1-0.32)^{12-1}$$

$$= 0.009\,775 + 0.055\,199 = \mathbf{0.064\,974}$$

*Question 3*    What is the probability that in a batch of 15 dolls at least 1 does not work?

*Solution*    The event 'at least one success out of 15 trials' can be interpreted directly as '1 or 2 or 3 or ... or 15 successes' and its probability found by adding together the 15 probabilities $P$ (1 success), $P$ (2 successes), ... $P$ (15 successes). However, as this involves 15 separate applications of the binomial formula, we shall employ a small trick to reduce the work. We argue as follows:

**P (at least 1 success out of 15 trials)**

$$= P \text{ (any number of successes except 0)}$$

$$= 1 - P \text{ (0 successes out of 15 trials)}$$

$$= 1 - \frac{15!}{(15-0)!\,0!}(0.32)^0(1-0.32)^{15-0}$$

$$= 1 - 0.003\,074 - \mathbf{0.996\,926}$$

The key to the reasoning is that 'at least 1 success' means 'not 0 successes' and as we saw in Question 3 of the Playing Card Example of Chapter 6, the probabilities of an event A and the event 'not A' add up to 1. Hence the probability of 'not 0 successes' is 1 minus the probability of 0 successes.

## Computer Program

Our program evaluates the binomial distribution formula for user-supplied values of the number of trials, $N$, and the probability of success on each trial, $P$. It can be used to verify the calculations in the last two examples or to apply the binomial distribution to other problems. More advanced uses of the distribution are discussed in the section on Further Reading and the program could be of help in implementing those.

```
10 PRINT "BINOMIAL DISTRIBUTION"
20 PRINT "---------------------"
30 PRINT
40 PRINT "NUMBER OF TRIALS";
50 INPUT N
60 PRINT "PROBABILITY OF SUCCESS";
70 PRINT " AT EACH TRIAL";
80 INPUT P
90 PRINT
100 PRINT "NUMBER          PROBABILITY    PROBABILITY"
110 PRINT "OF SUCCESSES    OF R           OF AT MOST"
120 PRINT "  (R)           SUCCESSES      R SUCCESSES"
130 A=(1-P)**N
140 S=A
150 PRINT "0",A,S
160 FOR R=1 TO N
170 A=(A*(N-R+1)*P)/(R*(1-P))
180 S=S+A
```

```
190 PRINT R,A,S
200 NEXT R
210 END
```

**Specimen Run**

```
BINOMIAL DISTRIBUTION
---------------------

NUMBER OF TRIALS ?5
PROBABILITY OF SUCCESS AT EACH TRIAL ?0.3

NUMBER          PROBABILITY     PROBABILITY
OF SUCCESSES    OF R            OF AT MOST
   (R)          SUCCESSES       R SUCCESSES
0               0.16807         0.16807
 1              0.36015         0.52822
 2              0.3087          0.83692
 3              0.1323          0.96922
 4              2.83500E-2      0.99757
 5              0.00243         1.
```

**Program Notes**

**1**  Lines 40 to 80 read the values of N and P from the user.

**2**  Line 130 calculates the probability of no successes at all. This is the first probability to be printed out and the program will successively modify its value in order to calculate all the other probabilities.

**3**  Line 140 initialises the variable S which will be a running total of all the probabilities as they are calculated. Its value is printed out in the column headed 'Probability of at most R successes' and updated by line 180.

**4**  Line 170 alters the value of A from being the probability of $(R-1)$ successes to be the probability of R successes using the equation

$$\underbrace{\frac{N!}{(N-R)!\,R!}P^R(1-P)^{N-R}}_{\substack{\text{P (R successes) from the} \\ \text{binomial formula}}} = \underbrace{\frac{N!}{(N-(R-1))!\,(R-1)!}P^{R-1}(1-P)^{N-(R-1)}}_{\substack{\text{P ((R}-1\text{) successes) from} \\ \text{the binomial formula}}} \underbrace{\left(\frac{P(N-R+1)}{(1-P)\,R}\right)}_{\substack{\text{Conversion factor used in} \\ \text{the program}}} \quad (7.2)$$

Hence the program, starting with the initial value of A equal to the probability of 0 successes, has a FOR loop to deal with R successes where R ranges from 1 to N. Each probability is calculated from the previous one by multiplying it by the conversion factor in equation (7.2). We shall use the same programming technique in the Poisson distribution program at the end of Chapter 8.

## Summary

**1**  A compound trial is a succession of simple trials whose outcome is a sequence of the outcomes of the simple trials. It is therefore possible to be part of the way through a compound trial with some of the simple trial outcomes known and others unknown.

**2**   A probability tree diagram has routes which represent the various outcomes a compound trial can have. The probability of a route is the product of the probabilities of the branches along the route.

**3**   Individual trials are said to be statistically independent if the probabilities of the outcomes of one of them are unaffected by the outcome of the other. The probability of a sequence of outcomes for a succession of such trials is the product of their individual probabilities.

**4**   The binomial distribution gives the probability of $r$ 'successes' when $n$ statistically independent and identical trials are performed each having probability $p$ of 'success'. Success is a technical word here and stands for one of the two possible outcomes each independent trial can have. Its precise meaning will depend on the problem in hand. The binomial distribution formula is

$$P (r \text{ successes out of } n \text{ trials}) = \frac{n!}{(n-r)! \, r!} \, p^r (1-p)^{n-r}.$$

## Further Reading

This chapter, like the previous one, contains topics which are of importance in both statistics and operational research. They are used and developed in other parts of the book, especially in the reliability theory of Chapter 11. Operational research texts like (6) and (13) and statistics books like (21), (22), (24), (25) and (28), contain work on the binomial distribution while reference (26) shows how it is used in non-parametric statistical hypothesis testing. References (21) and (24) also give introductions to statistical quality control in which the analysis of acceptance sampling involves the binomial distribution. Some of these applications are illustrated in the following exercises.

## Exercises

**1**   Four cards are chosen from a standard pack of 52 playing cards. After each one is chosen it is not replaced in the pack. Calculate the probability that (i) all four cards are aces, (ii) at least one of them is an ace.

**2**   80% of all the defendants appearing before a certain court are guilty. There is a 10% chance that an innocent person will be found guilty and a 5% chance that a guilty person will be found innocent. Calculate the probability that (i) a miscarriage of justice occurs, (ii) a person is guilty given that he or she has been found guilty.

**3**   A salesman is planning a journey. If he goes by train it will take $1\frac{3}{4}$ hours. He could go by car but Main Road Junction is often busy. If it is very bad he will turn off and take the By-Pass giving a journey time of 1 hour 40 minutes. If the Main Road Junction has a moderate amount of traffic he will take the City Route and the journey would then take 1 hour 30 minutes with a 25% probability that it will take 2 hours. Finally, if Main Road Junction is clear of traffic he would take the direct route giving a journey time of 1 hour exactly. If he estimates the probabilities of Main Road Junction traffic being heavy to be 0.2, moderate to be 0.5, and light to be 0.3, use expected journey times to determine whether he should go by train or car.

**4**   Two bad marksmen, Alf and Bob, fight a duel. The probability that Alf will shoot Bob at any attempt is 0.1 and the probability that Bob will shoot Alf at any attempt is 0.2. Alf shoots first and they then take turns to shoot at each other until either one of them is hit or they have fired six shots each. What is the probability that (i) Alf shoots Bob, and (ii) Bob shoots Alf?

**5**   In a certain country, 23% of the population are left handed. If a random sample of five people is chosen, find the probability that there are (i) exactly four, (ii) at most one, (iii) more than two, left-handed people in it.

**6**   A flower shop takes delivery of a large batch of daffodil bulbs. The owner selects 6 bulbs at random and plants them. After an appropriate time, only 4 have grown into flowers although the supplier claims that 95% of them are of good quality. (i) Use the binomial distribution to calculate the probability that at most 4 bulbs out of the 6 which were chosen are good assuming that the supplier's claim is true. (ii) Given that the event 'at most 4 bulbs are good' has actually occurred, do you believe the supplier's claim or is it more likely that the fraction of good bulbs in the batch is less than 95%?

**7**   A machine prints 4 identical electronic circuits onto one board. A hundred boards are manufactured and tested, the results being as follows:

| Number of working circuits per board | 0 | 1 | 2 | 3 | 4 |
|---|---|---|---|---|---|
| Number of boards | 3 | 10 | 26 | 38 | 23 |

(i) Calculate the number of working circuits out of the 400 which were manufactured and hence the probability that a circuit chosen at random is of good quality. (ii) Use the probability found in (i) and the binomial distribution to calculate the probabilities of 0, 1, 2, 3 and 4 working circuits on a board chosen at random. (iii) Multiply your answers to (ii) by 100 to obtain predictions for the data values observed. These forecasts are based on the appropriateness of the binomial distribution to describe the compound trial of testing a board. If the predictions are close to the observations then we can deduce that the individual circuits are statistically independent of each other, and we will have 'fitted a binomial distribution' to the data.

**8**   One twin from each of a set of 9 identical twins was given a new type of shampoo to use while the other twin from each pair was provided with an ordinary shampoo. Seven of the pairs correctly identified which one of them had been given the new, supposedly better, preparation. Now if the shampoos are indistinguishable from each other, then the probability of a correct identification by each pair of twins would be 0.5. Does the observed event of 7 or more correct identifications have a sufficiently large probability, when calculated on the basis of this hypothesis, to be likely to be due to statistical error? If the observed outcome to the experiment does not have a high probability of occurring as a consequence of the twins guessing which is which, then it forms evidence that the new shampoo is indeed significantly better than ordinary shampoo.

# 8 The Poisson and Normal Distributions

The reader can study either of these distributions separately although there are sections relating them to each other and to the binomial distribution of the last chapter.

## The Poisson Distribution

Many events occur at random in space or time. For example, the arrival of telephone calls or the incidence of scratches on the surface of plastic sheeting. The trial in this type of situation consists of observing a fixed time period or region of space and counting the number of occurrences of the random event concerned. The possible outcomes of the trial are therefore the whole numbers 0, 1, 2, 3, ...

If it can be assumed that the events are equally likely to happen at all points in time or space and that they are statistically independent of each other, then the Poisson distribution applies to them. Statistical independence means that the occurrence of the event at one time or place does not affect the probability of it occurring at some other time or place. We discussed this concept in the section on the binomial distribution.

The Poisson distribution formula (8.1) gives the probability of exactly $r$ events being observed in a fixed region of time or space when the average number for that time period or spatial region is $a$.

$$P\,(r \text{ events}) = \frac{e^{-a}a^r}{r!} \tag{8.1}$$

In this formula, the letter e denotes a certain constant of the universe, rather like $\pi$, whose value is approximately equal to 2.7183. Most scientific calculators have the exponential function $e^x$ built into them and they also have the factorial function, $r!$, which is another part of the formula. This is read as '$r$ factorial' and is the product of all the whole numbers from $r$ down to 1 with the convention that 0! is taken to be 1. So 4!, for example, is equal to $4 \times 3 \times 2 \times 1$ which is 24. For many problems the value of the average $a$ is large and formula (8.1) can then be difficult to evaluate accurately. Later in this chapter we see how the normal distribution can give approximate answers in such cases.

In operational research we use the Poisson distribution to describe the level of demand for goods or services in stock control and the arrivals in queuing problems. In the following example of a demand analysis for a coach hire company, we investigate the fraction of time the business is idle, the level of service it provides, and finally whether it should invest in an additional coach. A similar exercise is carried out for the casualty department of a hospital later in the chapter.

### The Coach Company Example
A coach hire company finds that over a period of 100 working days it receives 184

requests to supply coaches for one-day return journeys. There are no bookings which extend over more than one day and the likelihood of a request occurring is the same throughout the working day. We can use the Poisson distribution to describe the level of demand with the average $a$ being 184 divided by 100, which is 1.84 coaches per working day. The description of the pattern with which demand, or customers, arrive at a business or system is discussed more generally in Chapter 10 on Queues.

*Question 1*    For what fraction of time is the business idle?

*Solution*    This is the probability that there is 0 demand for coaches in a working day. Putting $r$ equal to 0 in the Poisson formula (8.1) together with $a$ equal to 1.84 we find that

$$P(0) = \frac{e^{-1.84} (1.84)^0}{0!} = 0.1588 \tag{8.2}$$

Readers who do not have access to a scientific calculator can check this result using printed tables of the exponential function and the facts that 0! is equal to 1 and any non-zero number raised to the power 0 is 1.

**Our answer, therefore, is that there is no demand, and so the business is idle, for about 16% of all working days.**

*Question 2*    The company has only two coaches. For what percentage of working days are they able to cope with demand?

*Solution*    Notice that 'supply' and 'demand' are not necessarily the same. The demand for coaches can be 0, 1, 2, 3, ... in any one working day and yet the supply can be only 0, 1 or 2 as the company has just two coaches. In general the supply of goods or services has a finite upper limit while the demand can theoretically reach any value and all non-negative whole numbers are given a probability by the Poisson formula (8.1). Obviously, when demand exceeds supply then the business provides all it can and the surplus demand is of no benefit at all. In the present example we can tabulate the supply and demand relationship.

**Table 8.1**

| Number of coaches demanded, $r$ | 0 | 1 | 2 | 3 | 4 | . . . . |
|---|---|---|---|---|---|---|
| Probability from Poisson formula $P(r)$ | 0.1588 | 0.2922 | 0.2688 | 0.1649 | 0.0759 | . . . . |
| Can supply cope with demand? | Yes | Yes | Yes | No | No | . . . . |

Hence the overall probability that the company has enough coaches to cope with demand is $P(0) + P(1) + P(2)$, which is 0.7198, and the answer is that **it copes with demand on 72% of all working days.**

*Question 3*    The company makes £15 profit per day when a coach is out on hire but loses £10 for each day a coach is not being used. Would it be profitable for the company to run an additional coach, assuming that the average demand for coaches remained at 1.84 per day?

*Solution*   We use the expected payoff per day of the additional coach as a measure of its profitability. If the expected payoff is positive then on average the extra coach will be of benefit to the company whilst if it is negative then the coach gives a net loss and is a liability.

As we saw in Chapter 6, to calculate an expectation we must tabulate the probabilities and payoffs and take the overall sum of their products (Table 8.2).

**Table 8.2**

| Number of coaches demanded, $r$ | 0 | 1 | 2 | 3 | 4 | . . . . |
|---|---|---|---|---|---|---|
| Probability from Poisson formula, $P(r)$ | 0.1588 | 0.2922 | 0.2688 | 0.1649 | 0.0759 | . . . . |
| Payoff from extra coach (£) | $-10$ | $-10$ | $-10$ | $+15$ | $+15$ | . . . . |

The sum of products is

$$P(0)(-10)+P(1)(-10)+P(2)(-10)+P(3)(+15)+P(4)(+15)+ . . . . \qquad (8.3)$$

which can be written as

$$[P(0)+P(1)+P(2)](-10)+[P(3)+P(4)+P(5)+ . . . .](+15) \qquad (8.4)$$

Now the first term in square brackets is the answer to Question 2 which we found to be 0.7198. One of the purposes of this example is to demonstrate the computation of infinite summations like the one in the second square bracket. The trick is to remember from Chapter 6 that all the probabilities in any distribution must add up to 1. Even though there are an infinite number of them in the Poisson distribution, their total is exactly 1. Hence we can write

$$P(0)+P(1)+P(2)+P(3)+P(4)+P(5)+ . . . . =1 \qquad (8.5)$$

from which it follows that

$$\begin{aligned} P(3)+P(4)+P(5)+ . . . . &=1-P(0)-P(1)-P(2)\\ &=1-0.1588-0.2922-0.2688\\ &=0.2802 \end{aligned} \qquad (8.6)$$

Substituting the numerical values for the square bracket terms in equation (8.4) we find the expected daily payoff of the extra coach to be

$$0.7198 \times (-10)+0.2802 \times (+15) \qquad (8.7)$$

which is $-£3.00$. **Hence it would not be profitable for the company to run a third coach given the existing level of demand.**

*Question 4*   Does the answer to Question 3 mean that the company should not buy another coach?

*Solution*   **Not necessarily.** A weakness of the above calculation from the decision-making point of view is that it is based on an average demand of 1.84 coaches per day. It is quite likely that by carrying advertisements for the company and generally enhancing the company's image, an extra coach would increase the average daily demand.

To allow for this in our analysis, we can calculate the expected profit of the additional coach for several different values of the average daily demand, searching for those which make it positive.

**Table 8.3**

| Average daily demand, $a$ | 1.84 as in Qu. 3 | 1.90 | 2.00 | 2.10 | 2.20 | 2.30 | 2.40 |
|---|---|---|---|---|---|---|---|
| Expected profit from extra coach (£ per day) | $-3.00$ | $-2.59$ | $-1.92$ | $-1.24$ | $-0.57$ | $+0.10$ | $+0.76$ |

Table 8.3 allows the manager to use his forecast of demand to predict the profitability of the third coach and is a much better management tool than the result of Question 3.

Note that an exact forecast of future daily demand is not necessary to predict simply whether another coach will be profitable or not. We can see from the table that if management feels that the enhanced demand with 3 coaches will be greater than about 2.3 requests per day then a third coach will be profitable and have an expected payoff greater than zero. Alternatively there could be a threshold value of profit below which the company does not want to risk running more coaches. The average daily demand necessary to generate this level of profit could be read from the table or from an extension of it.

Whilst expected payoff profiles like Table 8.3 are useful, it is emphasised, as in the Oil Company Example of Chapter 6, that a quantitative analysis is only one of several considerations involved in making a company decision. Our work relates the average profit of an extra coach to management forecasts, or speculations, about the future level of demand. This cannot by itself provide an infallible or complete measure of the benefit the vehicle would bring to the company.

## The Poisson Approximation to the Binomial Formula

It often happens that the binomial formula described in Chapter 7 is difficult to apply because the number of trials, $n$, is large. If the probability of success on each trial, $p$, is so small that $p^2$ is considered to be negligible, then the Poisson formula can be used to give approximations to the binomial probabilities. The approximation is purely mathematical and consists of using the Poisson formula with the value of $a$ set equal to $pn$. Here is an example to show how it is done.

### The Industrial Accident Example

One percent of all employees who ignore a 'Keep Out' sign in a part of a certain factory have an accident. What is the probability that when 50 people ignore the sign, all on separate occasions, less than 2 of them have accidents?

*Solution*    The number of accidents is described by the binomial distribution as there are 50 independent trials each with probability 0.01 of success. Here 'success' means 'having an accident' and the binomial formula (7.1) can be used.

$$P \text{ (less than 2 successes)} = P(0) + P(1)$$
$$= \frac{50! \, (0.01)^0 (1 - 0.01)^{50}}{(50 - 0)! \, 0!} + \frac{50! \, (0.01)^1 (1 - 0.01)^{49}}{(50 - 1)! \, 1!}$$
$$= 0.6050 + 0.3056 = \textbf{0.9106} \tag{8.8}$$

and so we obtain the answer, of about 91%.

Now the figures in this example are sufficiently small for the binomial formula still to be usable. They were chosen in this way so that the answer from the approximation technique can be compared with the exact result. It is not difficult to imagine larger values of $n$ and smaller values of $p$ which would make calculations like (8.8) overflow the arithmetic range of a calculator or computer. In those cases we have no choice but to try the Poisson approximation although this in turn might fail for the same reason. Later in this chapter we encounter the normal curve approximation to both the binomial and Poisson distributions and although that never fails it gives inaccurate results when applied to binomial situations for which the Poisson approximation can be used.

Continuing with our example, we calculate the expected number of successes $pn$ to be $0.01 \times 50$ which is 0.5. This figure is low enough to be used as the value of $a$ in the Poisson formula and we now have

$$P \text{ (less than 2 successes)} = P(0) + P(1)$$
$$= \frac{e^{-0.5}(0.5)^0}{0!} + \frac{e^{-0.5}(0.5)^1}{1!}$$
$$= 0.6065 + 0.3033 = \mathbf{0.9098} \tag{8.9}$$

This approximate solution is the same as the exact answer (8.8) to two decimal places. It should be clearly understood that the underlying situation of industrial accidents is described by the binomial, and not the Poisson, distribution. We have merely used the mathematical fact that in certain circumstances one formula, the Poisson, gives good approximations to the results obtained from another formula, the binomial.

## The Normal Distribution

This distribution is used to describe the different values which result from measuring some property of the members of a population. The property could be height or examination mark, or for non-human populations like electric light bulbs it could be working temperature or power consumption. In the general case we are interested in the trial of choosing an item at random from the population and measuring the particular value associated with it.

The frequencies with which different outcomes of this trial occur in a sample or in the whole population can be shown by drawing a **histogram** (Fig. 8.1).

This has the range of possible measurements subdivided into classes and drawn as the horizontal axis. The number of items whose values fall into a particular class is represented by the area of a rectangle with that class width as its base. Notice that areas and not heights are employed to indicate frequency as the visual impact of a rectangle lies in the size of its area and not in its height.

The histogram (Fig. 8.1) has the bell shape which arises from many different types of measurement data. The fact that most of the numbers are near to their average value with large deviations being relatively uncommon and symmetric is enough to warrant describing the histogram by a **normal curve.** The appropriate one for the above example is shown superimposed on the diagram and although the curves have a precise mathematical definition that need not concern us.

The name 'normal' originated because the curve was thought to fit all histograms of naturally occurring lengths, weights and ages. Anything else was 'abnormal' and required further explanation. Of course, we now think more scientifically and apply statistical tests to sample data to see if the use of the normal distribution is justified in a particular case.

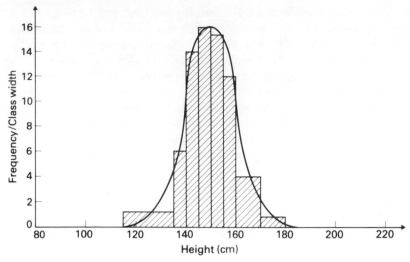

**Fig. 8.1**   Histogram of the heights of a sample of 385 men

The section on Further Reading quotes references which explain these tests of 'goodness of fit', as they are called. In this book we assume either that such a procedure has been carried out or that the histogram has such a strong resemblance to the normal shape that the testing is considered unnecessary. Such a resemblance occurs in our first worked example which is about the useful lifetime of torch batteries. This is related to the work of Chapter 11 where we deal with reliability in more detail. The last two worked examples illustrate the use of the normal distribution as an approximation to the binomial and Poisson formulae when they give rise to computational difficulties.

**The Battery Example**

A torch battery manufacturer tested a large sample of batteries to destruction and measured the length of each one's useful life. He found that the histogram of his data had a bell shape similar to that of diagram (8.1) and decided that a normal curve would give an acceptable description of its outline. He then used a scientific calculator to find that the sample mean of the lifetimes was 60.41 hours and the sample standard deviation was 2.2 hours. We study 4 types of question the manufacturer might be interested in, each one illustrating a different use of the normal tables on pages 137 and 138.

*Question* 1   Find the probability that a battery chosen at random will have a lifetime longer than 61.4 hours.

*Solution*   The mechanics of the solution are very simple. All we shall do eventually is put the 3 given numbers into formula (8.12) and look up the area corresponding to the resulting $z$ value in the table on page 137. However, we utilise this first question to develop some general concepts relating to the normal distribution.

**Population Mean and Standard Deviation**

Having made the qualitative decision that a normal curve gives an acceptable description of the shape of the histogram, we must determine which particular curve to use. For this purpose we require good estimates of the **population mean** and **population standard deviation** of the measurement in question. Readers unfamiliar with statistics need only be aware that the population mean is the average of all the population measurements while the standard deviation is a measure of the spread of the values about the mean, a small standard deviation indicating that all the population values are close to the mean and a large value indicating that they are spread away from it.

As these quantities depend on the entire population they are unknown in the vast majority of cases and therefore estimated by choosing a, hopefully large, sample. If the sample contains $n$ items and we call the measurement of interest an $x$ value, then the formulae for the **sample mean** and **sample standard deviation** are

$$\left.\begin{array}{l} \text{Sample Mean, } \bar{x} \text{ (read as `}x\text{ bar')} = \dfrac{\text{Sum of } x \text{ values}}{n} \\[2em] \text{Sample Standard Deviation, } s = \sqrt{\dfrac{\text{Sum of } x^2 \text{ values} - n\bar{x}^2}{(n-1)}} \end{array}\right\} \quad (8.10)$$

These formulae are incorporated into most scientific calculators which allow the $x$ values to be keyed in separately and then give the results when special buttons are pressed. An explanation of their use together with the dependence of their accuracy on the size of the sample, can be found in statistics books like (22), (24) and (25). For our purposes we assume that we have good estimates, either by using these formulae or otherwise, of the population mean, $\mu$ (Greek letter 'mu'), estimated by $\bar{x}$, and the population standard deviation, $\sigma$ (Greek letter 'sigma'), estimated by $s$. We shall not concern ourselves here with the validity of the estimation process as the theory of sampling forms a sizeable topic in statistics with only limited applicability in operational research. The general rules of thumb are to ensure that the sample is truly random in that every item in the population has an equal probability of being selected and to make that sample as large as possible. In fact the normal curve can be thought of as the limit of a sequence of histograms relating to larger and larger samples with smaller and smaller class widths.

In the present example, the manufacturer may have found the sum of the lifetimes, which are the $x$ values, to be 30 205 hours and the sum of their squares to be 1 827 099. If there were 500 batteries in the sample then formulae (8.10) give the results quoted in the problem.

$$\left.\begin{array}{l} \bar{x} = \dfrac{30\,205}{500} = 60.41 \\[2em] s = \sqrt{\dfrac{1\,827\,099 - 500\,(60.41)^2}{499}} = 2.2 \end{array}\right\} \quad (8.11)$$

We take these to be the estimates of $\mu$ and $\sigma$ respectively and obtain the sketch (Fig. 8.2) to describe the distribution of battery lifetimes throughout the population. There are no units on the vertical axis as the curve merely indicates the shape of the histogram.

Now the probability of a battery having a lifetime longer than 61.4 hours is the number of them which do have such lifetimes divided by the number of batteries altogether. As frequency is denoted by area in the histogram, we can measure this probability as the area under the curve to the right of 61.4 divided by the area under the whole curve. We have therefore reduced Question 1 to the problem of evaluating some areas in Fig. 8.2, the shaded area representing the number of batteries with lives greater than 61.4 and the whole area representing the total number of batteries.

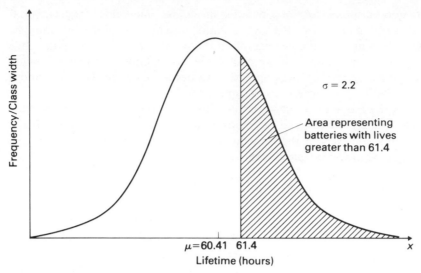

**Fig. 8.2**    Shape of histogram of battery lifetimes

Clearly it is impractical to tabulate areas under every normal curve arising from each possible combination of $\mu$ and $\sigma$ values. Fortunately all of these curves are scale versions of the **standard normal curve** which is the particular one with mean zero, standard deviation 1 and unit total area. A table of the areas under this curve can be found on page 137 of this book and we shall scale every problem on the normal distribution so that it can be used. Similar tabulations appear in specially published books of statistical tables such as (30).

The plan, therefore, is to scale Fig. 8.2 to become the standard normal curve and then look up any required areas in the table. The formula which scales $x$ values on the original graph of measurements to $z$ values on the standard normal curve is

$$z = \frac{x - \mu}{\sigma} \tag{8.12}$$

The $z$ **score** as it is sometimes called is simply the distance of any measurement $x$ from the mean $\mu$ expressed as a number of standard deviations, $\sigma$. It can be used in its own right to compare $x$ measurements from different normal situations with each other. A problem in the exercise at the end of this chapter gives a student's marks in two unrelated examinations. The student's performance in the two subjects can be compared using $z$ scores as these indicate how well he did relative to the mean and standard deviation of the class as a whole. In an extreme case a student can be bottom of the class with a mark of 90%, resulting in a negative $z$ score, and top in another subject with 3%, resulting in a positive $z$ score. A comparison of the $z$ scores, and not the unprocessed percentages, therefore gives a true indication of performance relative to the entire class.

In our problem we want to scale diagram (8.2) and so we put $x$ equal to 61.4, $\mu$ equal to 60.41 and $\sigma$ equal to 2.2. This results in $z$ being 0.45 and the standard normal curve corresponding to Fig. 8.2 is given in Fig. 8.3.

The vertical axis is 'probability density' because as the whole area under this curve is equal to one, we can interpret any area directly as a probability without having to divide by the total.

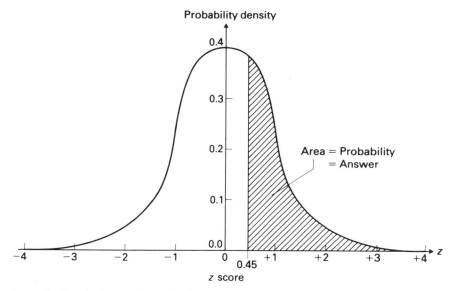

**Fig. 8.3**   Standard normal curve for Question 1 of the Battery Example

Now the event in Fig. 8.3 corresponding to '*x* greater than 61.4' is '*z* greater than 0.45' and the probability of this is the area to the right of 0.45. From the table on page 137 we see that this area is 0.3264 and so the answer to Question 1 is **33% of all batteries have a lifetime longer than 61.4 hours.**

The fact that every calculation of normal probabilities involves the determination of one or more areas under a curve might cause the more mathematical reader to think that integral calculus would be of help. Unfortunately it is impossible to perform the relevant integration, which for the standard normal curve is of the function $e^{-z^2/2}/\sqrt{2\pi}$, in terms of analytic functions. Numerical techniques are therefore used to produce the areas we have referred to above and a computer program which does this is listed on page 134.

*Question 2*   Find the probability that a battery chosen at random has a lifetime of 63 hours measured to the nearest whole number of hours.

*Solution*   As probabilities are given by areas under the normal curve, the probability of a specific *x* value, like 63 hours, is zero as the area corresponding to the event '*x* equals 63 exactly' is the 'area' of a straight line. This reflects the reality that it is virtually impossible to choose a battery at random and find its lifetime to be exactly 63 hours, not a microsecond more or a microsecond less. In everyday speech, however, we often measure age by saying, 'I am 25 years old' when we mean anything from 25 years and 1 day, which is the day after one's 25th birthday, up to 25 years and 364 days, the day before the 26th birthday. All these ages are reckoned as '25 years old'.

In Question 2 we see another common method of measurement. This is when an instrument registers a quantity to the nearest calibration its accuracy will allow. For example, the battery lifetimes could be measured by an electric clock which recorded only the nearest whole hour in which the battery failed. A reading of '63 hours' would then result from any lifetime between 62.5 hours and 63.5 hours. All measuring instruments

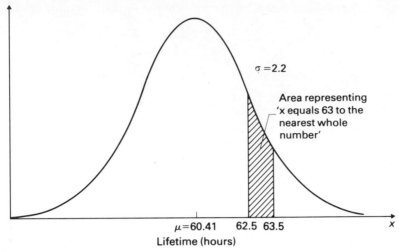

σ =2.2

Area representing
'x equals 63 to the
nearest whole
number'

μ=60.41   62.5 63.5   x

Lifetime (hours)

**Fig. 8.4**   Shape of histogram for Question 2 of the Battery Example

have restrictions on their accuracy and will give the nearest reading to the true value that their sensitivity allows.

The event '63 hours to the nearest whole number of hours' is therefore the same as the event '$x$ is between 62.5 and 63.5' and can be represented as an area under the normal curve (Fig. 8.4). We can reduce this graph to the standard normal curve using formula (8.12) and obtain Fig. 8.5. The detailed labelling of the axes is not shown in these diagrams although it was in Fig. 8.3 to give an idea of scale. In practice, sketch graphs like Figs 8.4 and 8.5 are drawn to contain only the essential numbers and areas of the problem.

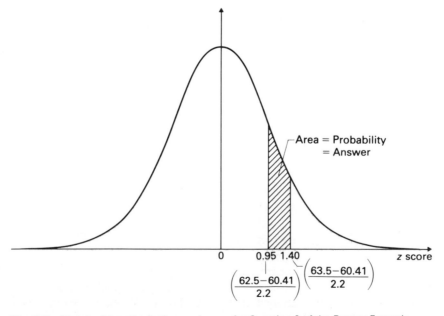

Area = Probability
= Answer

0   0.95 1.40   z score

$\left(\dfrac{62.5-60.41}{2.2}\right)$ $\left(\dfrac{63.5-60.41}{2.2}\right)$

**Fig. 8.5**   Sketch of the standard normal curve for Question 2 of the Battery Example

To evaluate the shaded area in Fig. 8.5 and hence complete the solution a subtle device is used. We have on page 137 a table of the areas to the right of all $z$ values while the area we want is between 0.95 and 1.40. Now the area to the right of 0.95 contains the required area but also includes the area to the right of 1.40 as an unwanted ingredient. We therefore look up the area corresponding to 0.95 in the table and subtract from it the area corresponding to 1.40.

$$\textbf{Answer} = P(x \text{ between } 62.5 \text{ and } 63.5)$$
$$= 0.1711 - 0.0808 = 0.0903 \simeq \textbf{9.0\%} \tag{8.13}$$

Notice in passing that $z$ scores are calculated to just two decimal place accuracy and, as in the rest of this book, answers, but not intermediate items of working, which are probabilities, are similarly treated. This is in keeping with the philosophy developed in Chapter 6 that probabilities are intended to convey general management information only. In view of their definition as relative frequencies whose values no two experimenters would agree upon, any undue accuracy we invest them with is quite inappropriate.

*Question 3*   Find the probability that a battery chosen at random will have a lifetime of less than 56.3 hours.

*Solution*   The probability of the event 'lifetime less than 56.3 hours' can be shown on the normal curve as an area (Fig. 8.6).

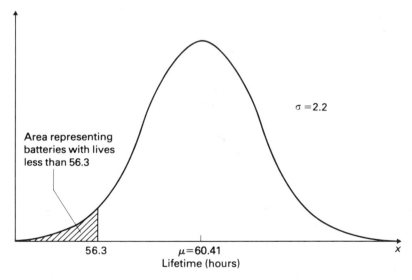

Area representing batteries with lives less than 56.3

$\sigma = 2.2$

56.3

$\mu = 60.41$
Lifetime (hours)

$x$

**Fig. 8.6**   Shape of histogram for Question 3 of the Battery Example

This can be scaled to the standard normal curve (Fig. 8.7) and again we need a suitable trick to evaluate the area concerned. This time we use the property that the normal curve is symmetric and the area to the left of $-1.87$ is a mirror-image of the area to the right of $+1.87$. From the table on page 137 this second area is 0.0307 and so the answer to Question 3 is that **the probability of a battery chosen at random lasting less than 56.3 hours is 3.1%.**

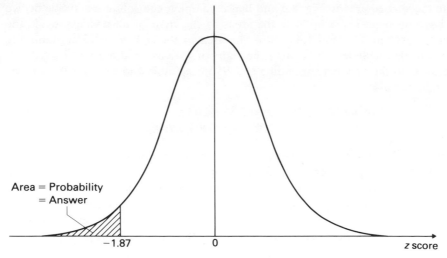

**Fig. 8.7**  Sketch of the standard normal curve for Question 3 of the Battery Example

*Question 4*  What lifetime should be guaranteed so that about 90% of all batteries last longer than the guarantee?

*Solution*  This question could arise if the manufacturer wanted to quote a guaranteed life for publicity purposes but did not wish to have more than 10% of the batteries returned under guarantee. In the solution to the previous question we found that setting the guaranteed life to 56.3 hours would result in only 3.1% being returned. A competitive sales manager, however, will want to set this latter figure as high as he can consistent with his costings in order to make the guaranteed life as long as possible. In this question we assume that the profit margin will allow 10% of the batteries to be brought back and replaced without affecting profitability.

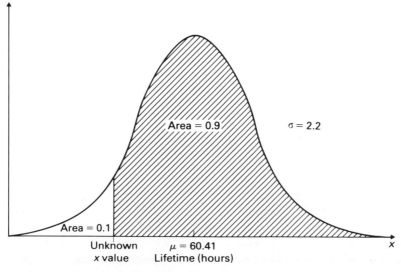

**Fig. 8.8**  Shape of histogram for Question 4 of the Battery Example

In terms of the normal curve, we are searching for an $x$ value such that 90% of all batteries have a longer lifetime than $x$ hours. This means that the area under the curve to the right of $x$ is 0.9, as in Fig. 8.8. This diagram can be scaled to be the standard normal curve and then reflected in the vertical axis so that the unknown $z$ value is positive (Fig. 8.9).

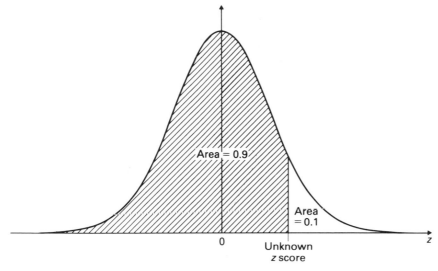

**Fig. 8.9**   Sketch of the standard normal curve for Question 4 of the Battery Example

Whatever $z$ score we find for this diagram will be given a minus sign before we work backwards to Fig. 8.8.

Perhaps the first method which springs to mind of finding the $z$ value in this diagram is to search for the area to the right, 0.1, in the answer columns of the normal table. This is inaccurate, however, as the specific area 0.1 does not appear in those columns and any attempt to use the table 'back to front' is unsatisfactory. On page 138 there is a table which gives the $z$ score corresponding to various values of the area to the right and we find that the required $z$ value is 1.2816.

Remembering that Fig. 8.8 was scaled and reflected to become Fig. 8.9, we now want to convert a $z$ score of $-1.2816$ into an $x$ value. To do this we use the formula

$$x = \mu + \sigma z \tag{8.14}$$

which is a rearrangement of equation (8.12) so that it can be used 'in reverse' to calculate $x$ values from $z$ scores. The $x$ value in Fig. 8.8 is therefore

$$x = 60.41 + 2.2(-1.2816)$$
$$= 57.59$$

Now before we give a recommended guaranteed battery lifetime to the manufacturer, consider the phrase 'about 90%' contained in the question. It implies that accuracy is not of paramount importance and we are really looking for a guarantee which can be expressed as concisely as possible. The manufacturer would surely not want to use our exact answer of 57.59 hours in the wording on his packaging and advertising. **We therefore suggest either guaranteeing 57 hours with just under 10% of batteries being returned or 58 hours with just over 10%.** He may even wish to use 60 hours as the final figure.

As an extra refinement to the solution we could imitate the method of Question 3 to calculate the exact percentage of batteries which will be brought back as a consequence of any of these guarantees being implemented.

## The Normal Approximation to the Binomial Formula

In the Industrial Accident Example of this chapter the binomial formula became difficult to evaluate as the number of trials was large. We used there the expected number of successes, which is the probability of success at each trial times the number of trials, as the average in the Poisson formula to obtain approximate answers.

It could be, however, that the expectation is itself so large that the Poisson formula cannot be computed easily. In such cases we can utilise the normal distribution as described in the next example.

### The Telepathy Example
A fair die is thrown 540 times and each time a woman volunteer is asked to guess the outcome.

*Question 1*    Assuming that she guesses at random, what is the probability that more than 110 of her answers are correct?

*Solution*    The probability of a random guess being correct when a fair die is thrown is 1/6. The sequence of 540 trials are statistically independent and every one has the same probability of success. Hence the probability of a specific number of successes is given by the binomial distribution with $n$, the number of trials, equal to 540 and $p$, the probability of success at each trial, equal to 1/6. In particular we can attempt to calculate the probability of more than 110 successes using formula (7.1).

$$P \text{ (more than 110 successes)} = P(111) + P(112) + \ldots + P(540)$$

$$= \frac{540!}{(540-111)!\ 111!} (\tfrac{1}{6})^{111}(1-\tfrac{1}{6})^{540-111} + \ldots + (\tfrac{1}{6})^{540} \qquad (8.15)$$

This expression is reminiscent of the Industrial Accident Example where we decided to use the Poisson formula to overcome the difficulties of the large factorials and powers. Adopting the same procedure here we find, as the expected number of successes, $pn$, is 90:

$$= \frac{e^{-90}(90)^{111}}{111!} + \frac{e^{-90}(90)^{112}}{112!} + \ldots + \frac{e^{-90}(90)^{540}}{540!} \qquad (8.16)$$

Unfortunately, in this case the resulting Poisson expression is not much easier to evaluate than the original binomial one. This is because most calculators and computers do not work to sufficient accuracy to distinguish between the infinitesimally small $e^{-90}$ and 0. Furthermore there are 410 terms in equation (8.16) so even if they could be obtained on a calculator it would be extremely tedious to add them together without the programmability of a computer.

When the Poisson approximation to the binomial distribution is unsuitable because the expected number of successes is too big for the Poisson formula, the normal distribution can be used instead. We begin by calculating the appropriate mean and standard deviation from the formulae:

$$\left. \begin{array}{l} \mu = pn \\[2mm] \sigma = \sqrt{np\,(1-p)} \end{array} \right\} \tag{8.17}$$

These are 90 and 8.660 25 respectively for the values of $n$ and $p$ in our example.

Now the outcomes in the original binomial distribution are constrained to be whole numbers as they are the various scores the woman can achieve in the experiment. The horizontal axis in the normal distribution, however, ranges over all values of $x$ and includes the whole numbers as points. It is not correct, therefore, to ignore those $x$ values which are not whole numbers as they do have a probability of occurring in the normal distribution. In fact they are overwhelmingly likely to occur and each whole number, being a single point, has zero probability because the area under the curve corresponding to it is zero.

The correct way to approximate a distribution with whole number outcomes using the normal curve is to identify every $x$ value with its nearest whole number. Thus the outcome '7 successes' in the binomial distribution corresponds to the section of the $x$ axis from 6.5 to 7.5 as all such values give 7 when rounded off to the nearest whole number. This **correction for continuity** means that we must always determine the range of $x$ values corresponding to the event of interest in the problem. This consists of all those $x$ values which give the required outcomes when rounded off to the nearest whole number.

In our example, 'more than 110 successes' implies the range '$x$ greater than 110.5' as these are all the $x$ values which round off to a whole number bigger than 110. The standard normal curve is therefore Fig. 8.10 and from the normal table **the required probability is 0.0089.**

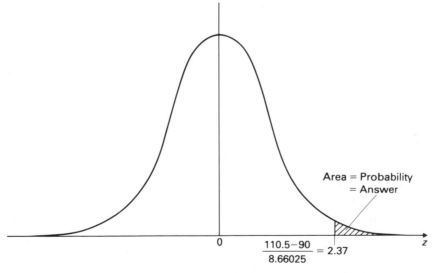

**Fig. 8.10**   Sketch of the standard normal curve for the Telepathy Example

*Question 2*   Does the answer to Question 1 suggest that the woman is telepathic or has similar extra-sensory perception?

*Solution*   It is not within the terms of reference of this book to consider the general problem of analysing the data observed in experiments. However, as statistics is a subject with a more than passing relationship to operational research, we take this opportunity of indicating the method. The argument adopted in **statistical hypothesis testing** runs as follows.

Suppose the treatment or property being investigated has no effect whatsoever. In this example we shall assume that the woman is not telepathic and is merely guessing the outcomes randomly. We calculate the probability of the observed data values based on this **null hypothesis** and examine the result.

(i) If the probability of the observations is low then we have a choice to make. Either we have witnessed an experiment which has a small probability of occurring simply by chance or the null hypothesis we used to calculate that probability is not true. It's like walking into the kitchen to find the remains of a chicken strewn over the floor and the cat licking his lips. The null hypothesis, that the events are unconnected, gives the observations a very low probability. It means that the chicken fell to the ground spontaneously, was half-eaten by some non-feline agency and the cat just happened to be licking his lips. Clearly the probability of this is so small that we dismiss the null hypothesis and blame the cat, but not all statistical hypothesis testing is as straightforward. In general we must decide how low the probability of the observations has to be before the null hypothesis is rejected as being unlikely to be true.

(ii) If the probability of the observations is not low then there is no reason to believe that the null hypothesis is untrue. This collection of negatives does not prove that the null hypothesis is true but simply states that the data to hand is consistent with it. In fact no amount of sample data can prove conclusively that a general statement about a population is true. Seeing a thousand white swans does not prove that all swans are white. Conversely, however, observing just one non-white swan proves that the statement 'all swans are white' is false.

This quirk of logic, that a generality can never be proved by sampling but can be disproved by a counter-example, has given rise to the method by which scientific progress is made. One scientist will perform certain experiments and propose a generalisation, or theory as it is called. The same or another scientist will then attempt to devise an experiment or otherwise make an observation which disproves some consequence of the theory. He in turn proposes a new theory and the process continues. This evolution of theories can be studied in the histories of such subjects as chemistry, physics and biology.

Returning to the telepathy problem, we must decide whether the probability of the observations, that is her score, is so low when based on the null hypothesis that we do not believe the truth of that hypothesis. The answer to Question 1 tells us that there is less than a 1% chance that she was guessing at random. As for the cat in the kitchen, we have a credible null hypothesis only if we accept that observations with a very low probability have occurred. **We therefore conclude this example by rejecting the null hypothesis that the woman was guessing at random.** There must be some other factor at work to explain her high score, but we have no positive evidence of what that factor could be.

## The Normal Approximation to the Poisson Formula

The Poisson distribution is often applied to situations where the average number of events occurring in a fixed time period or spatial region is large. As the appropriate formula (8.1), contains a combination of exponentials, factorials and powers, it may be too difficult to evaluate exactly because of calculator or computer limitations. The following example shows how the normal distribution gives an approximate answer in such cases.

**The Hospital Example**

Patients arrive at the casualty department of a hospital at an average rate of 138.44 per day. It is assumed that the arrivals are random in time and do not occur in batches, as they could in a real hospital. This enables the Poisson distribution to be used to give the probabilities of specific numbers of patients on any one day, as explained in connection with the demand for coaches earlier in this chapter. The identification of an 'arrival pattern' in systems like hospitals, banks, shops and so on is discussed in Chapter 10 on Queues.

*Question 1*   What is the probability that there are more than 130 arrivals in one particular day?

*Solution*   We begin by trying to apply the Poisson formula (8.1).

$$P(\text{more than } 130) = P(131) + P(132) + P(133) + \ldots$$
$$= 1 - P(0) - P(1) - P(2) - \ldots - P(130)$$
$$= 1 - \frac{e^{-138.44}(138.44)^0}{0!} - \frac{e^{-138.44}(138.44)^1}{1!} - \ldots - \frac{e^{-138.44}(138.44)^{130}}{130!} \tag{8.18}$$

In calculating the infinite summation in the first line we have used the trick explained in the solution to Question 3 of this chapter's Coach Company Example. This involves expressing a subtotal of probabilities as 1 minus all the other probabilities. It is of little value here, however, as the terms of the resulting finite sum contain combinations of large and small quantities which are awkward for calculators and computers alike. We therefore turn to the normal distribution as an approximation and use the formulae:

$$\left. \begin{array}{l} \mu = a \\ \sigma = \sqrt{a} \end{array} \right\} \tag{8.19}$$

For the value of $a$ in our example, 138.44, these quantities are 138.44 and 11.7661 respectively.

Having identified the particular normal curve with which to approximate the Poisson distribution, we must now determine the event on the $x$ axis of that curve corresponding to 'more than 130 arrivals'. Using the correction for continuity idea developed in the previous example, the event of interest is '$x$ greater than 130.5'. This is because any $x$ value greater than 130.5 becomes 'more than 130' when rounded off to the nearest whole number.

Figure 8.11 gives the standard normal curve for Question 1 and from the normal table the area and hence the probability is 0.7486. **We conclude that the hospital will experience more than 130 arrivals or 'demands for service' on 75% of all days.**

*Question 2*   How many patients should the department be able to deal with per day if they want to cope with demand on about 95% of all days?

*Solution*   A consequence of being able to deal with $N$ patients per day is that the casualty department copes whenever there are $N$ or less arrivals in one day. We want the probability of this event to be about 95% and so

$$P(0) + P(1) + P(2) + P(3) + \ldots + P(N) \simeq 0.95 \tag{8.20}$$

where the left hand side is the probability of $N$ or less arrivals.

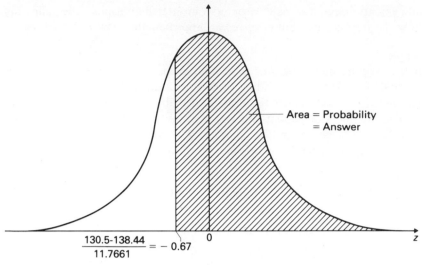

**Fig. 8.11**   Sketch of the standard normal curve for Question 1 of the Hospital Example

If the average number of arrivals were smaller we could find the value of $N$ by adding $P(0)$, $P(1)$, $P(2)$, .... until their total became 0.95. The number of arrivals described by the last probability included in the sum would be the answer, $N$. However, as in Question 1, the numerical difficulties of the Poisson formula when the average $a$ is large preclude this procedure and we use the normal distribution instead.

The particular normal curve we want has the mean and standard deviation calculated in the solution to Question 1, namely 138.44 and 11.7661. Equation (8.20) suggests that we find an $x$ value with the property that 95% of the area under the curve is to the left of $x$. In other words the probability of the number of arrivals being less than $x$ is 0.95.

The corresponding standard normal curve is given in Fig. 8.12 and from the Percentage

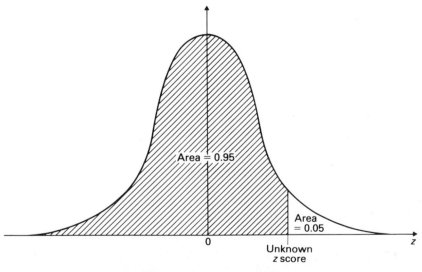

**Fig. 8.12**   Sketch of the standard normal curve for Question 2 of the Hospital Example

Points table on page 138 we see that the unknown $z$ score is 1.6449. Using formula (8.14), which converts $z$ scores back to $x$ values, this is scaled back to the $x$ value 157.794.

As in Question 4 of the Battery Example, we pause before quoting this answer to the manager concerned. It is impossible for a casualty department to arrange to cope with 157.794 patients per day. **Our advice, then, is that if they can deal with 157 patients they will cope on just under 95% of all days while if they allow for 158 patients that figure will be just over 95%.** The exact probability of being able to cope consequent upon either of these decisions can be calculated using the normal distribution and the working would be similar to that of Question 1.

*Question 3* A neighbouring hospital to the one we are considering has an average arrival rate to its casualty department of 64.21 patients per day. Assuming that the incidence of arrivals to both hospitals are unrelated to each other, what is the probability that the combined total of arrivals exceeds 200 in any one day?

*Solution* The Poisson and normal distributions are both **additive** in the sense that if two independent variables both have either distribution then their sum will also have that distribution. The overall mean and variance is the sum of the individual means and variances.

In this case, the combined total of arrivals has the Poisson distribution with mean $138.44 + 64.21$ which is 202.65. Working with this average in the normal approximation we find that

$$P \text{ (more than 200)} = P(x \text{ greater than } 200.5)$$
$$= P(z \text{ greater than } (200.5 - 202.65)/\sqrt{202.65})$$
$$= P(z \text{ greater than} - 0.151)$$
$$= \mathbf{0.5596}, \text{ from tables, which is about } 56\%. \qquad (8.21)$$

The additivity property of the normal distribution is used in PERT (see Chapter 5), to describe the time taken by a sequence of activities all of which have normally distributed durations.

## Computer Programs

Many books of statistical tables contain cumulative probabilities of the Poisson distribution. The method of tabulation, as indeed for the normal distribution, varies from book to book and usually each one contains an explanation on its use. Unfortunately it is often the case in practice that the average in the Poisson or the $z$ score in the normal distribution for a specific problem is not amongst those tabulated. This means accepting an approximate answer by reading from the nearest appropriate place in the tables. Here are three programs which can be used instead of tables or indeed to generate tables.

### Poisson Program

```
10 PRINT "POISSON PROGRAM"
20 PRINT "---------------"
30 PRINT "ENTER AVERAGE, A :";
40 INPUT A
50 PRINT "NUMBER OF   "," P(R) "," P(R OR LESS"
60 PRINT "OCCURRENCES, R"," "," OCCURRENCES)"
70 R=0
```

```
8Ø  S=Ø
9Ø  P=EXP(-A)
1ØØ  S=S+P
11Ø  PRINT R,P,S
12Ø  R=R+1
13Ø  P=P*A/R
14Ø  IF P>Ø.ØØØ1 THEN 1ØØ
15Ø  END
```

**Specimen Run**

```
POISSON PROGRAM
---------------
ENTER AVERAGE, A : ?Ø.86
NUMBER OF        P(R)            P(R OR LESS
OCCURRENCES, R                   OCCURRENCES)
    Ø           Ø.423162         Ø.423162
    1           Ø.363919         Ø.787Ø81
    2           Ø.156485         Ø.943567
    3           4.48591E-2       Ø.988426
    4           9.64471E-3       Ø.998Ø71
    5           1.65889E-3       Ø.99973
    6           2.37774E-4       Ø.999967
```

**Program Notes**

**1**  Lines 1Ø to 9Ø print the headings, read the value of the average, A, from the user, and initialise the number of occurrences, R, the probability of R successes, P, and the total probability S.

**2**  Lines 1ØØ to 12Ø increase S by the value of P, print the values of R, P and S, and increase R by 1.

**3**  Line 13Ø calculates each probability in the distribution from the previous one using the equation

$$P((R+1) \text{ occurrences}) = \frac{P(R \text{ occurrences}) \times A}{R} \qquad (8.22)$$

This relationship is a consequence of the mathematical structure of the Poisson formula (8.1) and avoids having to evaluate factorials and powers. As all the quantities are kept small and the exponential function is used just once in the whole program, this method ensures the highest possible accuracy from the computer.

**4**  Line 14Ø tests the last probability evaluated and continues the calculations only if it is greater than 0.0001. Clearly this 'cutoff' level of accuracy can be altered if required.

**Normal Area Program**

```
1Ø  PRINT "STANDARD NORMAL AREA PROGRAM"
2Ø  PRINT "----------------------------"
3Ø  PRINT
4Ø  PRINT "Z SCORE ";
5Ø  INPUT Z
6Ø  T=Z
```

```
7Ø  S=Z
8Ø  R=1
9Ø  T=(-T*Z*Z*(2*R-1))
1ØØ  T=T/((2*R+1)*2*R)
11Ø  S=S+T
12Ø  R=R+1
13Ø  IF  ABS(T)>Ø.ØØØ1  THEN  9Ø
14Ø  A=Ø.5-(S/SQR(8*ATN(1.Ø)))
15Ø  PRINT  "AREA TO THE RIGHT IS ";A
16Ø  END
```

### Specimen Run

```
STANDARD NORMAL AREA PROGRAM
---------------------------

Z SCORE   ?-2.1
AREA TO THE RIGHT IS   Ø.98214
```

### Program Notes

**1**   The program uses the series

$$\text{Area to the right of } Z = 0.5 - \frac{1}{\sqrt{2\pi}}(Z - \frac{Z^3}{3} + \frac{Z^5}{5.2^2.2!} - \frac{Z^7}{7.2^3.3!} + \frac{Z^9}{9.2^4.4!} - \cdots) \qquad (8.23)$$

This is obtained, incidentally, by integrating the Maclaurin series of the standard normal function $\dfrac{e^{-Z^2/2}}{\sqrt{2\pi}}$ from Z to infinity.

**2**   Lines 1Ø to 8Ø print the heading, read the value of Z from the user and initialise the variables R, which counts the terms in the brackets of equation (8.23), T, which is the value of the Rth term, and S, which is the sum of the first R terms.

**3**   Lines 9Ø and 1ØØ calculate the value of the (R + 1)th term from that of the Rth. Lines 11Ø and 12Ø update the values of S and R while line 13Ø sends control back to line 9Ø for the next term to be processed if the terms are still significantly large, otherwise control goes to the next instruction.

**4**   Line 14Ø calculates the area from equation (8.23) with the value of the series in brackets taken to be S. Notice that the value of $\pi$ needed in the calculation is obtained from the computer as 4 times the inverse tangent function of 1. This is preferable to supplying the program with our own approximation to $\pi$ as in evaluating it from a function the computer will work to its own maximum accuracy. Finally, line 15Ø prints out the answer.

### Normal Percentage Points Program

```
1Ø  PRINT  "PERCENTAGE POINTS PROGRAM"
2Ø  PRINT  "-------------------------"
3Ø  PRINT
4Ø  PRINT  "AREA TO THE RIGHT ";
5Ø  INPUT P
```

```
60 X=-5
70 Y=5
80 Z=(X+Y)/2
90 T=Z
100 S=Z
110 R=1
120 T=(-T*Z*Z*(2*R-1))
130 T=T/((2*R+1)*2*R)
140 S=S+T
150 R=R+1
160 IF ABS(T)>0.00001 THEN 120
170 A=0.5-(S/SQR(8*ATN(1)))   '
180 IF ABS(A-P)<0.0000001 THEN 220
190 IF A<P THEN Y=Z
200 IF A>P THEN X=Z
210 GOTO 80
220 PRINT "Z SCORE IS ";Z
230 END
```

**Specimen Run**

```
PERCENTAGE POINTS PROGRAM
-------------------------

AREA TO THE RIGHT  ?0.4
Z SCORE IS   0.253347
```

**Program Notes**

**1**   This program uses the last program on a trial and error basis to produce a Z value which results in a given area to the right. The numerical procedure used is known as the **binary chop** and consists of halving a range of values within which the answer is known to be. The new range is taken to be the half which contains the answer and the process repeated, thus generating a sequence of ranges, each half the size of its predecessor and all of them containing the answer. When the area resulting from the mid-point of one of these ranges is sufficiently close to the given area, then the value of that mid-point is printed out as the answer.

**2**   Lines 10 to 50 print the heading and read the value of the required area from the user. Lines 60 and 70 set the very first range of values to be from $-5$ to $+5$ thus including all possible answers.

**3**   Line 80 calculates the mid-point of the range from X to Y and lines 90 to 170 are the same as lines 60 to 150 of the last program. They calculate the area to the right of Z. Line 180 tests this area to see whether it is sufficiently close to the required value, P. If it is not then lines 190 and 200 redefine the range from X to Y according to whether it is too large or too small. Line 210 sends control back to line 80 for the new mid-point and area to be calculated. The halving procedure continues until the computed area and the required area are within 0.000 000 1 of each other; at this time control is sent by line 180 to line 220 where the current value of Z is printed out as the answer.

**Standard Normal Tables**

These tables are referred to in various parts of this book whenever the normal distribution

**Table 8.4** Area under the Standard Normal Curve

Area tabulated

| z | .00 | .01 | .02 | .03 | .04 | .05 | .06 | .07 | .08 | .09 |
|---|---|---|---|---|---|---|---|---|---|---|
| 0.0 | .50000 | .49601 | .49202 | .48803 | .48405 | .48006 | .47608 | .47210 | .46812 | .46414 |
| 0.1 | .46017 | .45620 | .45224 | .44828 | .44433 | .44038 | .43644 | .43251 | .42858 | .42465 |
| 0.2 | .42074 | .41683 | .41294 | .40905 | .40517 | .40129 | .39743 | .39358 | .38974 | .38591 |
| 0.3 | .38209 | .37828 | .37448 | .37070 | .36693 | .36317 | .35942 | .35569 | .35197 | .34827 |
| 0.4 | .34458 | .34090 | .33724 | .33360 | .32997 | .32636 | .32276 | .31918 | .31561 | .31207 |
| 0.5 | .30854 | .30503 | .30153 | .29806 | .29460 | .29116 | .28774 | .28434 | .28096 | .27760 |
| 0.6 | .27425 | .27093 | .26763 | .26435 | .26109 | .25785 | .25463 | .25143 | .24825 | .24510 |
| 0.7 | .24196 | .23885 | .23576 | .23270 | .22965 | .22663 | .22363 | .22065 | .21770 | .21476 |
| 0.8 | .21186 | .20897 | .20611 | .20327 | .20045 | .19766 | .19489 | .19215 | .18943 | .18673 |
| 0.9 | .18406 | .18141 | .17879 | .17619 | .17361 | .17106 | .16853 | .16602 | .16354 | .16109 |
| 1.0 | .15866 | .15625 | .15386 | .15150 | .14917 | .14686 | .14457 | .14231 | .14007 | .13786 |
| 1.1 | .13567 | .13350 | .13136 | .12924 | .12714 | .12507 | .12302 | .12100 | .11900 | .11702 |
| 1.2 | .11507 | .11314 | .11123 | .10935 | .10749 | .10565 | .10383 | .10204 | .10027 | .09853 |
| 1.3 | .09680 | .09510 | .09342 | .09176 | .09012 | .08851 | .08691 | .08534 | .08379 | .08226 |
| 1.4 | .08076 | .07927 | .07780 | .07636 | .07493 | .07353 | .07214 | .07078 | .06944 | .06811 |
| 1.5 | .06681 | .06552 | .06426 | .06301 | .06178 | .06057 | .05938 | .05821 | .05705 | .05592 |
| 1.6 | .05480 | .05370 | .05262 | .05155 | .05050 | .04947 | .04846 | .04746 | .04648 | .04551 |
| 1.7 | .04457 | .04363 | .04272 | .04182 | .04093 | .04006 | .03920 | .03836 | .03754 | .03673 |
| 1.8 | .03593 | .03515 | .03438 | .03362 | .03288 | .03216 | .03144 | .03074 | .03005 | .02938 |
| 1.9 | .02872 | .02807 | .02743 | .02680 | .02619 | .02555 | .02500 | .02442 | .02385 | .02330 |
| 2.0 | .02275 | .02222 | .02169 | .02118 | .02068 | .02018 | .01970 | .01923 | .01876 | .01831 |
| 2.1 | .01786 | .01743 | .01700 | .01659 | .01618 | .01578 | .01539 | .01500 | .01463 | .01426 |
| 2.2 | .01390 | .01355 | .01321 | .01287 | .01255 | .01222 | .01191 | .01160 | .01130 | .01101 |
| 2.3 | .01072 | .01044 | .01017 | .00990 | .00964 | .00939 | .00914 | .00889 | .00866 | .00842 |
| 2.4 | .00820 | .00798 | .00776 | .00755 | .00734 | .00714 | .00695 | .00676 | .00657 | .00639 |
| 2.5 | .00621 | .00604 | .00587 | .00570 | .00554 | .00539 | .00523 | .00509 | .00494 | .00480 |
| 2.6 | .00466 | .00453 | .00440 | .00427 | .00415 | .00403 | .00391 | .00379 | .00368 | .00357 |
| 2.7 | .00347 | .00336 | .00326 | .00317 | .00307 | .00298 | .00289 | .00280 | .00272 | .00264 |
| 2.8 | .00256 | .00248 | .00240 | .00233 | .00226 | .00219 | .00212 | .00205 | .00199 | .00193 |
| 2.9 | .00187 | .00181 | .00175 | .00169 | .00164 | .00159 | .00154 | .00149 | .00144 | .00139 |
| 3.0 | .00135 | .00131 | .00126 | .00122 | .00118 | .00114 | .00111 | .00107 | .00104 | .00100 |
| 3.1 | .00097 | .00094 | .00090 | .00087 | .00085 | .00082 | .00079 | .00076 | .00074 | .00071 |
| 3.2 | .00069 | .00066 | .00064 | .00062 | .00060 | .00058 | .00056 | .00054 | .00052 | .00050 |
| 3.3 | .00048 | .00047 | .00045 | .00043 | .00042 | .00040 | .00039 | .00038 | .00036 | .00035 |
| 3.4 | .00034 | .00032 | .00031 | .00030 | .00029 | .00028 | .00027 | .00026 | .00025 | .00024 |
| 3.5 | .00023 | .00022 | .00022 | .00021 | .00020 | .00019 | .00019 | .00018 | .00017 | .00017 |
| 3.6 | .00016 | .00015 | .00015 | .00014 | .00014 | .00013 | .00013 | .00012 | .00012 | .00011 |
| 3.7 | .00011 | .00010 | .00010 | .00010 | .00009 | .00009 | .00008 | .00008 | .00008 | .00008 |
| 3.8 | .00007 | .00007 | .00007 | .00006 | .00006 | .00006 | .00006 | .00005 | .00005 | .00005 |
| 3.9 | .00005 | .00005 | .00004 | .00004 | .00004 | .00004 | .00004 | .00004 | .00003 | .00003 |

**Table 8.5**   Percentage Points of the Standard Normal Distribution

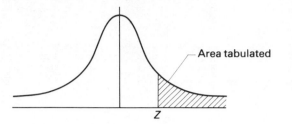

Area tabulated

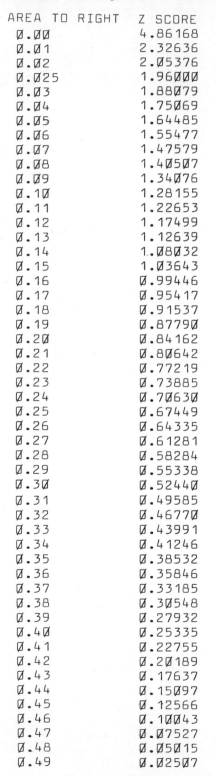

| AREA TO RIGHT | Z SCORE |
|---|---|
| 0.00 | 4.86168 |
| 0.01 | 2.32636 |
| 0.02 | 2.05376 |
| 0.025 | 1.96000 |
| 0.03 | 1.88079 |
| 0.04 | 1.75069 |
| 0.05 | 1.64485 |
| 0.06 | 1.55477 |
| 0.07 | 1.47579 |
| 0.08 | 1.40507 |
| 0.09 | 1.34076 |
| 0.10 | 1.28155 |
| 0.11 | 1.22653 |
| 0.12 | 1.17499 |
| 0.13 | 1.12639 |
| 0.14 | 1.08032 |
| 0.15 | 1.03643 |
| 0.16 | 0.99446 |
| 0.17 | 0.95417 |
| 0.18 | 0.91537 |
| 0.19 | 0.87790 |
| 0.20 | 0.84162 |
| 0.21 | 0.80642 |
| 0.22 | 0.77219 |
| 0.23 | 0.73885 |
| 0.24 | 0.70630 |
| 0.25 | 0.67449 |
| 0.26 | 0.64335 |
| 0.27 | 0.61281 |
| 0.28 | 0.58284 |
| 0.29 | 0.55338 |
| 0.30 | 0.52440 |
| 0.31 | 0.49585 |
| 0.32 | 0.46770 |
| 0.33 | 0.43991 |
| 0.34 | 0.41246 |
| 0.35 | 0.38532 |
| 0.36 | 0.35846 |
| 0.37 | 0.33185 |
| 0.38 | 0.30548 |
| 0.39 | 0.27932 |
| 0.40 | 0.25335 |
| 0.41 | 0.22755 |
| 0.42 | 0.20189 |
| 0.43 | 0.17637 |
| 0.44 | 0.15097 |
| 0.45 | 0.12566 |
| 0.46 | 0.10043 |
| 0.47 | 0.07527 |
| 0.48 | 0.05015 |
| 0.49 | 0.02507 |

is used. All the values tabulated can be found by running the programs just described and the reader might like to experiment with FOR loops in them in order to generate a complete table in a single run. The computer programs are preferable from the accuracy point of view when answers are required for values in between those tabulated.

## Summary

1  The Poisson distribution describes events occurring randomly in time or space. It is used to describe the demand pattern for goods or services in stock control, queuing and level of service problems. It is also used to describe the number of failures in reliability theory.

2  If the average number of events occurring within the time period or spatial region concerned is $a$, then

$$P(\text{exactly } r \text{ events}) = \frac{e^{-a} a^r}{r!}$$

3  Although there are an infinite number of possible outcomes for the number of events occurring, all their probabilities add up to 1. This enables infinite sums of probabilities to be calculated, as in Question 3 of the Coach Company Example.

4  The Poisson formula can be used as an approximation for the binomial formula if the number of trials, $n$, is large and the probability of success at each trial, $p$, is small. The method is to take $a$ equal to $pn$ in the Poisson formula.

5  The normal distribution describes populations of measurements whose histograms have a symmetric bell-like shape. The outline of the histogram is drawn with an $x$ axis scaled to the standard normal curve using the population mean, $\mu$, and the population standard deviation, $\sigma$, in the formula

$$z \text{ score} = \frac{x - \mu}{\sigma}$$

Probabilities about the original population are represented as areas on this graph and evaluated using tables like the one on page 137. The table on page 138 enables a $z$ score to be found when the area to its right is known. This is useful in problems like Question 4 of the Battery Example.

6  The normal distribution gives approximate probabilities for the binomial distribution when the number of trials, $n$, is large and the probability of success at each trial, $p$, is small but their product, $pn$, is too large for the Poisson approximation. The method consists of using a normal curve with mean $\mu$ equal to $pn$, and standard deviation $\sigma$ equal to $\sqrt{np(1-p)}$. Each whole number outcome of the binomial distribution is interpreted as being the range of $x$ values on the normal curve axis which round off to that number.

7  The normal distribution gives approximate probabilities for the Poisson distribution when the average, $a$, in that distribution is too large for the Poisson formula to be used. The method consists of using a normal curve with mean $\mu$ equal to $a$ and standard deviation $\sigma$ equal to $\sqrt{a}$. Each whole number outcome of the Poisson distribution is interpreted as being the range of $x$ values on the normal curve axis which round off to that number.

**8** The Poisson and normal distributions are both additive in the sense that if two independent variables have either of these distributions then their sum will also have that distribution. The overall mean and variance is the sum of the individual means and variances.

## Further Reading

The work of this chapter is used in the next three chapters and covered in many operational research textbooks like (6) and (7) as well as in statistics books like (22), (24), (25), (28) and (29). The Poisson distribution is used in operational research to describe demand for goods or services and arrivals to a system which are random in time. The normal distribution is important as an approximation to the Poisson and various lifetime distributions. Applications of the normal distribution to classical statistical sampling theory and hypothesis testing and the fitting of a normal curve to experimental data can be found in books like (25), (27) and (29).

## Exercises

**1** A company finds that on average 4.7 faults occur to their telephone system each year. It can be assumed that the faults occur randomly in time and are unrelated to each other. (i) Calculate the probability that exactly 3 faults occur in a given year. (ii) Calculate the probability that there are 4 or more faults in a given year. (iii) Calculate the average number of faults per month and hence the probability that at least two faults occur during a given month.

**2** An upholsterer experiences the demand for renovating fireside chairs to be 1.9 per day on average. Each chair requires one man working for one day and the chairs arrive at the beginning of the day. It costs the upholsterer £30 per day to employ a man and he charges customers £45 per day for the labour involved in working on their chair. (i) Calculate the upholsterer's expected daily profit if he employs just one man, himself. (ii) Determine by the use of expectations whether it would be profitable for him to employ another man.

**3** A botanist observes 54 dandelions growing inside a 1200 square metre area of grass. Assuming that the dandelions grow randomly throughout the area, use the average per square metre to calculate the probability that there are more than two in a given area of one square metre.

**4** A bicycle manufacturer finds that about 1 in every 600 bicycles are returned to him under guarantee. Calculate the probability that less than 3 are returned out of a batch of 1500 bicycles.

**5** A machine produces bolts with an average length of 4 cm and standard deviation 1.3 cm. Assuming that the bolt lengths are normally distributed, find the probability that a bolt chosen at random (i) is longer than 4.5 cm, (ii) has a length between 3.7 cm and 4.9 cm, (iii) is shorter than 4.2 cm. Use the binomial distribution to calculate the probability that there are more than 4 bolts shorter than 4.2 cm in a sample of 6 bolts chosen at random from the production line.

**6** Charlie Brown scores 74% for English in which the class average is 70.1% with standard deviation 2.2%. His chemistry mark is 84% and the class average in that subject is 80.1% with standard deviation 2.5%. His mother wants to buy him a chemistry set as he did so well in chemistry. Does his father, who happens to be a statistician, agree with her?

**7** An insurance company receives on average 406.3 claims of a certain type each year. Assuming the claims occur randomly in time, find the probability that (i) it receives more than 450 claims in a given year, (ii) it receives between 380 and 436 claims inclusive in a given year.

**8** In a certain town house prices can be assumed to be normally distributed with mean £63 000 and standard deviation £6000. The price of second-hand cars is also normally distributed with mean £2300 and standard deviation £230. Use the additivity of the normal distribution to find the probability that a house and car chosen at random have a total cost greater than £84 000. Remember that the variances should be added together, not the standard deviations.

**9** Out of a thousand patients, 770 responded to a certain drug. What is the probability that out of a further 120 patients, more than 93 respond?

# 9 Stock Control

Most companies are involved with the handling and storage of stock. This takes the form of raw materials or manufactured articles waiting to be sold or delivered. Poor control of stock levels can influence the profitability and efficiency of a company's operations and possibly affect its relationship with its customers and suppliers.

In this chapter we consider ways of determining the quantity of a certain item to be ordered and how often the orders should be placed. This can be done with the objective of either meeting demand for a sufficiently high proportion of the time or minimising the total handling cost. The latter expense includes the cost of placing an order or setting up a production run, delivery charges, warehousing expenses, penalty costs of being out of stock, and any interest payments on the value of the stock. The result of the analysis may be that the order quantity is zero and the item should not be stocked at all but bought in as and when required.

The first worked example serves to introduce some of the fundamental ideas of stock control when the demand for stock is constant, or **deterministic.** The next two examples extend these concepts to situations where the demand for stock is random in time, or **stochastic.** A full understanding of their solutions requires a knowledge of the work in Chapters 6 and 8 on probability, expectation, and the Poisson and normal distributions. The last worked example results in a simulation being performed and the reader might find it helpful to have read the simulation section of Chapter 6.

## Deterministic Demand

### The Ice Block Example
A fish shop needs a block of ice each day to decorate its window display. Blocks of ice are manufactured in a special freezer which can make up to 4 of them at a time. Each run of the freezer costs £4 irrespective of how many blocks are made while unused ones cost £1 each per day to keep frozen. We investigate how often the special freezer should be used to manufacture the blocks and how many should be made in order to minimise the overall cost.

*Solution*   We examine every possible strategy:
*Strategy A: Make 1 block every night.* The cost of this plan is £4 per day, that is each 24-hour period, and is the cost of running the special freezer every night. There are no storage costs in this plan.
*Strategy B: Make 2 blocks every 2nd night.* The cost of this policy is £4 to run the special freezer and £1 to store one of the blocks for one day. This gives a total cost of £5 over a two-day period which averages to £2.50 per day. This compares favourably with the

cost of strategy A but nevertheless we continue the investigation in the hope of finding something even cheaper.

*Strategy C: Make 3 blocks every 3rd night.* The cost of this strategy is £4 for a production run, £1 to store one of the blocks for one day and £2 to store one of the blocks for 2 days. This totals £7 but is spread over a 3-day period and so averages to £2.33 per day. This strategy is therefore cheaper to implement than either A or B.

*Strategy D: Make 4 blocks every 4th night.* The cost of this policy is £4 for a production run, £1 to store one block for 1 day, £2 to store a block for 2 days and £3 to store one block for 3 days. This totals £10 for a 4-day period giving an average of £2.50 per day.

As the special freezer cannot make more than 4 blocks at a time, A, B, C and D are the only strategies possible. Comparing their daily costs we see that C is the cheapest and **the fish shop manager should therefore make 3 ice blocks every 3 nights.**

This example illustrates the compromise between having large quantities of stock resulting in high storage costs, as in strategy D, and having small stock levels giving rise to high production run or ordering costs, as in strategies A and B. This compromise is a central feature of stock control and a formula is now developed which predicts the optimal strategy in the more general case. We begin by elaborating on the important parameters of the Ice Block Example.

### The Production Run or Ordering Cost, £*P*

In the example this was £4 and in general it is the cost of initiating a stock replenishment over and above the cost of the stock itself. For manufacturers it is the cost of setting up a production run, while if the item is not manufactured but bought by the company then it is the cost of placing an order. This includes any transport and administration charges not incorporated in the unit cost of the stock item itself.

The cost of placing an order is often underestimated by managers. They fail to realise that if ordering costs are truly zero then the least cost stock policy would be to place an order every day, or indeed every hour. This would reduce storage costs to zero and solve the problem. We must therefore quantify the ordering cost if we want to compare its effect with the cost of holding stock and find the optimal compromise between small orders with large ordering costs and large orders with large storage costs.

### The Storage Cost, £*S* per item per unit time

In the Ice Block Example this was £1 per block per day. In general it includes warehouse expenses, staff costs, interest on the cash tied up in the value of the stock, heating, refrigeration etc. It is averaged out to be a cost per stock item per unit time period.

### The Demand, *d* items per unit time

This was 1 per day in the last example and was constant from day to day. This is called **deterministic demand** but it is more usual for demand to be **stochastic** and vary randomly from one time period to another. A retail shop experiences random demand for goods and we shall consider such an example later in the chapter. Before that we generalise the Ice Block Example to any problem with constant demand.

## The Economic Order Quantity (EOQ)

When the demand for a stock item is constant, the graph of stock level against time looks ideally like Fig. 9.1.

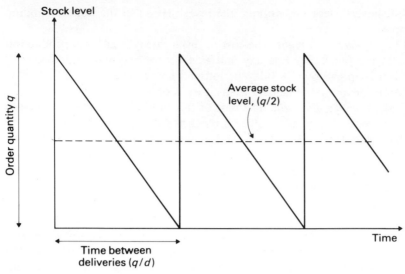

**Fig. 9.1**    Stock level against time graph with constant demand

This is the ideal state of affairs because new stock arrives just as the stock level falls to zero and there are no delays in its availability. We now calculate the stock handling cost per unit time.

As $q$ items are used at the rate of $d$ per unit time, the stock level will decrease to zero after $(q/d)$ time periods. For instance in the Ice Block Example a production run of, say, 4 blocks lasted (4/1) days as the demand was for 1 block per day. The production or ordering cost $P$ incurred at the beginning of this time averages out to $P/(q/d)$ per time unit.

We must add to this the storage cost and from the graph we see that the average stock level is $(q/2)$ items. As the storage cost is $S$ per item per time period, the cost is $(S \times q/2)$ per unit time. Hence the total stock handling cost per unit time is

$$\frac{Pd}{q} + \frac{Sq}{2} \tag{9.1}$$

Using calculus it can be shown that this cost is a minimum when $q$ is equal to the **Economic Order Quantity,** or **EOQ,**

$$\sqrt{\frac{2Pd}{S}} \tag{9.2}$$

As the quantity delivered is used at the constant rate of $d$ items per unit time, we can calculate the time interval necessary between placing orders. It is simply the Economic Order Quantity divided by $d$.

To illustrate the use of formula (9.2) we solve the Ice Block Example again. Putting $P$ equal to 4, $S$ equal to 1 and $d$ equal to 1 we obtain

$$\text{EOQ} = \sqrt{2Pd/S} = \sqrt{2 \times 4 \times 1/1} = \sqrt{8} = 2.8284 \tag{9.3}$$

As the nearest whole number to this answer is 3, we have found the same solution to the problem as we did before. However, using the EOQ formula is much quicker than evaluating the cost of every possible strategy.

Before leaving the Ice Block Example, it is instructive to look at the graph of the average stock handling cost (9.1), against the quantity ordered (Fig. 9.2).

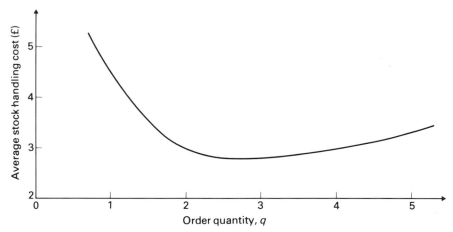

**Fig. 9.2** Average stock handling cost against order quantity

This curve shows the compromise between ordering costs and storage costs which a stock control policy has to achieve. If the quantity ordered, $q$, is small then the total cost is high because the ordering cost is high, while if $q$ is large then the cost is high because the storage cost is high. The intermediate value where the curve has a minimum is given by the EOQ formula as explained above. Although the costs in graph (9.2) are slightly higher than those in our original analysis because the former assumes an average storage cost, the resulting minimum occurs at the same point along the order quantity axis.

The EOQ formula is widely used even when the demand is not constant. In such cases $d$ is put equal to the average demand and the formula gives a rough idea of the best order quantity or replenishment level if the stock has to be brought back up to some predetermined amount.

## Stochastic Demand

Consider a typical stock level versus time graph when demand is not constant (Fig. 9.3). This is to be contrasted with Fig. 9.1 which relates to a constant demand situation, although the decisions to be made are the same, namely, how much stock should be ordered and when the order should be placed. We examine two systems which are in common use for optimising the effect of these decisions.

## Re-order Level (ROL) Systems

This involves placing an order whenever the stock level falls to a certain value called the **re-order level**. It is an easy system to implement and in industrial applications is known as the **two-bin** system. When there are no items left in the main bin an order is placed for more stock. While waiting for the order to be delivered or manufactured items are used from a second smaller bin. The number of items in this bin is therefore the re-order level and provided it contains enough items to supply demand during the waiting period, called

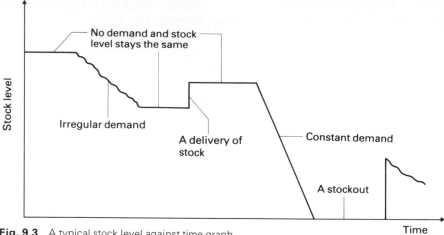

**Fig. 9.3**   A typical stock level against time graph

the **lead time**, the system will work satisfactorily. Naturally the order quantity is sufficiently large to replenish both bins.

The setting of the re-order level will provide a rule for when stock should be ordered. Ideally the arrival of the order should coincide with the stock level falling to zero and we can adopt Fig. 9.1 as an objective. This means that the quantity ordered can still be determined from the EOQ formula (9.2).

The following example illustrates this together with two methods for setting the value of the re-order level, one to give an acceptable service level and the other to minimise costs.

**The Radio Example**

The demand from customers at a shop for a certain type of radio set averages 1.4 per week. It costs the shop manager £2 to place an order and each radio costs 50p per week to store. If deliveries occur 3 weeks after an order is given, advise the manager on a stock policy.

*Solution*   The lead time here is 3 weeks and assumed to be known and constant. In practice it is unknown and random and the curse of any stock control system. The other parameters were discussed in the Ice Block Example and we use the EOQ formula (9.2) with $P$ equal to 2, $d$ equal to 1.4, and $S$ equal to 0.50.

$$\text{EOQ} = \sqrt{\frac{2Pd}{S}} = \sqrt{\frac{2 \times 2 \times 1.4}{0.5}} = \sqrt{11.2} = 3.35 \qquad (9.4)$$

We interpret this to mean that the manager should order 3 radio sets at a time to achieve the minimum cost compromise between the expense of ordering and storage. Note that this is independent of the decision of *when* to order.   We now examine two methods of selecting an appropriate re-order level to determine when orders are to be placed. One of them attempts to minimise the total stock handling cost as we did in the Ice Block Example while the other involves specifying how often stockouts can be tolerated.

**Method 1: Minimise the Expected Cost**

In developing the Economic Order Quantity formula using Fig. 9.1 we considered it forbidden to run out of stock. The quantity ordered was mathematically linked with the time period between orders so that, because demand was constant and predictable, stock-outs would never occur. When demand is stochastic, however, there is no amount of stock we can keep to be absolutely certain of not running out. Demand could, theoretically, exceed any predetermined level. It is therefore necessary to quantify the cost of being out of stock in order to find a compromise between stockouts on the one hand and storing and ordering too much on the other.

The **shortage cost** per item is the cost of not having an item in stock when it is demanded. This could be the profit that would have been made or it could be much greater because of the loss of customer loyalty and further business. If the stock item is one of a manufacturer's raw materials, a stockout can delay production and involve considerable expense. It is therefore often difficult to assign a cost to being short of a stock item and this inaccuracy is a weakness of minimum cost methods for stochastic demand.

The shortage cost mirrors the storage cost in the sense that one is the cost of not stocking an item when it is required while the other is the cost of having the item when it is not required. In this context, the re-order level, which is the stock in hand at the start of the lead time, is a compromise between holding large quantities of stock with high storage costs in order to avoid a stockout, or having low stocks with correspondingly high shortage costs.

In the Radio Example, suppose the manager estimates the cost of not having a radio when one is required to be £4.50. This shortage can occur only during the lead time as stock levels are always greater than the re-order level at other times. The alternative to being short of a radio set is to stock an extra one over the lead time at a cost of 3 weeks at 50p per week, or £1.50. In any one lead time, a stockout either occurs or does not occur, and using the concept of expectation described in Chapter 6, the expected payoff of stocking one extra radio is

$$
\begin{aligned}
\text{Sum of probability times payoff} &= P(\text{stockout}) \times (4.50) + P(\text{no stockout}) \times (-1.50) \\
&= P(\text{stockout}) \times (4.50) + (1 - P(\text{stockout})) \times (-1.50) \\
&= 6 \times P(\text{stockout}) - 1.5 \qquad\qquad (9.5)
\end{aligned}
$$

We shall use this expression in a subtle way. The probability of a stockout can be found from the Poisson distribution as the demand for radios during the lead time is a random number of events occurring within a fixed time period. The Coach Company Example of Chapter 8 showed how such demand situations can be described. We then determine the smallest re-order level, which is the stock in hand at the start of the lead time, which results in the value of (9.5) being negative. In other words, adding one radio to that level gives an expected loss and we therefore have the optimal quantity.

To implement this scheme we note that the expected demand during the lead time is 1.4 per week for 3 weeks, or 4.2. Using this average in the Poisson formula (8.1) we can construct Table 9.1 showing the consequences of different re-order levels.

The probabilities in the second column of Table 9.1 can be generated by the computer program on the Poisson distribution given at the end of Chapter 8. It is a useful table as it describes what will happen as a result of any chosen re-order level and in a way corresponds to the cost against order quantity graph (Fig. 9.2) for the deterministic demand case where we chose the minimum point.

**Table 9.1**

| Re-order level | P(no stockout) =P(demand during lead time ≤ re-order level) = P(0)+P(1)+ .. .. +P(re-order level) | P(stockout) =1−P(no stockout) | Expected payoff of extra item, (9.5) |
|---|---|---|---|
| 1 | 0.0780 | 0.9220 | 4.03 |
| 2 | 0.2102 | 0.7898 | 3.24 |
| 3 | 0.3954 | 0.6046 | 2.13 |
| 4 | 0.5898 | 0.4102 | 0.96 |
| 5 | 0.7531 | 0.2469 | −0.02 |
| 6 | 0.8675 | 0.1325 | −0.71 |
| 7 | 0.9361 | 0.0639 | −1.12 |

From our results we see that a re-order level of 5 radios is optimal in the sense that having one more in stock over the lead time has a negative payoff. The re-order level of 5 is the smallest with this property and our conclusion is that **the manager should order 3 radios, the Economic Order Quantity, whenever the stock level falls to 5 radios.**

In general the minimum expected cost method uses the smallest re-order level for which the probability of a stockout during the lead time is less than

$$\frac{\text{storage cost per item during the lead time}}{\text{storage cost per item during the lead time}+\text{shortage cost}} \qquad (9.6)$$

This is the expression one obtains by equating the expectation (9.5) to zero and making the probability of a stockout the subject of the equation. In our example this fraction is $1.5/(1.5+4.5)$, which is 0.25 and the re-order level for which the probability of a stockout is just less than this value in Table 9.1 is 5, as we found before.

It was mentioned above how unreliable estimates of the shortage cost can be in practice. There is another method for determining the re-order level to be implemented which ignores the costs of the operation and aims to provide a specified degree of 'customer satisfaction'.

**Method 2: Provide a Given Level of Service**
Suppose it is considered desirable to keep enough stock for the probability of not running out in any one week to be more than, say, 90%. This probability is called the **level of service** and the idea behind it was touched on in Question 2 of the Hospital Example in Chapter 8.

Table 9.1 displays the probability of not having a stockout resulting from each possible re-order level. We can therefore select the particular one which achieves the standard of service required and in this case using a re-order level of 7 radios gives a level of service equal to 0.9361, or about 94%.

**We conclude that if the shop manager places an order for more radios when the stock level falls to 7 then the probability of not running out while waiting for a delivery to arrive is greater than 90%.** We calculated earlier in equation (9.4) that the Economic Order Quantity is 3 radios and so this is the associated order quantity.

Notice that the expected demand during the lead time is 4.2 and yet we have set the re-order level as high as 7, an excess of 2.8. This is called the **safety** or **buffer stock** and its purpose is to cater for fluctuations in demand over and above the average in order to maintain the required level of service. In other words, whilst we expect to sell 4.2 radios during the lead time, we place an order when we still have 7 in stock to be more than 90% sure of not selling out.

## Re-order Cycle (ROC) Systems

The Radio Example was a typical application of the re-order level system of stock control. In many businesses, however, there are several different types of stock items which must be ordered at the same time. The re-order level system is not appropriate then as it involves placing separate orders for each stock item type at irregular intervals. If the items concerned are cheap or small then the ordering cost of such a system can be unacceptably high.

The re-order cycle system has a fixed time interval, called the **review period**, between successive operations of stock taking/ordering. A good example of the use of this system is in a supermarket where it is desirable to order all the different food 'lines' from one or two wholesalers at the same time each week or month. Stock taking of all the foods is done at the same time, possibly by a computerised system, and all the decisions on re-ordering are made together.

### The Beans Example

A supermarket sells on average 25 cases of baked beans each week. Stock taking and ordering for all tinned foods is carried out every second Thursday with orders placed one Thursday arriving as stock in hand for the following Thursday. If the storage cost of a case of beans is estimated to be 3p per week and the shortage cost is 7p per case per week, advise the supermarket manager on how to calculate the order quantity.

*Solution* We consider the same two criteria for optimising the stock control that were used for re-order level systems. One tries to minimise the expected stock handling cost while the other aims for a given level of service.

### Method 1: Minimise the Expected Cost

The technique for re-order level systems was to find the stock value which gave a negative expected payoff when increased by 1. The argument here is the same except that as stockouts can occur at any time during the whole review period and not just in the lead time, the review period replaces the lead time in formula (9.6) and the application of the Poisson distribution. Formula (9.6) becomes

$$\frac{\text{storage cost per item for the review period}}{\begin{array}{c}\text{storage cost per item} \\ \text{for the review period}\end{array} + \begin{array}{c}\text{shortage cost per item} \\ \text{for the review period}\end{array}} \qquad (9.7)$$

which in this example is $(3 \times 2)/(3 \times 2 + 7 \times 2)$, or 0.3. We now want to find a stock level which results in the probability of a stockout being just less than this value.

As usual we assume that the demand for stock has the Poisson probability distribution. During the review period the average demand is 2 weeks at 25 cases per week which is 50 cases. This is a large number for a Poisson mean and so we use the normal approximation described in the Hospital Example of Chapter 8 (Fig. 9.4).

From the Percentage Points Table on page 138, the $z$ score with area 0.3 to the right is 0.5244. This corresponds to a number of cases given by

$$x = \mu + \sigma z = 50 + 7.0711 \times 0.5244 = 53.7081 \qquad (9.8)$$

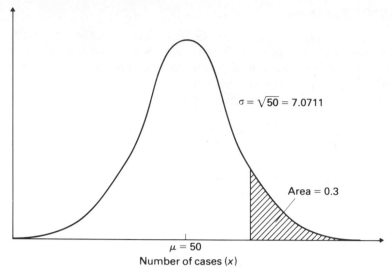

**Fig. 9.4**   Sketch graph of normal distribution for demand for baked beans during the review period

Having 54 cases in stock at the beginning of the review period therefore makes the probability of a stockout just less than 0.3, as required. This is the stock level which when increased by 1 gives a negative expected payoff and is thus optimal.

**The conclusion is that the supermarket manager should aim to replenish the stock level of baked beans to 54 cases when the new order arrives.** As he has to order in advance by one week, the lead time, he must add the expected demand for that time to the existing stock level. For example, if he finds there are 46 cases left at stock taking time, he should deduct 25 as the demand for the lead time and then order 33 cases to replenish the remainder to 54. Equivalently he can order the difference between what he has at ordering time and (54+25), which is 79. Of course, if he has less than 25 cases when he takes stock, he should order the entire 54 cases.

### Method 2: Provide a Given Level of Service
This was defined for re-order level systems as the probability of not having a stockout. We assume for argument's sake that the supermarket manager wishes to give an 80% level of service in this example.

The analysis is very similar to that of Question 2 of the Hospital Example of Chapter 8 and gives the normal curve shown in Fig. 9.5.

From the Percentage Points Table on page 138, we find that the $z$ score with 0.2 area to the right is 0.8416. This means that

$$x = \mu + \sigma z = 50 + 7.0711 \times 0.8416 = 55.9510 \tag{9.9}$$

**The conclusion we draw is that 56 cases are needed at the start of every review period.** As discussed above, the manager must allow for demand during the lead time, so he deducts 25 from the existing stock level. If the result is negative then he should order 56 cases while if it is positive he should order the difference between its value and 56.

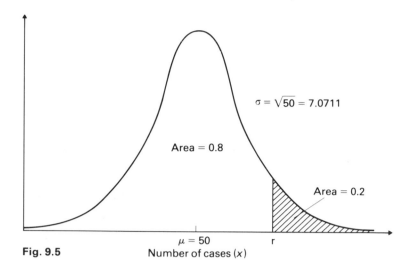

**Fig. 9.5**

$\sigma = \sqrt{50} = 7.0711$

Area = 0.8

Area = 0.2

$\mu = 50$     r

Number of cases $(x)$

## Simulation of Stock Control Systems

It is not unusual for a stock control problem to be impossible to analyse exactly. Many real situations have their own peculiarities which cannot be quantified or, if they can, do not result in solvable mathematics. As in Queues, Chapter 10, and Computer Modelling, Chapter 13, we can simulate the system in order to predict what will happen in practice. Here is an example.

### The Bakery Example

A bakery manager observes the demand for bread to be

| Demand (number of loaves) | 45–54 | 55–64 | 65–74 | 75–84 | 85–94 |
|---|---|---|---|---|---|
| Percentage of days | 15 | 23 | 27 | 32 | 3 |

Bread is baked overnight as a batch of 300 loaves and the cost of setting up the ovens with the extra labour is £30. The bakery has 4 freezers, each of which can store 100 loaves of bread at a cost of £2 per night per freezer. There is a discount on electricity if more than 2 of the freezers are working together. Taking all this into account gives the following storage costs

| Number of loaves stored overnight | 0 | 1–100 | 101–200 | 201–300 | 301–400 |
|---|---|---|---|---|---|
| Cost (£) | 0 | 2 | 4 | 5 | 6 |

As the manager can bake the bread on any night he decides, he wants to use the re-order level system of stock control. We investigate appropriate values to adopt for the re-order level in the light of the two criteria developed in this chapter.

*Solution*   **Method 1: Minimise the Expected Cost**
The expected demand is for 68.5 loaves per day. This means that bread will be baked every (300/68.5), or 4.4, days on average giving an ordering cost of £(30/4.4) per day. However, the expectation of the stock handling cost is not as easy to formulate in this problem as it was in the Radio and Beans Examples. The storage cost per loaf is not constant but depends on how many loaves are being stored and how many freezers are in use. We therefore simulate the daily stock level of bread and decide by trial and error which re-order level results in the minimum expected stock handling cost.

The technique of simulation was discussed in Chapter 6 and the topic forms a thread running through the chapters on stochastic modelling. This problem is a good example of a system suitable for simulation and we shall put many of the ideas developed elsewhere into practice. We begin by describing how the simulation can be run by hand and then consider a computer program which achieves the same results more quickly and with much less effort. As in computer programming generally, it is helpful to examine how a human would perform the computation before attempting to write a program.

In order to study the consequences of a particular value of the re-order level we need to record, for each day's operation of the simulated bakery:
*Variable 1: The Stock Level at the Start of the Day*. This is the stock level at the end of the previous day plus any loaves baked overnight. Its value on day 1 does not affect the long-term behaviour of the simulation and we can take this initial value to be, say, 200 loaves.
*Variable 2: The Demand for Bread During the Day*. This is simulated from the probability distribution given in the question, even though that distribution does not contain the precise outcome for demand but ranges of values. The plan is to interpret a random number as an outcome in a similar way to that in the Chef Example of Chapter 6. The mid-point of that range is then used as the demand for bread during the day. Another method of dealing with distributions containing ranges as outcomes is explained in the Bank Example simulation of Chapter 10 but here we obtain Table 9.2.

**Table 9.2**

| Demand for bread as given in the question | 45–54 | 55–64 | 65–74 | 75–84 | 85–94 |
|---|---|---|---|---|---|
| Probability, given as a percentage in the question | 0.15 | 0.23 | 0.27 | 0.32 | 0.03 |
| Mid-point of range, taken as the exact demand in the simulation | 49.5 $\simeq 50$ | 59.5 $\simeq 60$ | 69.5 $\simeq 70$ | 79.5 $\simeq 80$ | 89.5 $\simeq 90$ |
| Random number range having the same probability as the demand | 00–14 | 15–37 | 38–64 | 65–96 | 97–99 |

*Variable 3: The Stock Level at the End of the Day*. This is variable 1 minus variable 2 unless this gives a negative answer. In that case the shop has sold out of bread and the closing stock level is zero.

*Variable 4: The Overnight Storage Cost.* This is found from the table in the question according to the value of variable 3.

*Variable 5: The Production Setup Cost.* Baking takes place at the end of any day when the stock level is less than or equal to the re-order level. The production or ordering cost is therefore £30 or zero depending on the closing stock level.

After many days have been simulated the average daily stock handling cost can be calculated. This is the total of variables 4 and 5 over all the days of the simulation divided by the number of days. It is necessary to run the entire simulation many times for different re-order levels and select the one which makes this average a minimum.

Table 9.3 is a **time plot**, as it is called, of the first few days of a hand simulation for a re-order level of 50 loaves.

**Table 9.3**   Time Plot for the Bakery Example Simulation

| Day | Stock level at start of day (variable 1) | Two-digit random number | Demand during day from table 9.2 (variable 2) | Stock level at end of day (variable 3) | Storage cost (£) (variable 4) | Baking cost (£) (variable 5) | Total cost (£) | Average daily cost to date (£) |
|---|---|---|---|---|---|---|---|---|
| 1 | 200 | 24 | 60 | 140 | 4 | 0 | 4 | 4 |
| 2 | 140 | 55 | 70 | 70 | 2 | 0 | 2 | 3 |
| 3 | 70 | 85 | 80 | 0 | 0 | 30 | 30 | 12 |
| 4 | 300 | 91 | 80 | 220 | 5 | 0 | 5 | 10 |
| 5 | 220 | 20 | 60 | 160 | 4 | 0 | 4 | 9 |
| 6 | 160 | 49 | 70 | 90 | 2 | 0 | 2 | 8 |
| . | . | . | . | . | . | . | . | . |
| . | . | . | . | . | . | . | . | . |
| . | . | . | . | . | . | . | . | . |
| . | . | . | . | . | . | . | . | . |

The various criteria for deciding when to stop a simulation were discussed in Chapter 6. Clearly we cannot reproduce a full length time plot for reasons of space but the quantity of interest is in the last column and as the simulation proceeds this should tend to a limiting value. This is the average daily stock handling cost to be associated with the particular re-order level being used and running more simulations with different levels enables the one with the least cost to be identified.

Simulations in general are tedious and time-consuming to implement by hand in the way just described. At the end of this chapter there is a computer program which runs the Bakery Example one for any given re-order level. The user can therefore keep repeating the execution of the program for all different values of this level in a search for the one which minimises the average daily stock handling cost.

**Method 2: Provide a Given Level of Service**

This criterion for setting the re-order level of a stock control system was considered for the Radio and Beans Examples. As it ignores costings it is particularly simple to apply to the Bakery problem which is a good example of how expected costs can be difficult to estimate in practice. The technical difference between this case and the other two is that here we have an observed probability distribution for the demand instead of using the Poisson distribution. Nevertheless it is relatively easy to draw up a table like Table 9.1, except for the costings, from the information in the question. For example, consider the probability of not having a stockout when there are 74 loaves in the bakery at the start of a day. The figure '74' is chosen as it is one of those appearing in the tabulation of the demand pattern given in the question. We see there that on $(15+23+27)\%$ of all days demand is less than or equal to 74 loaves. Hence this is the probability of not having a stockout; it is equivalent to the level of service resulting from maintaining 74 loaves in stock. A complete analysis of the demand pattern in this way is shown in Table 9.4.

**Table 9.4**

| Stock level at start of day | Level of service $=P$(no stockout) $=P$(demand $\leq$ stock at start of day) |
|:---:|:---:|
| 44 | 0.00 |
| 54 | 0.15 |
| 64 | 0.38 |
| 74 | 0.65 |
| 84 | 0.97 |
| 94 | 1.00 |

From this table the bakery manager can decide how many loaves to plan on having in stock at the start of each day. He can then bake bread on those nights when there would not otherwise be enough for the following morning. For instance, if he wants to be 97% certain of satisfying demand, he should aim at having at least 84 loaves in stock each morning.

It is also possible to draw a graph of level of service against number of loaves from the information in this table. The manager could then specify any level of service and read from the graph the appropriate value of demand which has that probability of not being exceeded. Such graphs are called **cumulative probability** or **cumulative frequency** curves or **ogives** and are often used by statisticians.

## Computer Program

The following program carries out the simulation described in the Bakery Example. It should be compared with the simulation program in Chapter 6.

```
10  PRINT "BAKERY SIMULATION"
20  PRINT "-----------------"
30  PRINT "RE - ORDER LEVEL ";
40  INPUT L
50  FOR N=500 TO 2000 STEP 500
60  C=0
70  S=0
80  V1=200
90  FOR D=1 TO N
100 X=INT(100*RND)
110 V2=50
120 IF X<=14 THEN 200
130 V2=60
140 IF X<=37 THEN 200
150 V2=70
160 IF X<=64 THEN 200
170 V2=80
```

```
180 IF X<=96 THEN 200
190 V2=90
200 V3=V1-V2
210 IF V3>0 THEN 230
220 V3=0
230 V4=0
240 IF V3=0 THEN 320
250 V4=2
260 IF V3<=100 THEN 320
270 V4=4
280 IF V3<=200 THEN 320
290 V4=5
300 IF V3<=300 THEN 320
310 V4=6
320 V5=0
330 IF V3>L THEN 360
340 V3=V3+300
350 V5=30
360 C=C+V4+V5
370 IF V2<=V1 THEN 390
380 S=S+1
390 V1=V3
400 NEXT D
410 A1=C/N
420 A2=S/N
430 PRINT
440 PRINT "SIMULATION OF ";N;" DAYS"
450 PRINT
460 PRINT "AVERAGE STOCK HANDLING COST PER DAY IS ";A1
470 PRINT "FRACTION OF DAYS WHEN STOCKOUT OCCURS IS ";A2
480 PRINT
490 NEXT N
500 END
```

**Specimen Run**

```
BAKERY SIMULATION
-----------------
RE - ORDER LEVEL ?50

SIMULATION OF 500 DAYS

AVERAGE STOCK HANDLING COST PER DAY IS 11.93
FRACTION OF DAYS WHEN STOCKOUT OCCURS IS 0.042

SIMULATION OF 1000 DAYS

AVERAGE STOCK HANDLING COST PER DAY IS 11.835
FRACTION OF DAYS WHEN STOCKOUT OCCURS IS 0.026
```

```
SIMULATION OF 1500 DAYS

AVERAGE STOCK HANDLING COST PER DAY IS 11.832
FRACTION OF DAYS WHEN STOCKOUT OCCURS IS 0.036

SIMULATION OF 2000 DAYS

AVERAGE STOCK HANDLING COST PER DAY IS 11.8505
FRACTION OF DAYS WHEN STOCKOUT OCCURS IS 0.0305
```

**Program Notes**

**1** Lines 10 to 40 print a heading and read the value of the re-order level from the user. The consequences of different levels can be seen by repeated running of the program.

**2** Line 50 begins a FOR loop which runs the program for values of the number of days from 500 to 2000 in steps of 500.

**3** Lines 60 to 80 initialise the total cost, C, the total number of stockouts, S, and the stock level at the start of the day, V1. The names V1 to V5 correspond to the variables 1 to 5 defined in the Bakery Example simulation.

**4** Line 90 begins a FOR loop to count N days and the loop ends at line 400. Line 100 creates a random two-digit number by multiplying a random decimal by 100 and taking the whole number part. The appropriate way to do this may be different on a given computer.

**5** Lines 110 to 190 decide the value of V2, the daily demand for bread, on the basis of the value of the two-digit random number X. This is done in accordance with Table 9.2.

**6** Line 200 calculates the stock level at the end of the day, V3. Lines 210 and 220 have the effect of setting it to be zero if it is negative.

**7** Lines 230 to 310 calculate the overnight storage cost, V4. This is found using the table given in the question on the Bakery and depends on the value of V3.

**8** Lines 320 to 350 calculate the cost of an overnight baking session if it is necessary. Line 320 sets it to be zero while line 330 tests the stock in hand against the re-order level. If a stock replenishment is not needed then its cost, V5, is left equal to zero and control is sent to line 360. If on the other hand it is necessary to bake bread, then line 340 increases the stock level by the number of loaves baked and line 350 adjusts the baking cost from zero to 30.

**9** Line 360 adds the storage and baking costs to the total cost so far. Line 370 sends control to line 390 if the demand for bread has not exceeded the initial daily stock while if this is not so then line 380 records the occurrence of one more stockout day. Line 390 sets the following day's initial stock level equal to the current day's final stock level and line 400 returns control back to line 90 for the simulation of the next day.

**10** When N days have been simulated, lines 410 and 420 calculate the average daily cost, C/N, and the fraction of days on which a stockout occurred, S/N. Lines 430 to 480 print out these results and line 490 returns control back to line 50 for the next highest number of days, if there is one, for which the program is to run. When the program has executed the simulation for 2000 days, it stops.

**11** The program could print out the details of each day simulated. This would give a table like Table 9.3 but would be very long. It may be that summaries every few hundred days would be preferable.

**12** On many computers, running a simulation twice results in the same sequence of random numbers being used. It is often possible to 'scramble' the random number generator in between runs but the details of how to do this vary from machine to machine. It is necessary in a game program, like the one at the end of Chapter 13 or the same numbers emerge every time the game is played.

## Summary

**1** The main parameters of a stock control problem are:
   (i)  the production or ordering cost, £$P$ per order,
  (ii)  the storage cost, £$S$ per item per unit time,
 (iii)  the demand, $d$ items per unit time,
 (iv)  the lead time between ordering items and having them available in stock,
  (v)  the shortage cost per item,
 (vi)  the review period between regular stock taking sessions, if applicable.

**2** The Economic Order Quantity (EOQ) formula, $\sqrt{\dfrac{2Pd}{S}}$, gives the amount which should be ordered to minimise the stock handling cost assuming that the demand, $d$, is constant and the lead time is zero. The time between placing orders, called the Economic Review Period (ERP), is the economic order quantity divided by the demand, $d$.

**3** The Re-order Level (ROL) system involves placing an order for more items when the stock level falls to a predetermined value. The quantity ordered is often calculated using the economic order quantity formula.

**4** The Re-order Cycle (ROC) system involves reviewing the stock level at regular time intervals and ordering items to replenish the level to some predetermined value.

**5** We considered two methods for choosing values for the re-order level and the re-order cycle replenishment level. One attempted to minimise the total cost of handling stock while the other aimed for a given level of service, which is the probability that there will be enough stock to meet demand. In practice, managers pay attention to both criteria when deciding how to control stock levels.

**6** Simulation is a very powerful means of testing a stock control policy before implementing it. The flexibility of simulation enables the programmer to 'fine tune' the simulated system by changing the decision rules for ordering more stock. This was illustrated in the Bakery Example where the re-order level can be found by examining the simulated consequences of it having various values.

## Further Reading

There are several books devoted entirely to the subject of stock control, like references (32) and (33). Most general operational research books have at least one chapter on the topic and references (6), (7) and (13) contain useful sections.

    Sometimes stock items are classified according to the cash flow they represent when they are used or sold. Strict control is exercised over those items which correspond to large amounts of money moving quickly while control of those which are either cheap to replace or slow moving is less stringent. Reference (32) deals with this aspect of the subject, called Pareto analysis.

There are situations where the decision of which items to keep in stock is part of the stock control problem. This is considered in references (1) and (14). It is a consequence of increased computerisation that stock control, like cash flow analysis, is becoming part of the overall data processing operation of companies. The stock levels and stock movements which enable managers to decide on which items to stock are being reported on regularly alongside bank balances and other financial information. Many systems incorporate point-of-sale data entry whereby the stock level is updated by a computer when the cashier rings up the sale of the item on the cash register, which is really a computer terminal.

Mathematically speaking, problems of stock control, queuing and replacement and maintenance can all be formulated as what are known as stochastic processes. Reference (36) is relevant to this approach.

## Exercises

**1**   A supermarket sells roughly 500 packets of cornflakes each week. It estimates that the shelf space for a packet costs 0.72p per week, and that it costs £4 to place an order for more cornflakes and have them delivered. Use the economic order quantity formula to advise on how many packets to order and how often an order should be placed so that the stock handling cost is a minimum.

**2**   Robin Hood uses exactly 4 arrows every day because he never misses a shot. It costs 16 shillings to make any quantity of arrows and Robin estimates that each arrow costs him half a shilling a day to carry around with him. Use the economic order quantity formula to determine how many arrows he should make at a time and how often he should do a production run.

**3**   In a certain building an average of 1.4 electric light bulbs need replacing every week. Using the Poisson probability distribution (i) calculate the probability of running out of bulbs during a particular week if there are two spares in stock at the beginning of the week, (ii) it is required to keep the probability of running out of spare bulbs during each week to below 0.05. As you can see from your answer to (i), having just two spare bulbs does not achieve this objective. Would having 3 spare bulbs in stock at the start of each week be sufficient? If not, what is the least number of spares which will be?

**4**   A lighthouse keeper likes chewing gum and uses on average 12.8 packets per week. If the supply ship visits the lighthouse every two weeks, use the normal approximation to the Poisson distribution, as in the Baked Beans Example, to calculate the re-order replenishment level which results in a lower than 5% chance of him running out of gum.

**5**   Ruritania recruits more soldiers whenever the size of the army falls to a certain level. It takes 3 months to train a new recruit and it costs 13 ducats a month to feed and clothe each man. The country is permanently at war and loses on average 33.2 soldiers per month in battle. If it runs out of soldiers it hires mercenaries at a cost of 20 ducats per month per man. Identify the storage cost, shortage cost and average demand during the lead time in this manpower stock control problem. Hence calculate the size the government should allow the army to fall to before taking on new recruits in order to minimise the expected costs.

**6**   A television manufacturer depends on another manufacturer to supply him with special wooden cabinets for his luxury model. At the beginning of each working week of 5 days, he decides to make 65 such models, that is 13 per day, during that week provided there are at least 50 cabinets in stock. If there are less than 50 at the start of the week, then he will make only 30 luxury models, that is 6 per day. The lead time for the delivery of any number of cabinets is equal to 3 days with probability 0.5, 5 days with probability 0.4, and 8 working days with probability 0.1. (i) Calculate the expected lead time and the demand during the expected lead time if 13 luxury televisions are manufactured each day. (ii) If the ordering cost is £2 and the overnight storage cost is 2p per cabinet, calculate the economic order quantity assuming that demand is for 13 cabinets per day. (iii) In view of the answers to (i) and (ii), the manufacturer decides to use a re-order level stock control system and order 100 cabinets whenever there are 60 or less of them in stock. Use a simulation to estimate the average daily cost of this strategy if the 'penalty' for being out of stock is £13 per day. If you have access to a computer you might like to program the simulation so that various values of the re-order level and the re-order quantity can be used on successive simulations so that those which result in the smallest average daily cost can be found by experimentation.

# 10 Queues

The flow of people or items through a system often results in the formation of a queue. Whilst we are all familiar with human queues, non-human ones occur all around us in the movement of documents, stock, vehicles and raw materials. Consider a housewife queuing in a supermarket to pay for her groceries. There could be a can of baked beans in the shopping which itself waited in the warehouse before being put out for sale. The lorry which delivered it from the factory almost certainly queued in traffic and would have been sent only when the supermarket's order reached the top of the order form queue. Sheets of metal wait in the factory to be cut and made into cans while beans queue to be baked and packed, not to mention the labels which are glued to the can and all the other flows of items which result in the can being in the housewife's shopping. Only a fraction of all queues consist of people and most businesses contain queues of one sort or another as part of their operations.

A knowledge of where queues occur in a system and of how they behave is of obvious benefit to the manager. It is often necessary to have the formation of queues in mind when designing a system. For instance, an architect must assess how many checkouts to install in a supermarket or how large the lorry park of a warehouse should be.

Every queue has three distinguishing characteristics and we discuss these in general terms before examining specific examples.

## I  The Arrival Pattern

This is the way in which people or items arrive at the system being considered. The times at which the arrivals occur can be **deterministic**, regular, or **stochastic**, random. In the chapter on Stock Control we studied methods of regulating the arrival of stock items to the queue of those waiting to be used or sold. Those arrivals were deterministic and the objective was to keep the queue length, or stock level as it was called there, at an optimum value.

In more general queuing situations, arrivals are at random in time and form a queue spontaneously, like people in a shop or order forms in a mail order company. There are two ways of describing how these arrivals occur. Firstly we can measure the number of them happening in a unit time period like '3 per hour', as we did in stock control for the demand for goods. The Poisson distribution applies to the special case where this rate of arrival is constant in time and we follow that approach up in the section on Simple Queues later in the chapter.

The second method of describing the arrival pattern is to measure the **inter-arrival time**, which is the time between two successive arrivals. This can be deterministic or stochastic, the latter case resulting in there being a probability distribution over the various possible inter-arrival times. In everyday speech we use phrases like 'every half-hour' to describe the arrival of trains or buses and this is really an inter-arrival time.

Inter-arrival times can give a more accurate description of the arrival pattern in cases where successive arrivals are related. For example, if people are given appointments to see a doctor at 15 minute intervals, then we expect their arrival times to be 15 minutes apart on average. The rate of arrival is not constant but has peaks every 15 minutes and so its use is limited in such situations.

A common feature of the arrival pattern is that arrivals can come from more than one population. A hairdresser's shop, for example, might cater for both men and women but the arrivals do not form a single queue and are not waiting for the same service. At traffic lights, cars and lorries queue together but members of each of the two populations occupy different lengths of road space and move at different speeds when the lights turn green. These differences cannot be ignored and each population's arrival pattern must be described separately in an analysis of traffic flow.

## II   Queue Discipline

An arrival is usually confronted by other people or items who arrived earlier and have formed one or more queues for service. The **queue discipline** is the order in which members of the queue are processed. For human queues we expect a **First In First Out (FIFO)** arrangement although in hospitals an accident casualty might go to the head of the queue for the operating theatre. Non-human queues can have similar **priority** mechanisms and a factory manager might suspend some work in progress in order to do a 'rush job' urgently. In the control of food stocks it can be important to sell items on a FIFO basis and it is then called 'rotating the stock'.

Another discipline is **Last In First Out (LIFO)** but this is used mainly for non-human queues. For example, the documents in an 'in' tray on an office desk are usually processed from the top one, which arrived last, downwards. Queues of raw materials, like nuts and bolts waiting to be used in a factory, frequently follow this discipline.

A consideration allied to queue discipline is **queue behaviour**. A person will sometimes refuse to join a queue if he considers it to be too long. This is called **balking** and is not restricted to humans. A warehouse may be unable to accept delivery of goods because it does not have enough space to store them. The incoming items have therefore balked and do not join the queue of waiting stock as it is too long.

Sometimes an item or person leaves a queue because of the amount of time they have already spent there. This 'renegade' behaviour is called **reneging** and again is not confined to human queues. Perishable food which rots in storage has effectively left the queue of goods for sale because of the length of time it has been there.

As a final example of queue behaviour consider **jockeying**. This occurs when a person leaves one queue and joins another one, usually because it is shorter. We are all familiar with this phenomenon in human queues and it is one of the reasons why they are so difficult to analyse exactly. All queue behaviour is stochastic in the sense that we can describe it mathematically only by the use of probabilities.

## III   The Service Pattern

This is the rate at which items or people are dealt with by a **service channel** and hence leave the system. The exact nature of the channel or the service it provides is not important as far as the behaviour of the queue is concerned. It is merely the *rate* at which service occurs which affects the way the queue grows or shrinks in size.

The service pattern can be deterministic or stochastic in a similar way to the arrival pattern and there can be one or more service channels fed by one or more queues. In many banks for instance, there is just one queue of customers for several cashiers, who are the service channels. An example of several queues for one service channel occurs at an airport where various types of aircraft, arrivals from different populations of aircraft, form 'queues' in the air waiting to land. Large aircraft take longer to pass through the 'service channel' of the airport as they need the use of tractors, terminal buildings etc. and so in between their arrival smaller aircraft can be allowed to land on the same runway. In fact an airport is a queue fanatic's paradise with people, luggage and machinery queuing for flights, maintenance, refreshments, etc. The reason for this concentration of queues is that service channels like runways and aircraft are expensive to operate and require highly skilled labour. The optimum use of such resources may well involve neglecting considerations which cannot be directly costed, like customer satisfaction.

Some service channels process items or people in batches. When a bus arrives at a bus stop it takes a number of people from the queue, or possibly all of them, simultaneously. Incidentally, a bus is a good example of a mobile service channel, the service itself being transportation. Other service channels need recycling between dealing with arrivals. For instance a dentist sterilises his instruments after treating one patient and before seeing the next.

The three characteristics outlined above, arrival pattern, queue discipline and service pattern, must be identified before a given system can be analysed. The arrival pattern describes how the queue grows, the queue discipline specifies how the items or people are taken from it to be processed while the service pattern determines how fast it diminishes. We must not lose sight of the fact that the queue is the central feature of interest in the system. The arrivals to it and the services, or departures from it, are simply the way it interacts with the outside world.

There are very few types of queue which can be analysed exactly and so most of them are studied by simulation methods. These allow all the quirks of queue discipline, priorities and behaviour to be modelled as we shall see in the first two worked examples of this chapter. They form an extension of the treatment of simulation contained in Chapter 6, as did the Bakery Example of Chapter 9. The third example of this chapter is of a queue which can be formulated and solved mathematically. The discussion of that problem assumes some knowledge of the Poisson probability distribution covered in Chapter 8.

### The Bank Example

The time between the arrival of successive customers at a small bank has the following observed probability distribution.

| Inter-arrival time (nearest whole number of minutes) | 0 | 1 | 2 | 3 |
|---|---|---|---|---|
| Probability | 0.04 | 0.13 | 0.45 | 0.38 |

It is also found from observations on customers that the service time is described by this table.

| Service time per customer (nearest whole number of minutes) | 1 or 2 | 3, 4 or 5 | 6, 7, 8 or 9 |
|---|---|---|---|
| Probability | 0.36 | 0.42 | 0.22 |

At present the bank has only one cashier and customers are complaining that they have to wait too long for service. The manager would like to introduce a system whereby there are two cashiers and a single queue of customers. The next available cashier, or cashier 1 if they are both free, would serve the person at the head of the queue.

Naturally he does not wish to waste an employee's time and measures the cost of the proposed scheme as the fraction of time the second cashier is idle. We perform a simulation of the new system in order to estimate this fraction together with the average length of the queue created. The latter quantity is an indication of the benefit the change will bring to the customers and may help the manager in deciding whether to implement the plan or not.

*Solution*   Before organising the simulation we can gain a useful overview of the situation using expectations. The expected inter-arrival time is 2.17 minutes, calculated from the distribution in the question in the way described in Chapter 6. The expectation of the service time, however, is 3.87 minutes so that customers are arriving at an average rate of one every 2.17 minutes but are being served in the present system at the slower rate of one every 3.87 minutes. Common sense tells us that a queue will form and become longer and longer all the time. No wonder the customers are complaining!

If there are two cashiers as the manager suggests then the average service time would be halved to one customer every (3.87/2) or 1.935 minutes. This is shorter than the average time between arrivals and means that the queue will not grow without limit as in the present case. It will shrink as people are served, faster than it grows as people arrive. According to this superficial analysis the manager's plan could solve the problem of an ever-increasing queue and deserves further investigation.

It is wrong to conclude that a queue will not form simply because the service rate is higher than the arrival rate. A queue is the result of *fluctuations* in the arrival and service rates from their expected values. It forms whenever there is an abnormally large number of arrivals or an unusually long delay in the service channel. The expectations alone do not enable us to predict the details of the behaviour of the queue length as it is a function of the interaction between the arrival and service patterns. An example of a so-called 'simple queue' where a mathematical analysis is in fact possible can be found later in this chapter. The queue in the bank does not fall into this category and so we shall simulate its behaviour in order to advise the manager.

We begin by simulating the inter-arrival time distribution given in the question. The probabilities there are quoted to two decimal place accuracy and so it is logical to choose two-digit random numbers as an analogous trial for this purpose. An appropriate allocation of such numbers to the outcomes is given in Table 10.1.

The important property of the ranges of numbers in this table is that they give the various outcomes the same probability of occurring in the simulation as they have in the real system. As there are 100 two-digit numbers and each one is equally likely to arise, we take the range 17 to 61, for example, to represent '2' because there are 45 numbers in that range which give it the same probability as '2' in the real system. Hence for each customer arriving at our simulated bank we shall choose a number at random and use Table 10.1 to simulate their arrival time.

**Table 10.1**

| Inter-arrival time (nearest whole number of minutes) | 0 | 1 | 2 | 3 |
|---|---|---|---|---|
| Probability | 0.04 | 0.13 | 0.45 | 0.38 |
| Range of two-digit random numbers | 00–03 | 04–16 | 17–61 | 62–99 |

The second distribution to be modelled is the service pattern. This has a different form from the arrival pattern in that the outcomes are ranges of service times rather than exact values. One way of simulating such distributions takes the mid-points of the ranges as the outcomes and was used in the Bakery Example of Chapter 9. Here a more precise method is adopted and as the simulation will proceed on a minute-by-minute basis we examine the probability of every possible outcome for the service time when that time is measured to the nearest whole number of minutes.

The range '1 or 2' minutes has probability 0.36 according to the question. As we have no information to the contrary, we assume that the two outcomes within this range, 1 and 2, are equally likely so each of them has probability 0.18, which is half of 0.36. Continuing this argument for all possible whole number service times we obtain their probabilities and can allocate ranges of random numbers to them in preparation for the simulation (Table 10.2).

**Table 10.2**

| Service time per customer (nearest whole number of minutes) | 1 | 2 | 3 | 4 | 5 | 6 | 7 | 8 | 9 |
|---|---|---|---|---|---|---|---|---|---|
| Probability | 0.18. | 0.18 | 0.14 | 0.14 | 0.14 | 0.055 (0.05) | 0.055 (0.06) | 0.055 (0.06) | 0.055 (0.05) |
| Range of two-digit random numbers | 00–17 | 18–35 | 36–49 | 50–63 | 64–77 | 78–82 | 83–88 | 89–94 | 95–99 |

Notice that the probabilities of 6 and 9 minutes are rounded down to two decimal places while those of 7 and 8 minutes are rounded up. Mathematical rounding would result in all four of them being rounded to 0.06 but that would make the total of all the probabilities in the distribution bigger than 1. We compromise in 'cooking' this to be exactly 1 by assuming that within the range '6 to 9' the extreme values 6 and 9 are less common than the mid-range ones and fiddle the probabilities accordingly.

Having decided how to model the various random events occurring in the system we are now in a position to simulate a succession of customers. Table 10.3 is a specimen list of such arrivals with each one designated by a letter of the alphabet for reference. Random numbers are chosen to determine each customer's inter-arrival and service times, for instance the values 10 and 35 for customer C correspond to an inter-arrival time of 1 minute from Table 10.1 and a service time of 2 minutes from Table 10.2. The last column of Table 10.3, the 'clock time of arrival', is the time the previous customer arrived plus the present customer's inter-arrival time. This is the actual, as opposed to the relative, time that the customer entered the bank and we shall need it to chart his progress through the system.

**Table 10.3**

| Customer reference | Random number | Inter-arrival time | Random number | Service time | Clock time of arrival |
|---|---|---|---|---|---|
| A | — | — | 86 | 7 | 1 |
| B | 08 | 1 | 63 | 4 | 2 |
| C | 10 | 1 | 35 | 2 | 3 |
| D | 33 | 2 | 46 | 3 | 5 |
| E | 98 | 3 | 36 | 3 | 8 |
| F | 31 | 2 | 57 | 4 | 10 |
| G | 93 | 3 | 42 | 3 | 13 |
| H | 05 | 1 | 25 | 2 | 14 |
| I | 90 | 3 | 68 | 5 | 17 |
| . | . | . | . | . | . |
| . | . | . | . | . | . |
| . | . | . | . | . | . |

There are two points discussed in the section on simulation in Chapter 6 which are relevant here. Firstly the way a simulation is started does not materially affect the values of any long-term averages or probabilities measured from it. In Table 10.3 the very first customer, A, is made to enter the bank at the beginning of minute 1. We have to start the sequence of customers somehow and choosing minute 1 rather than 2 or 3 will not influence the long-term behaviour of the simulation and is of no consequence. We do not therefore simulate an inter-arrival time for customer A.

The second point from Chapter 6 concerns the generation of the random numbers to use in the table. These should not be 'dreamed up' but obtained from statistical tables, calculators or computers. Humans tend to have a bias when thinking up lots of digits and in a lengthy simulation this will show itself.

We now trace the progress of the simulated arrivals through the system in order to see how the queue develops and how busy the service channels become. Each minute of the simulation is recorded on a **time plot** which shows the status of each relevant part of the system. We also keep track of any costs or other quantities of interest which can later be averaged or otherwise interpreted as a result. In this example a suitable set of column headings can be seen in Table 10.4.

Customers are entered onto the time plot one by one and Table 10.4 is started with customer A who arrives at the bank at the beginning of minute 1. There is no queue and so he moves straight to cashier 1 and as his service time is 7 minutes we enter his letter, A, in the 'cashier 1' column for times 1 to 7. Once customer A's effect on the system has been plotted we can deal with customer B. He arrives at the start of minute 2 and as there is no queue, and cashier 1 is busy, goes to cashier 2. His service time is 4 minutes so we enter the letter B in the cashier 2 column for times 2 to 5.

Repeating this procedure for each simulated customer we can extend the time plot for as long as we like, Table 10.4 being only the beginning of a full-length solution. The criteria for deciding when to stop a simulation were explained in Chapter 6 and it seems sensible here to continue the exercise until the 'fraction of time cashier 2 is idle' figure does not change, as more minutes are simulated. The average length of the queue could then be found by adding together all the queue lengths in the last column and dividing by the number of minutes simulated.

By considering the results of a full simulation, and possibly by looking at a time plot as well, the bank manager can decide whether to employ a second cashier or not. It should be emphasised that, as with all stochastic analyses, the conclusions are at best as

**Table 10.4**   Time Plot for the Bank Example

| Time (minutes) | Customers in queue | Customer at cashier 1 | Customer at cashier 2 | Number of minutes to date cashier 2 is idle | Fraction of minutes to date cashier 2 is idle | Length of queue |
|---|---|---|---|---|---|---|
| 1 | None | A | None | 1 | 1.00 | 0 |
| 2 | ,, | A | B | 1 | 0.50 | 0 |
| 3 | C | A | B | 1 | 0.33 | 1 |
| 4 | C | A | B | 1 | 0.25 | 1 |
| 5 | C,D | A | B | 1 | 0.20 | 2 |
| 6 | D | A | C | 1 | 0.17 | 1 |
| 7 | D | A | C | 1 | 0.14 | 1 |
| 8 | None | D | E | 1 | 0.13 | 0 |
| 9 | ,, | D | E | 1 | 0.11 | 0 |
| 10 | F | D | E | 1 | 0.10 | 1 |
| 11 | None | F | None | 2 | 0.18 | 0 |
| 12 | ,, | F | ,, | 3 | 0.25 | 0 |
| 13 | ,, | F | G | 3 | 0.23 | 0 |
| 14 | H | F | G | 3 | 0.21 | 1 |
| 15 | None | H | G | 3 | 0.20 | 0 |
| 16 | ,, | H | None · | 4 | 0.25 | 0 |
| 17 | ,, | I | ,, | 5 | 0.29 | 0 |
| . | . | . | . | . | . | . |
| . | . | . | . | . | . | . |
| . | . | . | . | . | . | . |

reliable as the data they are derived from. In practice, improving the service given to customers in the bank might lead to an increase in their numbers. This would alter the inter-arrival time distribution given in the question and distort the simulation.

This highlights one of the problems of analysing proposed changes in the future using data observed in the past. Usually the very objective of such changes is to enhance the arrival rate to the system and yet the amount by which this will occur cannot be predicted. We should therefore analyse these changes for different levels of demand. There was a similar dilemma in the Coach Company Example of Chapter 8 where the decision to buy another coach depended on the level of demand and the level of demand depended to a certain extent on the number of coaches the company owned. In that example we tabulated the expected profit of an extra coach for all different levels of demand. This enables the manager to use his intuition about future demand in order to estimate the benefit of an additional vehicle. The equivalent approach in the Bank Example would be to run the simulation several times for all different inter-arrival time probability distributions. These could take into account a possible increase in the number of customers using the bank by giving arrivals a smaller expected inter-arrival time. The 'what if' potential in simulation was discussed in general terms in Chapter 6.

There is another way of assessing the results of simulating proposed changes in a system based on historical data. The arrival pattern or demand level observed in the past can be thought of as representing the minimum demand on the system for the future. In other words we assume that any alteration in the system will increase demand or at worst leave it unaffected. If, then, the simulation shows that the proposed changes are cost beneficial for existing levels of demand, they will surely be so for an enhanced level of demand.

The Bank Example used the ideas of Chapter 6 to simulate the arrival pattern, queue discipline and service pattern of a queue system. The flexibility of simulation as an investigative tool has been mentioned many times in this book and before studying exactly analysable queues we illustrate this property with a more complicated example.

### The Filling Station Example

Arrivals at a filling station are from two populations, petrol vehicles and diesel vehicles. The number of petrol vehicles arriving in any one minute is described by the following probability distribution.

| Number of petrol vehicles arriving in any one minute | 0 | 1 | 2 or more |
|---|---|---|---|
| Probability | 0.29 | 0.51 | 0.20 |

The time between the arrival of successive diesel vehicles can be assumed to be normally distributed with mean 4.7 minutes and standard deviation 1.4 minutes.

There is one pump for diesel fuel and whenever there is a queue for it all the 6 petrol pumps in the station become inaccessible. Petrol vehicles form a single queue and move to the first available pump when their turn comes. There is, however, a 12% chance that a petrol vehicle parked badly at a pump will block access to all the other pumps.

The service time at the pumps is observed to have the following distributions.

| Service time (minutes) | 1 | 2 | 3 | 4 | 5 | 6 |
|---|---|---|---|---|---|---|
| Probability for petrol vehicle | 0.20 | 0.22 | 0.18 | 0.16 | 0.14 | 0.10 |
| Probability for diesel vehicle | 0.08 | 0.15 | 0.24 | 0.25 | 0.19 | 0.09 |

The manager is thinking of rebuilding the forecourt of the filling station so that only 4 petrol pumps remain but there is more space for diesel vehicles to queue. They will then not prevent access to the petrol pumps unless there are more than 3 of them queuing. We simulate the operation of the proposed changes to estimate the average number of vehicles of each type in their respective queues.

*Solution* In the last example we performed a preliminary analysis by calculating the expectations of the arrival time and service time distributions. The values of these quantities relative to each other indicated whether a queue would form or not. In this example, the expected number of petrol vehicles arriving is 1.11 per minute, assuming that the category '2 or more' in the distribution can be interpreted as 'exactly 3' for want of further information. Hopefully the average effect of all such large numbers of arrivals will be adequately reflected by this completely ad hoc estimate. Similarly the expectation of the service time at a petrol pump is 3.12 minutes which means that on average (1/3.12) vehicles can be served per minute by one pump. As there are 4 pumps in the proposed system, we multiply this by 4 to find that the filling station will be able to deal with an average of 1.28 petrol vehicles per minute. As they are arriving at an average rate which is less than this, the queue will not grow indefinitely and the new arrangement of pumps has some chance of success as far as the petrol side of the business is concerned. The diesel vehicles arrive with a mean time of 4.7 minutes between them while their expected service time is 3.59 minutes. As the latter is less than the former we conclude that the queue for the diesel pump will similarly not grow without bound and we cannot dismiss the proposed rebuilding plan on the basis of this preliminary analysis. Notice that in this superficial treatment we have not been able to incorporate the 12% chance that a petrol vehicle, or a long queue of diesel vehicles, blocks all the pumps. It may be that either or both of these complications result in enormously long queues forming for petrol and only a simulation will tell us whether this is so.

The method used is essentially the same as that of the last example. Vehicles are simulated first and then their progress through the filling station and interactions with each other recorded on a time plot. Before doing that we must decide how to simulate each individual trial described in the question.

The number of petrol vehicles arriving in any one minute can be obtained by choosing a random number and interpreting it as shown in Table 10.5.

**Table 10.5**

| Number of petrol vehicles arriving in one minute | 0 | 1 | 2 or more (taken as 3) |
|---|---|---|---|
| Probability | 0.29 | 0.51 | 0.20 |
| Random number range | 00–28 | 29–79 | 80–99 |

The arrival of diesel vehicles is not described by an observed distribution in the question but by a theoretical one, the normal. As we shall perform a minute-by-minute simulation, we want the inter-arrival times measured to the nearest whole number of minutes. The method of Question 2 of the Battery Example in Chapter 8 is used to calculate the probabilities of these outcomes from the normal distribution. The results of the calculations, together with appropriate assignments of random number ranges for use in the simulation, are shown in Table 10.6.

**Table 10.6**

| Diesel vehicle inter-arrival time (minutes) | 2 | 3 | 4 | 5 | 6 | 7 | 8 |
|---|---|---|---|---|---|---|---|
| Probability | 0.05 | 0.14 | 0.25 | 0.27 | 0.19 | 0.08 | 0.02 |
| Random number range | 00–04 | 05–18 | 19–43 | 44–70 | 71–89 | 90–97 | 98–99 |

Notice that probabilities of whole numbers of minutes outside the range 2 to 8 are zero to 2 decimal places and so are not included in the table.

**Table 10.7**

| Outcome | Vehicle blocks other pumps | Vehicle does not block other pumps |
|---|---|---|
| Probability | 0.12 | 1−0.12=0.88 |
| Random number range | 00–11 | 12–99 |

We have now organised the modelling of the arrival patterns of the two types of vehicle. There is an element of randomness in the queue behaviour of the petrol vehicles and we can model the 12% chance that such a customer blocks all the pumps by choosing a random number and interpreting its value as follows (Table 10.7).

Finally, we can simulate the service pattern, as in Table 10.8.

**Table 10.8**

| Service time (minutes) | 1 | 2 | 3 | 4 | 5 | 6 |
|---|---|---|---|---|---|---|
| Probability for petrol vehicle | 0.20 | 0.22 | 0.18 | 0.16 | 0.14 | 0.10 |
| Random number range | 00–19 | 20–41 | 42–59 | 60–75 | 76–89 | 90–99 |
| Probability for diesel vehicle | 0.08 | 0.15 | 0.24 | 0.25 | 0.19 | 0.09 |
| Random number range | 00–07 | 08–22 | 23–46 | 47–71 | 72–90 | 91–99 |

Using the last four tables, we can simulate a sequence of petrol and diesel vehicles. This is analogous to the sequence of customers in the Bank Example (Table 10.3). A specimen succession of petrol vehicles is given in Table 10.9.

**Table 10.9** Simulated Petrol Vehicle Arrivals for the Filling Station Example

| Clock time (minutes) | Random number | Number of arrivals from Table 10.5 | Reference | Random number | Service time from Table 10.8 | Random number | Blocks pumps? (Table 10.7) |
|---|---|---|---|---|---|---|---|
| 1 | 21 | 0 | — | — | — | — | — |
| 2 | 71 | 1 | P1 | 24 | 2 | 04 | Yes |
| 3 | 90 | | P2 | 78 | 5 | 94 | No |
| | | 3 | P3 | 21 | 2 | 69 | No |
| | | | P4 | 01 | 1 | 45 | No |
| 4 | 31 | 1 | P5 | 03 | 1 | 25 | No |
| 5 | 07 | 0 | — | — | — | — | — |
| 6 | 53 | 1 | P6 | 29 | 2 | 21 | No |
| 7 | 82 | | P7 | 17 | 1 | 19 | No |
| | | 3 | P8 | 42 | 3 | 84 | No |
| | | | P9 | 64 | 4 | 60 | No |
| 8 | 45 | 1 | P10 | 77 | 5 | 09 | Yes |
| 9 | 52 | 1 | P11 | 13 | 1 | 24 | No |
| 10 | 92 | | P12 | 28 | 2 | 34 | No |
| | | 3 | P13 | 73 | 4 | 62 | No |
| | | | P14 | 39 | 2 | 94 | No |

A specimen sequence of diesel vehicles is shown in Table 10.10.

**Table 10.10**

| Reference | Random number | Inter-arrival time from Table 10.6 | Clock time of arrival | Random number | Service time from Table 10.8 |
|---|---|---|---|---|---|
| D1 | — | — | 1 | 46 | 3 |
| D2 | 79 | 6 | 7 | 85 | 5 |
| D3 | 15 | 3 | 10 | 70 | 4 |
| D4 | 29 | 4 | 14 | 99 | 6 |
| D5 | 55 | 5 | 19 | 50 | 4 |

As for the Bank Example, we have chosen to start the simulation with a clock time of '1' and assume that the first vehicles arrive then. The manner in which a simulation is begun does not influence its long-term behaviour and so this is of no consequence but enables us to 'get the system going'.

Entering the two sequences of simulated vehicles onto a time plot shows the complete evolution of the system (Table 10.11).

**Table 10.11**

| Clock time (minutes) | Queue for petrol | Petrol pump | | | | Queue for diesel | Diesel pump |
|---|---|---|---|---|---|---|---|
| | | 1 | 2 | 3 | 4 | | |
| 1 | — | — | — | — | — | — | D1 |
| 2 | — | P1* | — | — | — | — | D1 |
| 3 | P2, P3, P4 | P1* | ← blocked → | blocked | | — | D1 |
| 4 | — | P2 | P3 | P4 | P5 | — | — |
| 5 | — | P2 | P3 | — | — | — | — |
| 6 | — | P2 | P6 | — | — | — | — |
| 7 | P9 | P2 | P6 | P7 | P8 | — | D2 |
| 8 | — | P2 | P9 | P10* | P8 | — | D2 |
| 9 | P11 | blocked | P9 | P10* | P8 | — | D2 |
| 10 | P12, P13, P14 | ↓ | P9 | P10* blocked | | D3 | D2 |
| | | | | etc. | | | |

Petrol vehicles which park in such a way as to block access to all other pumps are identified in Table 10.9 and starred in the time plot. They prevent other vehicles from leaving the queue and are seen in this short and possibly unrepresentative simulation as an important cause of delay. The main purpose of the simulation, however, was to estimate the average lengths of the two queues in the proposed filling station. This can be done by counting the number of vehicles queuing in a much longer time plot than the one above, and dividing by the number of minutes simulated. It is often the case in performing a simulation that hitherto unsuspected features of the proposed system have a profound effect on its behaviour. The filling station manager may have thought that the petrol pumps being blocked by diesel vehicles would account for much of the unnecessary queuing. In fact it seems that the petrol pumps are badly positioned and even when the diesel queue problem is resolved the petrol vehicles themselves obstruct each other to a significant extent. If this conclusion is borne out by a longer, and hence theoretically more accurate, simulation then the manager should rethink the whole filling station design and not just change the way in which the diesel vehicles queue.

## Simple Queues

The last two examples showed how simulation methods can provide a model of systems with queues. For the majority of those systems there is no alternative to simulation as an analytical tool but there are some useful results for what are called **simple queues**. These have one service channel with a single queue governed by the First-In-First-Out (FIFO) discipline. Arrivals and services are assumed to occur randomly in time with an average of $\lambda$ (Greek letter 'lambda') arrivals and $\mu$ (Greek letter 'mu') services taking place in a unit time period.

The assumptions of random arrivals and services are often invalid for real queues. For instance, items might join the queue in groups rather than individually, like cars arriving together at a traffic light queue because they were all delayed behind a slow-moving lorry. The examples studied earlier in this chapter were not assumed to have random arrivals or services but were described by observed probability distributions. Events occurring randomly in time are modelled by the Poisson distribution covered in Chapter 8 and for this reason a simple queue is said to have **Poisson arrivals**.

Before illustrating the analysis of a simple queue, or indeed any queue which can be thought of as 'simple' to gain a rough idea of how it behaves, we use the Poisson distribution to examine its arrival and service patterns in more detail. The inter-arrival time and the service time both have the same type of probability distribution which we shall now derive.

## The Negative Exponential Distribution

If items or people arrive at an average rate of $\lambda$ per unit time then in $t$ time periods the average number of arrivals is $\lambda t$. Using this average in the Poisson formula (8.1) we find the probability of no arrivals in time $t$ to be

$$P(0 \text{ occurrences}) = \frac{e^{-\lambda t}(\lambda t)^0}{0!} = e^{-\lambda t} \qquad (10.1)$$

Now the probability of no arrivals in time $t$ is the probability that the inter-arrival time is greater than $t$. In the section of Chapter 8 on the normal distribution we saw that the probability of a continuous variable being greater than a given value can be represented as the area under a curve. It was appropriate in that chapter to use tables of areas because we were dealing with the standard normal curve but here we have formula (10.1) instead. The probability distribution which has this expression as its 'area to the right' is not the normal but the **negative exponential distribution**. The value of $\lambda$ is called its **parameter**. Figure 10.1 is the diagram corresponding to the normal curve.

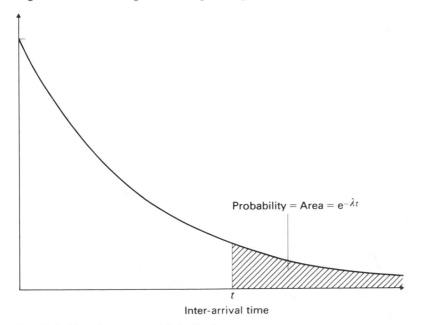

Probability = Area = $e^{-\lambda t}$

Inter-arrival time

**Fig. 10.1** Negative exponential distribution curve

Formula (10.1) can be used to answer questions for this distribution similar to those in the Battery Example of Chapter 8 on the normal distribution.

The relationship between the Poisson and the negative exponential distributions is that when an event occurs randomly in time the Poisson formula gives the probabilities of the various *numbers* of occurrences while the negative exponential describes the length of time *between* successive occurrences. For this reason the latter distribution is sometimes called the **waiting time distribution** as it models the length of time spent waiting for the first incidence of a random event.

The expectation of the time between successive occurrences of the event in question can be deduced mathematically from the negative exponential formula or argued out. The argument is short and runs as follows. If an event is happening on average $\lambda$ times in one time unit, then its occurrences divide that time unit into $(1/\lambda)$ time intervals. Hence the expected time between them is $(1/\lambda)$. For example, if lightning flashes on average 10 times per hour then the expected time between flashes is $(1/10)$ hour or 6 minutes.

As it is assumed in a simple queue that both arrivals and services are random in time, our conclusions about the arrival pattern and the negative exponential distribution can be interpreted to apply to the service pattern as well. Thus the length of each service, which is the time to the first incidence of a random service, is described by the negative exponential distribution with $\lambda$ replaced by the rate of service, $\mu$. For this reason a simple queue is said to have **negative exponential service time** with the probability of service taking longer than $t$ time units being $e^{-\mu t}$. It also follows that the expected service time is $(1/\mu)$ time units.

Having identified the arrival and service patterns for a simple queue as being 'Poisson arrivals, negative exponential service' we consider an example of the analysis of such a system.

**The Secretary Example**
A director dictates on average 4.2 letters per hour onto a cassette recorder. His secretary can type an average of 5.3 letters per hour.

*Question 1*   What is the probability that the secretary takes longer than 10 minutes to type a letter?

*Solution*   The service time is modelled by the negative exponential distribution with the probability of service being longer than $t$ time units equal to $e^{-\mu t}$, where $\mu$ is 5.3 in this example. Putting $t$ equal to $(10/60)$ hours we obtain **the answer 0.4134, or 41%**. We can use other results relating to the arrival and service patterns to find, for example, the expected time taken to dictate a letter $(1/4.2)$, or the expected time taken to type a letter $(1/5.3)$ hours.

*Question 2*   What is the probability that at a given time the secretary is idle?

*Solution*   The question does not concern the arrival and service patterns individually, as the first one did, but deals with their interaction and how the arrivals, dictated letters, feed the service channel, the secretary, via a queue. Before proceeding with the analysis of this interaction it is important to check that the arrival rate is less than the service rate. If this is not the case then the queue length will grow indefinitely and the system does not settle down with random fluctuations about a finite average queue length.

In our example, the service channel can deal with 5.3 letters per hour and so the arrival rate of 4.2 letters per hour accounts for the fraction (4.2/5.3) or 0.7925 of its time. As this fraction is less than 1 the condition for long-term stability of the queue length is satisfied and our analysis can proceed. Furthermore, this fraction is the probability of the service channel being busy and in general is $(\lambda/\mu)$, called the **traffic intensity**, $\rho$ (Greek letter 'rho'). The probability that the service channel is idle is 1 minus the probability that it is busy and so the answer to Question 2 is $1 - 0.7925$, **which is 0.2075, or 21%**.

The above argument quantifies a conclusion which is really implied by common sense. For a fixed arrival rate, the faster the service channel operates, the greater the fraction of time it stands idle. Mathematically, the larger the service rate, $\mu$, the smaller the traffic intensity which is also the probability of the channel being busy. This means that the designer of a system to deal with humans must decide on a compromise value of the traffic intensity. It must not be too large as it is the probability of the service channel being busy and customers will be deterred by having to queue. On the other hand, it must not be too small as 1 minus its value is the fraction of time the channel will be idle and any costs associated with keeping it on standby, like employees' wages, will be wasted.

*Question 3* What is the average time that a letter spends in the queue waiting to be typed and the expected number of letters in that queue?

*Solution* Textbooks like (34), (35) and (37) contain derivations of the distribution of probability over the different numbers of items in a simple queue. We do not study such derivations here as they are mathematically complicated and give no useful insight into simple queue behaviour over and above the formulae they yield. We can therefore quote their results without proving them in the knowledge that we do not lose any intuitive grasp of the subject by so doing. The main formulae are given in Table 10.12.

**Table 10.12** Simple Queue Results

| | In queue | In service channel | In complete system |
|---|---|---|---|
| P($r$ items) | $1 - \rho^2$    if $r=0$ <br> $(1-\rho)\rho^{r+1}$ if $r \geqslant 1$ | $1 - \rho$ if $r=0$ <br> $\rho$ if $r=1$ <br> 0 if $r \geqslant 2$ | $(1-\rho)\rho^r$ |
| P($r$ or more items) <br> where $r \geqslant 1$ | $\rho^{r+1}$ | $\rho$ if $r=1$ <br> 0 if $r \geqslant 2$ | $\rho^r$ |
| Expected number of items | $\dfrac{\rho^2}{1-\rho}$ | $\rho$ | $\dfrac{\rho}{1-\rho}$ |
| Expected time spent by each item | $\dfrac{\rho}{\mu-\lambda}$ | $\dfrac{1}{\mu}$ | $\dfrac{1}{\mu-\lambda}$ |

where $\rho =$ traffic intensity $= \dfrac{\text{arrival rate}}{\text{service rate}} = \dfrac{\lambda}{\mu}$ and should be less than 1 for the formulae to be valid

It turns out that the length of time spent in the system, just like the inter-arrival time and the service time, also has the negative exponential distribution. The appropriate parameter is $(\mu - \lambda)$.

The formula for the probability of the number of items in the complete system defines the **geometric distribution** of probability over the outcomes 0, 1, 2, ... . It is so named because its probabilities form a geometric progression and the more mathematically inclined reader can verify that all the other probabilities in the table are derived from it.

Table 10.12 provides the answers to Question 3 as follows:

**Expected time spent in the queue** $=\dfrac{\rho}{\mu-\lambda}=\dfrac{(4.2/5.3)}{5.3-4.2}=$ **0.7204 hours or about 43 minutes,**

**Expected number of items in the queue** $=\dfrac{\rho^2}{1-\rho}=\dfrac{(4.2/5.3)^2}{1-(4.2/5.3)}$

$$=\textbf{3.0257, which is about 3 letters.}$$

The formulae of Table 10.12 describe many aspects of a simple queue and can be used to design such systems and make predictions about their behaviour.

## Computer Program

The programs in Chapters 6 and 9 showed how a computer can help in conducting simulations. As we have seen in this chapter, simulation is an important tool in the analysis of queues and so computers are often used in this way. The program which follows, however, evaluates the formulae for a simple queue and illustrates how a computer can assist in the application of collections of results like those in Table 10.12.

```
10  PRINT "SIMPLE QUEUE RESULTS"
20  PRINT "--------------------"
30  PRINT
40  PRINT "ARRIVAL RATE ";
50  INPUT L
60  PRINT "SERVICE RATE ";
70  INPUT M
80  T=L/M
90  IF T<1 THEN 120
100 PRINT "QUEUE LENGTH TENDS TO INFINITY"
110 STOP
120 PRINT "PROBABILITY OF EXACTLY"
130 PRINT "ITEMS","IN QUEUE","IN SYSTEM"
140 R=0
150 Q=1-T*T
160 S=1-T
170 PRINT R,Q,S
180 R=R+1
190 S=S*T
200 Q=S*T
210 IF Q>0.0001 THEN 170
220 PRINT
230 PRINT "PROBABILITY OF AT LEAST :"
240 PRINT "ITEMS","IN QUEUE","IN SYSTEM"
250 R=1
260 S=T
270 Q=S*T
280 PRINT R,Q,S
290 R=R+1
300 S=Q
```

```
310 Q=Q*T
320 IF Q>0.0001 THEN 280
330 PRINT
340 N3=T/(1-T)
350 N1=T*N3
360 PRINT "EXPECTED NUMBER"
370 PRINT "IN QUEUE",N1
380 PRINT "IN SERVICE CHANNEL",T
390 PRINT "IN SYSTEM",N3
400 PRINT
410 T3=1/(M-L)
420 T1=T*T3
430 T2=1/M
440 PRINT "EXPECTED TIME"
450 PRINT "IN QUEUE",T1
460 PRINT "IN SERVICE CHANNEL",T2
470 PRINT "IN SYSTEM",T3
480 END
```

**Specimen Run**

```
SIMPLE QUEUE RESULTS
--------------------

ARRIVAL RATE   ?2.4
SERVICE RATE   ?6.7
PROBABILITY OF EXACTLY
ITEMS          IN QUEUE         IN SYSTEM
  0            0.871686         0.641791
  1            8.23506E-2       0.229895
  2            2.94987E-2       8.23506E-2
  3            1.05667E-2       2.94987E-2
  4            3.78509E-3       1.05667E-2
  5            1.35585E-3       3.78509E-3
  6            4.85678E-4       1.35585E-3
  7            1.73974E-4       4.85678E-4

PROBABILITY OF AT LEAST :
ITEMS          IN QUEUE         IN SYSTEM
  1            0.128314         0.358209
  2            4.59631E-2       0.128314
  3            1.64644E-2       4.59631E-2
  4            5.89769E-3       1.64644E-2
  5            2.11261E-3       5.89769E-3
  6            7.56755E-4       2.11261E-3
  7            2.71076E-4       7.56755E-4

EXPECTED NUMBER
IN QUEUE          0.199931
IN SERVICE CHANNEL                0.358209
IN SYSTEM         0.55814
```

```
EXPECTED TIME
IN QUEUE        8.33044E-2
IN SERVICE CHANNEL          0.149254
IN SYSTEM       0.232558
```

**Program Notes**

**1**  Lines 10 to 70 print a heading and read the values of the arrival and service rates from the user.

**2**  Line 80 calculates the value of the traffic intensity while line 90 checks that it is less than 1. If it is not, then an error message is printed by line 100 and the program stops. This validation of the input data is necessary to ensure that the formulae for a simple queue are suitable to describe the system. They are valid only if the traffic intensity is less than 1 and the queue tends to have an equilibrium behaviour.

**3**  Lines 120 to 160 print a heading and initialise R, the number of items, Q, the probability of R items in the queue, and S, the probability of R items in the system. Lines 170 to 210 print out R, Q and S, increase R by 1 and multiply each probability by the traffic intensity to obtain their values for R + 1 items. This is the relationship between successive probabilities implied by the first line of Table 10.12. Control is repeatedly sent back to line 170 for printing and recalculating until, in line 210, the probabilities are found to have become small.

**4**  Lines 220 to 270 print a heading and initialise the same variables as above in preparation for dealing with the second row of formulae in Table 10.12. Lines 280 to 320 then generate probabilities again until they become too small to be of interest.

**5**  Lines 330 to the end of the program calculate and print out the various results in the bottom two rows of Table 10.12.

## Summary

**1**  A queue has three main characteristics. The arrival pattern is the way in which people or items arrive and can be deterministic or stochastic. It can be described either by using the time between successive arrivals, the inter-arrival time, or the number of arrivals per unit time period. The second characteristic of a queue is the queue discipline. This is usually first in first out (FIFO) for human queues but can be last in first out (LIFO) for items. Sometimes there is a priority mechanism in force or the items or people exhibit some form of behaviour in the queue which must be taken into account. The third characteristic of a queue is the service pattern. Like the arrival pattern this can be deterministic or stochastic and also there can be one or more service channels.

**2**  Relatively few queues can be analysed exactly and so simulation is widely used. Arrivals to the queue have their time of arrival simulated and any other properties, like the length of time they will occupy the service channel, predetermined by simulation or otherwise. The interaction of the arrivals to form a queue is then traced on a time plot where any quantities of interest, like the fraction of time the service channel is idle, are recorded.

**3**  A 'simple queue' has 'Poisson arrivals' because the number occurring in a given time period is described by the Poisson probability distribution. It also has the FIFO queue discipline with a single service channel and 'negative exponential service times' which means that the service time is described by the negative exponential probability distribution. This distribution has $P$ (service time being greater than $t$) equal to $e^{-\mu t}$ where $\mu$ is the average number of services per unit time period, the service rate. The expectation of the negative exponential probability distribution is $(1/\mu)$.

**4** The traffic intensity is defined to be the ratio of the arrival rate to the service rate. When it is less than 1, a simple queue will tend to be stable in its behaviour and can be described by means of the formulae in Table 10.12.

## Further Reading

References (34), (35) and (37) deal exclusively with queues but are rather mathematical in nature. Reference (36) also includes relevant material. Most general operational research books have a section on queues and often include a simulation of a suitable system like the Filling Station Example. Airports and seaports are popular for this purpose.

As the majority of queuing problems are solved by simulation methods, references (46), (49), (50) and (52) are of use. There are also subjects like traffic engineering and production line design which involve the theory of queues and so contain work on them in their literature. From the mathematical point of view the behaviour of a queue is an example of what is called a stochastic process. It is considered using a 'birth death' population model or a Markov chain approach. The mathematical analogy with population modelling arises because a population is simply a queue of items, with births representing arrivals, waiting to die!

## Exercises

**1** Bees arrive at a colony randomly in time with an average rate of 1.7 bees per minute. As there is a narrow passage leading to the honeycomb only one bee can pass through and discharge its nectar at a time. This operation takes an average of 32.5 seconds per bee. (i) Assuming that the time taken at the honeycomb has the negative exponential distribution, calculate the average number of bees that can be serviced per minute and the probability that a particular bee takes over 45 seconds. (ii) Assuming that the bees form a simple queue, use your first answer to part (i) to calculate the traffic intensity, the average queue length and the average time a bee is in the system.

**2** An out-patient clinic has 2 doctors who see patients separately and spend 15 minutes with each one. The receptionist allocates 2 appointments every 15 minutes but finds that 32% of the patients are up to 10 minutes late while a further 13% are either too late to be seen or do not keep the appointment at all. Patients form a single queue and are dealt with by either doctor on a first-in-first-out basis. (i) Use two-digit random numbers to simulate whether each of a sequence of 24 patients is on time, 5 minutes late, 10 minutes late, or does not attend at all. Assume that being 5 minutes late and being 10 minutes late are each 16% likely to occur, that is half each of the 32% probability of being late. (ii) Use the sequence of patients generated in part (i) to simulate a 3-hour session of the clinic. Take 5 minutes as the unit of time so that patients are scheduled to arrive at time periods 1, 4, 7, 10 and so on. Your time plot should show the status of the queue and each of the two doctors' surgeries at each 5-minute period. (iii) Estimate from your simulation the average time a patient spends in the clinic. (iv) It is envisaged that the doctors will be put on standby for the duration of the clinic. In order to assess the impact of this on the operation of the system, perform the simulation again assuming that one of the doctors is called away to an emergency at the end of the first hour of the session.

If he does not return, estimate the length of time it takes to deal with all the patients and the average time a patient spends in the system.

**3**   A supermarket has 2 cashiers and customers form 2 queues for service. They arrive at the checkout area with the following arrival pattern:

| Inter-arrival time (minutes) | 0 | 1 | 2 |
|---|---|---|---|
| Frequency (%) | 16 | 52 | 32 |

It is assumed that an arrival will join the shorter of the two queues, or, if both are the same length, go to either of them with probability 0.5. The service time distribution is observed to be:

| Service time (minutes) | 1 | 2 or 3 | 4 |
|---|---|---|---|
| Probability | 0.5 | 0.4 | 0.1 |

(i) Calculate the expected inter-arrival time and the expected service time from the given distributions. Verify that as there are two cashiers and so the service time is roughly halved, they can cope with the arrivals.

(ii) Simulate a sequence of 50 arrivals to the checkout area. Assume that the probability of the service time being 2 is the same as the probability of it being 3; as the total of these two numbers is given in the question as 0.4, they are each equal to 0.2. Your time plot should include the status of both queues and both cashiers for each minute of simulated time.

(iii) Estimate from your simulation the average time a customer spends queuing.

(iv) The supermarket manager is considering introducing a system whereby customers with a special credit card will have their service time reduced to 2 minutes irrespective of how much shopping they have. Perform your simulation again assuming that 20% of all customers have such a credit card. Obtain a new estimate of the average time a customer spends in the queue.

# 11 Replacement, Maintenance and Reliability

All operations involve the use of some sort of equipment or machinery. Whether this is as humble as a ball-point pen or as sophisticated as an aircraft it is desirable to reduce the time it is out of service to a minimum and keep its costs as low as possible. This means deciding when to overhaul or inspect the equipment, possibly renewing it as a preventative measure, and, when it does fail, deciding whether to repair it or replace it.

The first two worked examples in this chapter deal with items whose age directly affects the replacement decision. In the Pen Example it is assumed that failure does not occur at random but whenever the equipment reaches a certain age. In this case the operating costs can be calculated exactly and the decision of which brand of machinery to buy can be based on their average replacement costs.

In the Lorry Example the running costs of the system increase as it grows older. In fact the vehicle is never considered to have failed completely but becomes progressively more expensive to operate while being worth less money and there is therefore an optimum age at which it should be replaced.

The Keyboard Example concerns a system, the keyboard of a computer terminal, whose components, the keys, can fail at any age with various degrees of probability. It is possible to replace the failures as and when necessary or to carry out a repair together with a preventative maintenance procedure. This latter may include the replacement of items which have not yet failed and is a feasible course of action when the labour costs of making a replacement are much higher than the value of the item itself. It may then be cost beneficial to replace many similar items while the system is being overhauled rather than wait for them to fail individually.

The final section of the chapter uses the expected lifetime, or time between failure for an item which can be repaired, and the number of failures per unit time as measures of the reliability of a system. This enables us to calculate probabilities concerning the equipment's lifetime and to relate the overall reliability of a large system to that of its component parts. The results are applied to making the decision of whether to overhaul a printing press before an important run and to calculating, amongst other things, the expected lifetime of a dinner service.

Each section of the chapter can be studied separately although the last two topics use ideas covered earlier in the book. The discussion in Chapter 1 on estimating future costs is particularly relevant to the whole of this chapter, as costings over the life of a system, which can be many years, are used to determine an optimum replacement or maintenance strategy. The resulting decision can be very sensitive to the values of those costings and appropriate sensitivity analyses, as described in Chapter 1, can be carried out.

## Replacement

### The Pen Example

The Standard pen costs 60p and needs replacing, on average, every 3 weeks. The Deluxe pen costs £1 but lasts for about 4 weeks. Assuming that they are both equally acceptable in all other respects, which one represents better value?

*Solution*    There are two possible strategies to consider. Either we keep buying replacement Standard pens or we keep buying replacement Deluxe pens. Any strategy which involves buying first one type and then the other cannot be optimal as if one of them is indeed cheaper to 'run' than the other we should stick with it all the time. The costs per week of these strategies are

Expected weekly cost of Standard pen $=(60/3)$ pence $=20$p
Expected weekly cost of Deluxe pen $=(100/4)$ pence $=25$p

**Hence if there are no considerations other than cost influencing the decision of which pen to buy, then the Standard pen represents better value.**

Apart from enabling the costs of different brands of equipment to be compared with each other, the calculation of a weekly expense tells the manager how much needs to be allocated in the weekly budget in order to meet the replacement cost when it arises. It is sensible from the accounting point of view to consider the 'provision for replacement' cost of equipment as a regular item of expenditure rather than as a possibly large 'one off' expense when the replacement is actually made.

The method of this Example was to examine every possible strategy, that is buying the Standard pen or buying the Deluxe pen, and choose the one having the lowest average cost. This technique, which is often used in replacement problems, is also employed in analysing stock control strategies as in the Ice Block Example of Chapter 9. It has the weakness that it is sensitive to any errors in estimating future costs and ways of dealing with this were discussed in Chapter 1.

The decision to buy the Standard pen was made on the sole basis of its average cost. The Deluxe pen may in fact have a nicer appearance and we may be prepared to pay 5p per week more in order to own it. It could also be more reliable in operation, as its longer expected lifetime seems to indicate, thus giving less 'down time' when it is unavailable for use.

Considerations like these which cannot be easily quantified as costs must be incorporated into the decision-making process after the calculations have been performed. It is then possible to assess on a subjective basis whether these factors warrant the resulting difference in costs and persuade us to choose a strategy which is not the one based on just minimising the cost.

Non-quantifiable aspects of replacement decisions are perhaps nowhere more pronounced than in the buying of a motor vehicle. As individuals we tend to do this on impulse and choose a car because of its shape or colour rather than for its expected operating cost alone. A company, however, even if it is replacing its fleet of cars simply as a reward to the salesmen, needs to have some idea of the future cost of the new vehicles. Such a calculation for a single vehicle is the subject of the next example and can be performed for any piece of equipment which depreciates in value and has increasing maintenance costs. There is then an optimum time to replace it but even if this strategy is not adhered to the analysis gives an estimate of the subsequent costs.

**The Lorry Example**

The costs of replacing and maintaining a certain type of lorry are thought to be as follows (Table 11.1).

**Table 11.1**

| Age of lorry (years) | 1 | 2 | 3 | 4 | 5 | 6 |
|---|---|---|---|---|---|---|
| Maintenance costs during the year (£) | 200 | 450 | 680 | 850 | 1300 | 1600 |
| Resale value at the end of the year (£) | 10000 | 8000 | 7000 | 5000 | 2000 | 1000 |

If the lorry costs £15 000 to buy, how long should it be kept so that the average yearly costs of replacing and maintaining it are minimised?

*Solution*   The type of information given in the question is often based on how much it costs to run lorries of various ages now. The expenses can therefore be compared directly with each other although in practice they will be incurred in different years of the lorry's life. Alternatively we can estimate the expenditure in the future and use the net present value concept described in Chapter 1 to relate them to each other. The analysis we shall perform assumes that the relevant costs apply not only to the current vehicle but to its replacement in the future. We can then spread the cost of the lorry's replacement over its entire lifetime to estimate the average yearly cost.

There are 6 strategies available in this problem as the owner can choose to keep the lorry for any whole number of years between 1 and 6 inclusive. Table 11.2 shows the financial consequences of each of those strategies.

**Table 11.2**

| Replace at end of year | Capital cost =15 000 − resale value | Total maintenance cost over vehicle's lifetime | Total of last 2 columns | Average cost per year of life |
|---|---|---|---|---|
| 1 | 5000 | 200 | 5200 | 5200 |
| 2 | 7000 | 650 | 7650 | 3825 |
| 3 | 8000 | 1330 | 9330 | 3110 |
| 4 | 10000 | 2180 | 12180 | 3045 |
| 5 | 13000 | 3480 | 16480 | 3296 |
| 6 | 14000 | 5080 | 19080 | 3180 |

Each line of this table is calculated from the given data with, for example, the strategy of running the lorry for 3 years being costed as the replacement cost at the end of that time, 15 000 minus 7000, plus the total maintenance costs over its whole lifetime. This is 200 + 450 + 680 giving a total in the 4th column of 9330 which is divided by 3 to obtain the average yearly cost of that particular strategy.

The last column of Table 11.2 shows that **the cheapest strategy is to replace the lorry at the end of every 4 years** but, as discussed earlier, the replacement decision is not usually taken on purely financial considerations. In particular, the poor reliability of old equipment may be unacceptable in an operation and whilst the expected cost of 'down time' when repairs are carried out can be incorporated into the maintenance estimate, the inconvenience and possible loss of customer good-will that such breakdowns cause cannot be readily quantified. In fact the analysis is sensitive to the costings that we use and it is wise to review the whole calculation at different points in the lorry's lifetime for updated costs. It is also sensible to perform a sensitivity analysis as outlined in Chapter 1 and rework the table for pessimistic and optimistic costs to see whether the decision is affected by them.

The technique of the Lorry Example can also be used to compare the relative costs of two or more different makes of equipment. Assuming that each one is operated for its optimum lifetime before being replaced, the average annual costs can help in deciding which one to buy.

## Maintenance

The decision of when to replace a piece of equipment, considered in the last section, is just one aspect of maximising its benefit to our operations. It may be possible to repair the item rather than renew it or overhaul it either regularly or before some crucial stage in our activities, like overhauling an aircraft before a long flight. It may even be cost beneficial to replace it as a preventative measure although it has not yet failed.

The next example shows how expected costs, or expected down time if that is considered to be more important, can be used to compare different strategies for maintaining a piece of equipment in a serviceable condition.

### The Keyboard Example
The keys on a computer terminal cost £3 each to replace and their lifetime has the following probability distribution:

| Life (nearest number of years) | 1 | 2 | 3 | 4 |
|---|---|---|---|---|
| Probability | 0.20 | 0.25 | 0.42 | 0.13 |

*Question 1*   What is the expected yearly cost of replacing a key whenever it fails?

*Solution*   We use the concept of expectation developed in Chapter 6 to calculate the average lifetime of a key from the data given in the problem. The 'sum of probability times payoff' is $0.2 \times 1 + 0.25 \times 2 + 0.42 \times 3 + 0.13 \times 4$ which is 2.48 years. As a replacement key costs £3, this means an average expenditure of £3 every 2.48 years or equivalently £(3/2.48) every single year, which is **£1.21, to the nearest penny.**

*Question 2*   It is possible to repair a key instead of replacing it with a new one. A repair costs £4 but the key then has an expected life of 3.1 years afterwards. Is it cost beneficial to repair failed keys rather than replace them?

*Solution*   We use the same method of analysis as in the Pen Example and compare expected average costs. The amount of £4 for repairing a failure can be thought of as being spread over the life of the repair, 3.1 years. This averages to £(4/3.1) for each year of its life, or about £1.29. As this is higher than the expected annual cost of replacing the key found in the solution to Question 1, **we conclude that it is cheaper to replace keys than it is to repair them.**

Although this decision is based on comparing costs over the various expected lifetimes, it seems likely that a repaired key is more reliable than a new one as its expected lifetime is longer. This factor could well affect the repair or replace decision and we shall discuss the connection between expected lifetime and failure rates in the next section of the chapter. We also deal with reliability aspects in later questions on the present example.

*Question 3* The complete keyboard contains 48 keys. The skilled labour necessary to fit the keys is expensive and the work of removing the keyboard from the terminal and re-assembling it afterwards is the same whether one key is being replaced or several are being dealt with. In fact it costs only £45 to replace all the 48 keys together in what is called a **group replacement**. This may involve the fitting of 48 keys individually or simply the replacement of the whole keyboard unit with a new one. In either case it is, typically, cheaper than the appropriate number of single replacements and is an option which is available on a regular basis as a preventative measure or instead of an emergency repair. We consider it here as a routine maintenance procedure and determine how often, if at all, it should be performed so that with individual replacements still being made as and when necessary, the overall cost of maintaining the keyboard is at a minimum.

*Solution* As usual for situations in which there are several possible strategies, we examine each of them in turn and select the one which optimises the given criterion, in this case the cost.

*Strategy A: No group replacements.* In the solution to Question 1 we calculated the expected cost of replacing one key as and when necessary due to failure. As the keyboard has 48 keys, the expected cost of this strategy is 48 times the answer we obtained there, or £58.08 per year.

*Strategy B: Group replacements every year.* If all 48 keys are replaced every year then, from the information given in the problem, 0.2 of them will fail in between the times when the replacements are carried out. Hence the total cost of this strategy is £45 for the group replacement at the start of a year plus $0.2 \times 48 \times £3$ for individual replacements during the year. This comes to £73.80 and is the yearly cost for this strategy.

*Strategy C: Group replacements every 2 years.* As for strategy B, there will be $0.2 \times 48$, or 9.6, individual replacements during the first year and we call this number $R_1$. The number of emergency replacements necessary during the second year, again working from the given data, is 0.25 of the original 48 and 0.2 of the replacements fitted in the first year as these are now 1 year old. Hence if $R_2$ is the number of replacements in the second year, then $R_2$ is equal to $0.25 \times 48 + 0.2 \times R_1$, which is 13.92. Now the total expected number of replacements required for this strategy is $R_1 + R_2$, which is 23.52, and as they cost £3 each there is an overall expenditure, including the group replacement cost, of £115.56. This amount is spent over a period of 2 years and so the yearly cost is £57.78.

*Strategy D: Group replacements every 3 years.* In the third year any original keys are 3 years old and so 0.42 of them fail. Any that were replaced during the first year are now 2 years old and so 0.25 of those fail while any that were fitted in the second year are 1 year old so 0.2 of those fail. The numbers replaced in previous years were calculated as $R_1$ and $R_2$ and so the number of individual replacements needed in year 3, $R_3$, is equal to $0.42 \times 48 + 0.25 \times R_1 + 0.2 \times R_2$, which is 25.344. Hence the total number of individual replacements over the 3-year period is $R_1 + R_2 + R_3$, 48.864, and as each one costs £3 with the initial group replacement costing £45, the overall outgoings for this strategy are £191.59. This averages to £63.86 for each of the 3 years for which the strategy runs.

*Strategy E: Group replacements every 4 years.* Using a similar argument as for the previous strategies, $R_4$, the number of individual replacements in year 4, is $0.13 \times 48 + 0.42 \times R_1 + 0.25 \times R_2 + 0.2 \times R_3$, which is 18.8208. The total cost is £45 + 67.6848 × £3, or £248.05, because $R_1 + R_2 + R_3 + R_4$ is 67.6848. This results in an average annual cost of £62.01.

As the required criterion for deciding when to institute group replacements is the cost, we conclude that **Strategy C should be adopted with a yearly cost of £57.78** and this is our answer to Question 3. As for the Lorry and Pen Examples, whichever strategy is finally implemented, even if it is not optimal, the analysis gives the annual cost of every strategy and not just the cheapest one. This in itself can be useful even if the strategic decision is not made on the basis of cost.

The approach of Question 3 is suitable for equipment whose availability is less important than the cost of its maintenance. Any expense incurred while the equipment is out of service should be incorporated in the cost of the individual replacement but sometimes it is difficult to quantify the effect of such breakdowns on the activity for which the equipment is used. In an extreme case there may be safety aspects to failures which make it essential to minimise the number of emergency replacements whatever the cost. When reliability considerations are more important than financial ones, the sequence of expected annual replacements can still be used to choose an optimum strategy, as we see in the next question.

*Question 4*   The least cost solution of Question 3 results in a failure rate for the keyboard in every second year, 13.92, which is unacceptably high. Which of the strategies examined earlier gives the best reliability in that the number of failures in any one year is minimised?

*Solution*   The sequence of expected annual replacements for strategies involving a group replacement was calculated to be 9.6, 13.92, 25.344 and 18.8208. The sequence can in general be increasing or decreasing depending on the probability distribution of the lifetime but in this case the first value has turned out to be the smallest. This means that Strategy B, which includes a group replacement every year, avoids the higher incidence of failures which can occur in the later years of a long group replacement cycle. Before coming to the conclusion that Strategy B provides us with the most reliable keyboard, we check that it is better than Strategy A in which no group replacements are made at all. To estimate the number of failures for this strategy we use the following argument.

It was found in the solution to Question 1 that each key has an expected lifetime of 2.48 years. This represents 1 failure every 2.48 years or equivalently (1/2.48) failures per year. As the keyboard contains 48 keys the overall number of failures will be $48 \times (1/2.48)$, which is 19.35 per year. This is much higher than that of Strategy B and so does not affect the conclusion that **Strategy B is best if reliability is considered to be important.** Clearly if group replacements were possible at more frequent intervals than one year, they would give better reliability still, but of those strategies that were examined, B is the best. It is necessary with many pieces of equipment to make a compromise between improving the reliability with regular and frequent overhauls and losing time while the machinery is out of service being maintained. We have ignored the time lost and inconvenience caused by having to make replacements, although when cost is the criterion rather than reliability, the effect of such disruptions is assumed to be incorporated into the replacement cost.

## Reliability

The probability distribution of the lifetime of a piece of equipment and its expected duration were used above in deciding on optimum replacement strategies. In this section of the chapter we see how the reliability aspects of a system's behaviour can be quantified in more detail and in this context the expected lifetime is called the **Mean Time Between Failures, MTBF,** or the **Mean Time To Failure, MTTF**.

Engineers and others involved in the life testing of equipment or individual components find it convenient experimentally to measure the **failure rate**. This is the fraction of all similar systems of the same age which fail at that age for the first time. It can be measured for all ages and has a graph which is typically like Fig. 11.1.

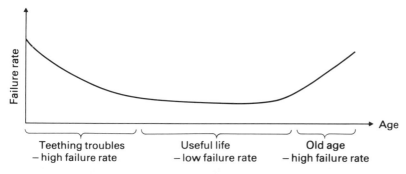

**Fig. 11.1**   Typical failure rate against age curve

The central flat portion of the curve defines the useful lifetime of the system and the whole graph is sometimes referred to as a **bath tub curve** because of its shape.

## Systems With Constant Failure Rate

Various mathematical assumptions can be made about the precise nature of the failure rate. It can be assumed to be such that the resulting lifetime has the normal probability distribution, as in the Battery Example of Chapter 8. The more usual assumption, made for all sorts of items ranging from humans to electronic components, is that the failure rate is constant with age. This means that we are describing the item's 'middle age' range, as indicated in Fig. 11.1, which is often observed experimentally to give a constant failure rate. In fact the theory which follows, just like that on Simple Queues studied in Chapter 10, is applied in many cases where the underlying assumptions are not strictly valid. This is because a lot of systems have almost constant failure rates and also the results are easy to use, again a similar situation to that of the theory of queues.

We begin by deriving the **reliability function, $R(t)$,** for such systems, which is the fraction of items lasting longer than $t$ time units. If the failure rate is denoted by $\lambda$ (Greek letter 'lambda') then in $t$ time units there will be an average of $\lambda t$ failures. Using the Poisson distribution of Chapter 8, the probability of no failures in that time is $e^{-\lambda t}$ which is therefore the probability that the life of the item is greater than $t$ units. This is the negative exponential distribution which was obtained in a similar way in Chapter 10 on Queues and we reproduce its graph in Fig. 11.2.

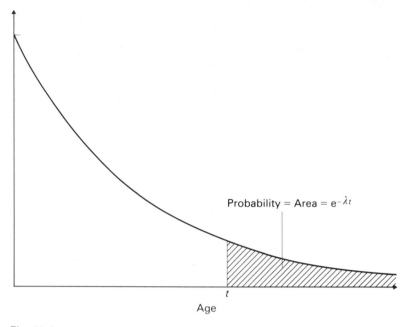

Probability = Area = $e^{-\lambda t}$

Age

**Fig. 11.2**

The expectation of the negative exponential distribution was found in Chapter 10 to be $(1/\lambda)$ and so this is the mean time between failures. Hence for systems with a constant failure rate the value of that rate and the expected lifetime are the reciprocals of each other.

**The Printing Example**

A printer finds from experience that the average time between failures of his press is 10.7 days. He believes that the failure rate will not change significantly in the foreseeable future.

*Question 1*  Every week the printer uses the machine on a very important job for a continuous period of 17 hours. He estimates that if it fails during the run he loses £300 in raw materials and lost time. Is it worth having the press overhauled at a cost of £15 before each of these long jobs in order to ensure that it does not fail?

*Solution*  The failure rate, $\lambda$, assumed constant, is $(1/10.7)$ per day in this example and so the probability of no failures in a time interval of length $t$ days is $e^{-\left(\frac{1}{10.7}\right)t}$.  The time period of interest is 17 hours which is $(17/24)$ days and we can draw up Table 11.3 showing the probabilities and payoffs when the machine works and does not work.

**Table 11.3**

| Outcome | Press works for 17 hours | Press fails during 17 hours |
|---|---|---|
| Probability | $e^{-\left(\frac{1}{10.7}\right)\left(\frac{17}{24}\right)}$ $=0.9359$ | $1-e^{-\left(\frac{1}{10.7}\right)\left(\frac{17}{24}\right)}$ $=0.0641$ |
| Cost(£) | 0 | 300 |

The expectation of this cost is $0.9359 \times 0 + 0.0641 \times 300$ which is £19.23. As this is bigger than £15, **it would be cost beneficial as a matter of weekly policy to buy overhauls for £15 and save an average of £4.23 per week.**

As well as assessing overhaul or maintenance costs, which should include the cost of the associated inconvenience and down time, this method can be used to appraise an insurance or servicing scheme. Of course the analysis depends on our estimate of the equipment's failure rate and, as in this question, it is perhaps easier to calculate it as the reciprocal of the mean time between failures, a quantity with which managers are all too familiar.

*Question 2*   The manufacturer of the press claims that an inspection and preventative maintenance scheme that he runs will reduce the average failure rate to 2.2 per month. If each inspection takes 2 hours and a failure causes about 3 hours of lost production time, does the inspection scheme give a reduction in the expected down time of the press?

*Solution*   Any evaluation of expected down time is similar to that of replacement or repair costs because both quantities are proportional to the number of failures which occur. We examine the two possible strategies in this case, not investing in the scheme and investing in it.

*Strategy A: No inspections.*   As there are on average $(1/10.7)$ failures per day, the monthly number is $(30/10.7)$ assuming for the sake of argument that there are 30 days in a month. If each failure results in the loss of 3 hours of production, then the expected down time per month for this strategy is $(30/10.7) \times 3$, which is about 8.4 hours.

*Strategy B: Regular inspections.*   According to the manufacturer the failure rate for this strategy is 2.2 per month and so the expected down time is the 2 hours for the inspection procedure plus $2.2 \times 3$ hours for the failures. This results in a total of 8.6 hours per month and as this is greater than the expected down time for Strategy A, **the conclusion is that the inspections are not worthwhile.**

The very purpose of preventative maintenance or inspection is to reduce the system's failure rate and so any appraisal of such a scheme must involve estimating what that rate will be. This is often difficult and the above analysis can be used instead to give a 'breakeven' value for it which makes the expected down time, or cost for that matter, the same as for Strategy A. The manager can then decide whether to adopt the scheme on the basis of the likelihood of the improvement. If he believes that this breakeven failure rate can be achieved with the proposed maintenance scheme then he should implement it, otherwise he should not. A similar breakeven analysis was performed in order to make a decision in the Oil Company Example of Chapter 6.

## Systems With Component Subsystems

Having discussed the reliability properties of a single item or piece of equipment we now consider the behaviour of several subsystems which together form a complete system. An example of this is a motor vehicle which depends for its operation on the correct functioning of the engine, brakes, steering and so on. Some subsystems can have a completely disabling effect on the whole system when they fail while others, like the car radio for instance, do not have such a vital importance.

We begin by examining three ways in which a complete system can depend on its subsystems. The worked example used to illustrate these configurations is about equipment which fails not because it malfunctions internally but because of an accident which may occur to it with equal probability at any time. Such systems do not age and have a failure rate which does not change in time. After the Dinner Service Example, the Television Example shows how the 3 basic configurations of subsystems can themselves be arranged within a piece of equipment.

### The Dinner Service Example

*Question 1*   A dinner service contains 10 plates and 10 soup bowls. Due to accidental breakages, each plate has an expected lifetime of 11.4 years and each soup bowl an expectation of 9.3 years. How long can the plates and bowls be expected to survive as a complete set?

*Solution*   The system consisting of the plates and bowls will fail if any one of the individual pieces of crockery fails. This arrangement can be represented by a **reliability diagram** (Fig. 11.3).

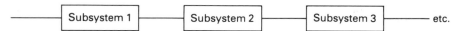

**Fig. 11.3**

The diagram shows the 'life line' of the system passing through every component subsystem with the failure of any one of them destroying its continuity. Items of equipment arranged like this are said to be in **series** and because the configuration fails whenever any one of the components fails, the overall failure rate is the sum of the individual component failure rates.

Now the functioning or failure of a set of components over $t$ time units forms a compound trial as described in Chapter 7. As the probability that a subsystem lasts longer than this time is its reliability function, $R(t)$, the probability tree diagram can be drawn as Fig. 11.4.

This diagram is similar to those of the Firework and Aircraft Engines Examples of Chapter 7. As for those examples, we assume here that the failures of the various subsystems are statistically independent of each other although in practice the failure of one component can induce the failure of another component somewhere else in the system.

The overall reliability function of the series configuration is the probability that the system, and hence *all* the subsystems, lasts longer than $t$ time units. This event is represented by the topmost route through the tree diagram (Fig. 11.4) and therefore, as the probability of a route through a tree is the product of the probabilities of its branches, the overall reliability function is the product of the individual subsystem reliability functions. This is a useful general result and in the special case where the component failure

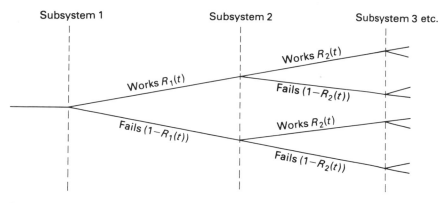

**Fig. 11.4**

rates are constants, say $\lambda_1$, $\lambda_2$, $\lambda_3$, ..., then as the individual reliability functions are of the form $e^{-\lambda t}$ we see that the corresponding system function is $e^{-\lambda_1 t}e^{-\lambda_2 t}e^{-\lambda_3 t}$ ..... which is $e^{-(\lambda_1+\lambda_2+\lambda_3+.....)t}$. This means that the overall system has its lifetime described by the negative exponential probability distribution just like those of the components. We can apply this result to Question 1 together with the fact that when the failure rate is constant in time it is the reciprocal of the expected lifetime. Hence the failure rates of the plates and bowls individually are (1/11.4) per year and (1/9.3) per year respectively and adding all 20 of them together because the items are in series, we obtain the overall failure rate to be $10 \times (1/11.4) + 10 \times (1/9.3)$, which is 1.9525 per year. We now take the reciprocal of the total failure rate to obtain **the expected system lifetime (1/1.9525), or about 0.51 years.**

The method of assuming constant failure rates, adding them together for all the subsystems and taking the reciprocal to obtain the expected lifetime of the system is called doing a **parts count**. It is often performed at the design stage of very complicated pieces of equipment which are considered to fail whenever any one of their components has failed. Clearly a parts count can predict an unacceptably low level of reliability when there are many subsystems, as measured by the expected lifetime or by some probability calculated from the resulting reliability function. This weakness can sometimes be improved by having backup components which are either normally active and work together with the original ones or are normally passive and are 'switched in' only when the original ones fail. We now examine these arrangements separately.

*Question 2*  The dinner service has 3 sugar bowls which are in use together. If each one has a life expectancy of 3.7 years, what is the probability that at least one of the bowls is left after 5 years?

*Solution*  A system can sometimes remain operational even though some of its subsystems have failed. The reliability diagram for this possibility is given in Fig. 11.5. Here the 'life line' of the system can remain unbroken even if some of the subsystems fail, instead of being dependent on all of them as in the series configuration. The arrangement is called **parallel with active redundancy**, the word 'active' indicating that the backup components are in operation all the time and are not held in reserve until they are needed. A good example of this configuration is a four-engined aircraft which is still able to fly with only two engines working; we examined a similar system in the Aircraft Engines Example of Chapter 7. The tree diagram (Fig. 7.7) used there resembles (Fig. 11.3) with the reliability

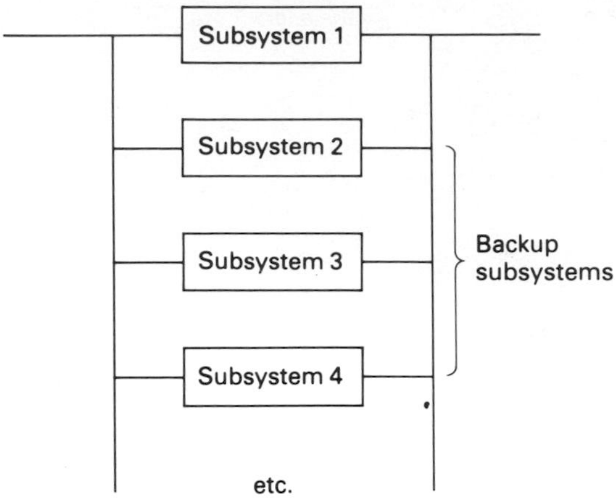

Fig. 11.5

function, $R(t)$, equal to 0.95. That example showed how the binomial distribution can describe the various levels of reliability and is appropriate if $R_1(t)$, $R_2(t)$, $R_3(t)$, ... are all the same. In other words, the subsystems are all duplicates of each other or just happen to have the same reliability function. Even when this is not the case and the binomial distribution cannot be used, the tree diagram (Fig. 11.4) shows how the probabilities that some components work while others fail can be calculated, as in the Fireworks Example of Chapter 7.

The overall reliability function can be derived from the tree diagram by adding together the probabilities of all the routes which represent the functioning of the system. In Question 2 each subsystem has the reliability function $e^{-t/3.7}$ as its failure rate is $(1/3.7)$ per year. Now the probability that the whole system survives to time $t$ years is the probability that at least one bowl lasts longer than $t$ years. This is the sum of the probabilities of all the routes through the tree diagram except the one for which all 3 of them fail. As all the probabilities add up to 1, this sum can be written as $1-(1-e^{-t/3.7})^3$, the bracketed term cubed being the probability of all 3 bowls failing which corresponds to the bottom route in Fig. 11.4. **The answer to Question 2 is found by putting $t$ equal to 5 in this reliability function and it is therefore 0.5930.**

It is important to note that the reliability function of a parallel configuration of constant failure rate components is not itself of negative exponential form. This in turn means that the failure rate of such a system is not constant in time, and the expected lifetime cannot therefore be found by taking its reciprocal as for the series arrangement. We discuss the calculation of expected lifetimes for systems with non-constant failure rates in the next example.

*Question 3* It is possible to buy a spare teapot with the dinner service. If one is bought and stored until the original one breaks, what is the probability that the total life of both teapots is greater than 9 years if the average life of each is 4.8 years?

*Solution* The advantage of having inoperative or 'passive' spare components is that they are not brought into use and hence liable to failure themselves until the original component has failed. Fig. 11.6 is the reliability diagram for items in **parallel with passive or 'switch in' redundancy**. The dotted lines represent connections which are not made until

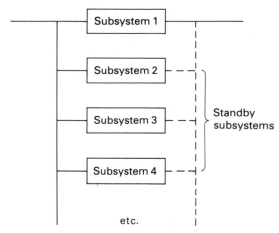

**Fig. 11.6**

they are necessary for the functioning of the system. Such links can be activated automatically, as when a new layer of paint comes into use whenever the top coat is worn away, or manually, for instance the spare wheel on a car has to be fitted to the hub before it can replace the failed original. In fact the process of replacing or renewing an item which is subject to failure, considered earlier in this chapter, can be thought of as the result of having an infinite number of standby components in parallel with switch in redundancy.

Ideally the down time of the system due to component failure in either of the parallel configurations should be a minimum. If the failed subsystem can be repaired while the back up one allows the main system to function, then very high degrees of reliability are possible. The spare wheel carried by a motor vehicle is again a good example as it is needed only while the original wheel is being repaired. Once that has happened the system is restored to its pre-failure state with the minimum of lost time. It is also advisable to carry out preventative maintenance or inspections on standby components. Motorists are always urged to check the roadworthiness of their spare wheel and test its air pressure along with that of the other tyres. There is a measure of reliability which is appropriate when a system or component is out of action because repairs are being performed. The **availability** is the fraction of time, on average, the item is available for use and can be predicted by considering a useful life/repair cycle.

$$\text{Availability} = \frac{\text{Mean Time Between Failures}}{\text{Mean Time Between Failures} + \text{Mean Time To Repair}} \qquad (11.1)$$

The existence of standby components which switch in automatically and can be repaired, or replaced altogether, without the main system failing, means that an overall availability of 1 is possible with the mean time to repair for the system being zero.

The obvious property of a system where standby items are used one after another and not simultaneously is that their expected lifetimes can be added together to give the total expected life of the whole system. In Question 3, for example, the expected time for which the two teapots will, between them, provide service to their owner is the sum of their lifetimes, 9.6 years.

The failure rate for the arrangement we are studying, unlike the expected lifetime, is not readily expressible in terms of the individual component rates. There is also no easy way of deriving the system's reliability function in the general case. The survival of the configuration to time $t$ units depends on if and when the original item fails and whether the standby, or standbys, function from that time up to $t$. However we can use the Poisson probability distribution to deal with systems whose components all have the same constant failure rate.

If the individual subsystems each have failure rate $\lambda$, then there will be, on average, $\lambda t$ failures in a period of $t$ time units. If there are $r$ standby components then the system can survive at most $r$ failures and so the probability of its lifetime being greater than $t$ is the probability of $r$ or fewer failures. Using the Poisson distribution, which is applicable in such situations as discussed in Chapter 8, we have

$$R(t) = P(r \text{ or fewer failures in time } t) = e^{-\lambda t} + \frac{e^{-\lambda t}(\lambda t)^1}{1!} + \frac{e^{-\lambda t}(\lambda t)^2}{2!} + \dots + \frac{e^{-\lambda t}(\lambda t)^r}{r!} \quad (11.2)$$

The failure rate $\lambda$ for the teapots of Question 3 is $(1/4.8)$ and the value of $t$ is 9. As there is just 1 standby, equation (11.2) reduces to the first two terms on the right hand side which give the result

$$e^{-1.875} + \frac{e^{-1.875}(1.875)^1}{1!} = 0.4409.$$

**and so the answer to Question 3 is 44%.**

We end this chapter by showing how the analyses of the 3 configurations examined above can be combined in stages to describe the overall reliability of a complicated piece of equipment.

**The Television Example**

Figure 11.7 is the reliability diagram for a completely fictitious television receiver.

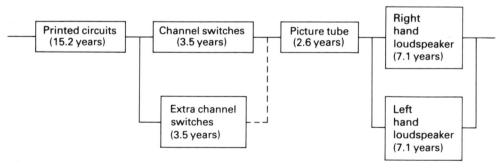

**Fig. 11.7**

The numbers in brackets are the expected lifetimes of the various components and it is assumed that all their failure rates are constant. Notice that the extra channel switches are not brought into use until the original ones fail while the two loudspeakers are in use all the time.

*Question 1*   What is the probability that the television does not fail for two years? The answer to this question could enable the manufacturer to calculate the expected number returned under a two-year guarantee, a similar analysis to that of the Battery Example in Chapter 8.

*Solution*  The reliability functions for each of the four subsystems within the television can be derived using the arguments developed in the last example (Table 11.4).

**Table 11.4**

| Subsystem | Reliability function | Value when $t=2$ |
|---|---|---|
| Printed circuits | $e^{-t/15.2}$ | 0.8767 |
| Channel switches | $e^{-t/3.5}(1+(t/3.5))$ | 0.8874 |
| Picture tube | $e^{-t/2.6}$ | 0.4634 |
| Loudspeakers | $1-(1-e^{-t/7.1})^2$ | 0.9397 |

As these four subsystems are themselves in series, their reliabilities can be multiplied together to give the overall reliability function for the whole system. **This product is 0.3388 and is the probability of the television functioning for two years.**

*Question 2*  What is the expected lifetime of the loudspeaker subsystem?

*Solution*  We saw in the last example that the expected lifetime of a parallel configuration of constant failure rate items with switch in redundancy is the sum of the individual expected lifetimes. The loudspeakers, however, are in parallel but have active redundancy.

The reader who is prepared to tackle some algebra and cook-book calculus can in fact evaluate the expected lifetime of many systems. It is shown in textbooks like (38) that this lifetime is the definite integral of the reliability function between the limits 0 and infinity. For systems whose components have constant failure rate, however, the reliability function is usually a linear combination of negative exponential functions, possibly multiplied by powers of $t$. For instance, the loudspeaker subsystem in the present example has reliability function, from Table 11.4

$$R(t) = 1 - (1 - e^{-t/7.1})^2$$
$$= 2e^{-t/7.1} - e^{-2t/7.1} \tag{11.3}$$

We can effectively perform the necessary integration to calculate the expected lifetime by replacing $t^n e^{-at}$ by $n!/a^{n+1}$ in this function. The first exponential in equation (11.3) has $n$ equal to 0 and $a$ equal to $1/7.1$ while the second has $n$ equal to 0 and $a$ equal to $2/7.1$. The complete integral is therefore

$$\frac{2 \times 1}{(1/7.1)} - \frac{1}{(2/7.1)} = 10.65 \tag{11.4}$$

**Hence the expected lifetime of the loudspeaker subsystem is 10.65 years.**

*Question 3*  What is the expected lifetime of the complete television?

*Solution*  The television's reliability function is the product of the reliabilities given in Table 11.4 because all the subsystems are in series. After some simplification we obtain

$$2e^{-0.877t} - e^{-1.018t} + \frac{2te^{-0.877t}}{3.5} - \frac{te^{-1.018t}}{3.5} \tag{11.5}$$

Applying the integration rule to this reliability:

$$\text{Expected lifetime} = \frac{2}{0.877} - \frac{1}{1.018} + \frac{2}{3.5 \times (0.877)^2} - \frac{1}{3.5 \times (1.018)^2}$$
$$= 1.77 \tag{11.6}$$

**We therefore conclude that the television has an expectation of life of 1.77 years.**

## Computer Program

The following program generates a sequence of expected annual replacements like the one used in the solution to Question 3 of the Keyboard Example. It assumes that replacements are made as and when necessary and calculates the expected number of failures in each year using the lifetime probability distribution of the items.

```
10 PRINT "REPLACEMENT PROGRAM"
20 PRINT "-------------------"
30 PRINT
40 DIM P(10),R(10)
50 K=0
60 K=K+1
70 PRINT "P(FAILURE DURING PERIOD ";K;") ";
80 INPUT P(K)
90 S=S+P(K)
100 IF S<1 THEN 60
110 PRINT
120 PRINT "HOW MANY ITEMS ARE IN"
130 PRINT "THE SYSTEM AT THE START ";
140 INPUT R(10)
150 PRINT "HOW MANY TIME PERIODS ";
160 INPUT N
170 PRINT "TIME","REPLACEMENTS","AVERAGE SO FAR"
180 K=1
190 A=0
200 FOR J=1 TO N
210 T=0
220 IF K=1 THEN 260
230 FOR L=1 TO K-1
240 T=T+P(L)*R(K-L)
250 NEXT L
260 FOR L=K TO 10
270 T=T+P(L)*R(10+K-L)
280 NEXT L
290 R(K)=T
300 A=A+T
310 PRINT J,T,A/J
320 K=K+1
330 IF K<11 THEN 350
340 K=1
350 NEXT J
360 END
```

**Specimen Run**

```
REPLACEMENT PROGRAM
-------------------

P(FAILURE DURING PERIOD  1 )   ?0.2
P(FAILURE DURING PERIOD  2 )   ?0.25
P(FAILURE DURING PERIOD  3 )   ?0.42
P(FAILURE DURING PERIOD  4 )   ?0.13
```

```
HOW MANY ITEMS ARE IN
THE SYSTEM AT THE START  ?100
HOW MANY TIME PERIODS  ?30
TIME            REPLACEMENTS  AVERAGE SO FAR
   1            20            20
   2            29            24.5
   3            52.8          33.9333
   4            39.21         35.2525
   5            35.822        35.3664
   6            42.9129       36.6242
   7            40.8703       37.2307
   8            39.0448       37.4575
   9            40.7068       37.8185
  10            40.6468       38.1014
  11            40.018        38.2756
  12            40.338        38.4475
  13            40.4356       38.6004
  14            40.2633       38.7192
  15            40.3059       38.825
  16            40.3539       38.9205
  17            40.3144       39.0025
  18            40.314        39.0754
  19            40.3298       39.1414
  20            40.3225       39.2005
  21            40.3197       39.2538
  22            40.3239       39.3024
  23            40.3231       39.3468
  24            40.3218       39.3874
  25            40.3228       39.4248
  26            40.3228       39.4594
  27            40.3224       39.4913
  28            40.3226       39.521
  29            40.3227       39.5487
  30            40.3226       39.5744
```

**Program Notes**

**1** Lines 10 to 40 print a heading and dimension arrays to store the probability distribution of lifetime and the number of replacements expected each year. The maximum possible life that an item can have is taken to be 10 time periods but clearly that can be adjusted if necessary.

**2** Lines 50 to 100 read the lifetime distribution from the user. A running total of the probabilities, S, is tested in line 100. If it has not yet reached the value 1, control is sent back to line 60 so that more probabilities can be read.

**3** Lines 110 to 160 read the initial number of items in the system and the number of time periods over which the calculations should extend from the user. Notice that the initial number of living items is stored as R(10). The program uses the array R to store the replacements as if its elements are arranged in a circle, like numbers on the face of a clock. The number of replacements at time 1, R(1), is calculated from R(10), R(9), ... to R(2), the number at time 2, R(2), from R(1), R(10), R(9), ... R(3), the number at time 3, R(3), from R(2), R(1), R(10), R(9), ..., R(4) and so on. The use of a 'circular' array is advantageous as the items have a maximum possible life of 1∅ time units and so the program needs to remember only the last 1∅ numbers of replacements. Each calculated R value displaces the one relating to a time 11 units before.

**4**   Lines 17∅ to the end of the program implement the scheme described above to perform similar calculations to those of Question 3 of the Keyboard Example. The variable K is a pointer indicating whereabouts the program has reached on the clock face memory. It begins by being equal to 1, is increased by 1 in line 32∅ for each new time period, but reset to 1 by lines 33∅ and 34∅ whenever it exceeds 1∅. The variable A keeps a record of the total number of replacements while the variable T is the total for the year J which is being processed.

**5**   The specimen run implies that the number of replacements per time period tends to the limit 4∅.3226 or thereabouts. We can verify this result by a calculation similar to that of Question 4 of the Keyboard Example and obtain the value $1∅∅ \times (1/2.48)$, which is also 4∅.3226. The number 1∅∅ in the specimen run is used instead of the 48 of the example so that the replacement numbers can be thought of as percentages of the original population. Its results can then be applied, pro rata, to any population size.

## Summary

**1**   A piece of equipment whose failure is terminal or whose repair and maintenance costs can be estimated in advance, can be costed as an average expense over each year of its useful life. As the number of years the equipment is kept for increases, so the maintenance costs increase and the average increases. Conversely, if equipment is kept for a relatively short period, the capital replacement cost becomes excessive. In general, there is an optimum time to replace the equipment and this can be determined by examining average annual costs. Clearly it is necessary to discount future cash flow into net present value terms before this is done.

**2**   When there is a population of items subject to wear and failure, the possibility of a group replacement may exist. Often the labour costs associated with replacing small inexpensive components make this a feasible consideration. The optimum time to perform a group replacement is again found by attempting to minimise the average annual cost of the overall maintenance of the population.

**3**   The reliability of an item or system is measured by its failure rate and expected lifetime. The failure rate is the fraction of all similar systems of the same age which fail at that age for the first time. It is typically constant over the useful 'middle age' life of the system. It may also be possible to carry out inspections or preventative maintenance to improve reliability.

**4**   Systems with a constant failure rate have their lifetimes described by the negative exponential probability distribution. The expected lifetime, or mean time to failure or mean time between failures, is the reciprocal of the failure rate.

**5**   A system often depends for its overall reliability on the reliability of its components. There are three main configurations in which component subsystems can be arranged as far as their composite reliability is concerned. Subsystems in series must all function correctly for the whole configuration to function. Subsystems in parallel with active redundancy provide backup for each other and are all in use simultaneously. They are all ageing even though they are not all needed to maintain the satisfactory operation of the whole system. Subsystems in a parallel configuration with passive redundancy, however, are not brought into use until they are needed, that is, until the one or more which are being used develop some fault. These subsystems can be thought of as being on standby rather than backup.

**6** The reliability of a system composed of many subsystems grouped in various configurations and inter-linked with each other can be determined. The reliability function, which is the probability that the system works beyond a given time, can be built up in stages by considering the configurations of subsystems separately and then combining them into larger and larger arrangements. It can be integrated by formula or numerically to give the system's expected lifetime.

**7** Engineers like to measure the availability of a system. It is the ratio of the mean time to failure to the sum of the mean time to failure and the mean time to execute a repair. In other words, it is the fraction of time that the equipment is available for use rather than being repaired.

## Further Reading

Replacement, maintenance and reliability are three aspects of the cost effectiveness of operating a piece of machinery. References (38) and (39) are specialist mathematical sources which deal with a wider range of problems than we have been able to do in this chapter.

The behaviour of a piece of equipment, queues and stock levels can all be formulated mathematically as special cases of stochastic processes. They are often analysed as such in the literature which is therefore highly mathematical. This common theoretical base gives rise to some interesting analogies between the subjects. For example, just as a stock level can be thought of as a queue of items waiting to be used or sold, so a collection of pieces of equipment can be thought of as a queue of items waiting to break down. Certainly items which do fail join a queue for attention and repair. There is an interesting analogy between the interdependency of subsystems and statistics. Consider the various subsystem lifetimes as forming a statistical sample. The lifetime of their series configuration is the minimum of the sample, that of the active parallel arrangement where $r$ subsystems are needed is the $r$th sample value when they are ranked in descending numerical order, and that of the passive parallel configuration is the sum of the sample values. These relationships are of use in evaluating overall system reliability from those of the subsystems.

The operation of replacing or repairing a piece of equipment whenever it fails is called a renewal process in the literature. It can be formulated as a passive parallel arrangement with an infinite number of standbys and is dealt with in the references cited above. Finally the ubiquitous method of simulation can be used to model the incidence of failure with the subsequent queuing of machines for attention or in fact to model any other aspects of the work of this chapter.

## Exercises

**1** Two pieces of equipment each cost £10 000. Their re-sale values and running costs over a 5-year period, expressed in net present value terms, are

| £ (thousands) | Year | | | | |
|---|---|---|---|---|---|
| | 1 | 2 | 3 | 4 | 5 |
| Re-sale value of type A at end of year | 9 | 9 | 8 | 7 | 5 |
| Running cost of type A during year | 1 | 1 | 2 | 3 | 3 |
| Re-sale value of type B at end of year | 8 | 7 | 7 | 6 | 6 |
| Running cost of type B during year | 1 | 2 | 2 | 3 | 4 |

(i)  Calculate the optimum time to replace type A based on average annual cost.

(ii)  Calculate the optimum time to replace type B based on average annual cost.

(iii)  Use your answers to (i) and (ii) to determine which piece of equipment represents better value.

(iv)  If it is company policy to replace equipment at the end of every 5 years, which model should be bought?

2  An illuminated sign has 50 electric light bulbs, each one having the following lifetime probability distribution.

| Life to the nearest month | 1 | 2 | 3 | 4 |
|---|---|---|---|---|
| Probability | 0.1 | 0.3 | 0.4 | 0.2 |

(i)  The bulbs cost 12p each to replace individually. Use the expected lifetime of the bulbs to calculate the expected monthly cost of replacing them as and when they fail.

(ii)  Because of the labour involved in testing each bulb to see which one has failed whenever the sign malfunctions, it is much cheaper per bulb to replace them all as a group. If this costs £1.30, determine whether group replacements should be performed as a matter of routine and if so whether they should be done every 1, 2, 3 or 4 months.

3  A video-cassette recorder is observed to fail on average 8.8 times per year. The time between failures is assumed to be described by the negative exponential distribution. What is the probability that the machine will not fail while it is recording a 3-hour programme, given that it is working at the start of the programme?

4  A coat has 5 buttons on it and they each last on average 3.26 years before falling off. Assuming that they are likely to fail at any time, find the reliability function for the coat if it is considered to be functioning satisfactorily if 3 or more buttons are still in place. What is the expected life of the coat?

# 12 Forecasting

In the planning or appraisal of any business activity it is necessary to make forecasts of one sort or another. Even the assumption that conditions will remain unchanged in the future is really a forecast and a wise manager might wish to justify it. The mere fact that rival companies are engaged in market research and other crystal ball gazing exercises will also encourage the manager to take action. In addition to this regular appraisal there are operations, like the ordering of stock, which require forecasts to be made as a matter of routine.

Operational research in general attempts to quantify the consequences of a proposed strategy or course of action and so each one of its various branches has a forecasting function. Other disciplines can also be a source of quantitative or qualitative predictions, like economics for an investment analysis or geology for mineral exploration. The art of good planning is to bring together all these 'assessments of the unknown' in order to form an optimal corporate policy.

It is usually quantities which originate outside his or her organisation that a manager will have difficulty in forecasting. These externally generated variables like the bank interest rate or the demand for the company's services are not within the manager's direct control and can inhibit the success of operations. In previous chapters of this book, such quantities were assumed to be known and were used as inputs to the various mathematical models and analyses performed. We have seen on many occasions how variables which are internal to an organisation, like its level of stock, can be related to external ones, like the level of demand, by using operational research techniques or even by simple arithmetic. It is therefore important to understand the behaviour of the external variables relevant to a particular company, in the same way that it is vital to have a weather forecast when sailing a yacht.

In this chapter we concentrate on analysing a single variable by examining either a sequence of its previous values, called a **time series**, or a correlated quantity which can be used to indicate its size. The first worked example concerns a variable with no significant upward or downward trend and with no variability due to seasonal effects. It is assumed here that the data simply fluctuates randomly about some fixed value and we use a technique called exponential smoothing to estimate that value.

The time series in the second example has a linear trend but again no seasonal variability. In this case exponential smoothing is used twice, once to estimate the rate of change of the data, which is the slope of the trend line, and then to estimate the data value itself.

The third example deals with a series containing both a trend and seasonality. A 'decomposition' is performed to estimate the mathematical nature of the trend and seasonal adjustments calculated as percentage deviations from the trend.

The last section of the chapter, with a worked example on correlation and regression, is about the derivation of an algebraic relationship between two variables which enables the value of one of them to be predicted from the value of the other.

Forecasting is an art as well as a science. Each method we study works best for data of a specific nature and incorporates its own theoretical model of how the time series behaves. Consequently we have to decide which model to adopt in a particular case and also how to apply it. For instance, before quantifying the trend of a series it may be necessary to transform the data so that it has a straight line graph. There are no rules for doing this and the choice of a transformation depends on the manager's intuitive understanding of the variable in question.

The suitability of a particular forecasting method to a given situation can be assessed by applying it to a sequence of historical data values. If this retrospective appraisal of the model is unsatisfactory then new models can be tested until an appropriate one is found. The process of tuning a model in this way to provide a description of a real system was discussed in Chapter 1 and applies especially to forecasting as in many cases we do not know the mechanism underlying the behaviour of the time series. We therefore build an empirical model based on the data values rather than a theoretical one and use the tuning procedure as an integral part of the modelling itself.

Having developed a suitable model, we assume that it will continue to function in the future with the same degree of accuracy that it would have had in the past. Clearly this is a dubious assumption and an assessment of its results should be carried out periodically as more data values of the time series become available.

## Smoothing

The first step in analysing a time series is to identify any overall upward or downward movement in the data values. A graph of the series should be drawn to gain a qualitative idea of this 'drift' or **trend**. In particular we want to know whether the trend can be approximated by a straight line or not and, if that is the case, whether the line has a significantly large slope or can be considered to be horizontal.

Depending on the conclusions drawn from the graph, an appropriate **smoothing** technique is used to generate a series of values which describes the trend. The next three examples deal with arithmetical ways of smoothing a time series while a statistical method, called regression, is covered later in the chapter.

### The Trombone Example
The manager of a music shop records the number of trombones sold each year.

| Year | 1975 | 1976 | 1977 | 1978 | 1979 | 1980 | 1981 | 1982 |
|------|------|------|------|------|------|------|------|------|
| Sales of trombones | 80 | 75 | 82 | 78 | 76 | 79 | 78 | 81 |

He would like a forecast of the sales for 1983.

*Solution*    Figure 12.1 illustrates the need to smooth the data in order to eliminate the fluctuations, or **noise**, and estimate its average behaviour, the trend. There seems to be a very slight upward trend with no seasonal or other cyclical patterns and so we assume a model for the series which states that each yearly sales figure is a constant, which we do not know, plus or minus random noise. We can either average all the data values to

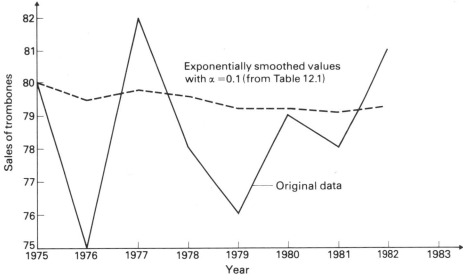

**Fig. 12.1**   Graph for the Trombone Example

estimate the value of the constant or use a method called **exponential smoothing**. Whereas averaging gives equal weight or importance to every data value, exponential smoothing is preferable as it ascribes more importance to those in the recent past than to those in the distant past. We shall return to its advantages later.

Exponential smoothing is rather like firing missiles at a moving target, which is the analogy of the time series. We know where the target is now but not where it will be when the next missile arrives. This is therefore aimed at a point in space where we believe the target will be in the future. For example, suppose that the previous shot had been 5 metres to the right of the target. If the next missile is aimed a full 5 metres to the left then it will certainly miss because the target is moving and will be elsewhere by the time it arrives. It makes more sense to adjust the direction of the next missile by some fraction, say 50%, of the error so that there is a chance of hitting the target as it moves back from its last known position. In fact heat- and metal-seeking missiles do this by automatically correcting their course using radar information. They do not respond to the full correction needed until they are close to the target aircraft to avoid being 'shaken off'.

We apply this idea to smoothing a time series by adjusting the previous smoothed value (the point of impact of our last missile) by some fraction, $\alpha$ (Greek letter 'alpha'), called the **smoothing constant**, of its deviation from the latest observation. This can be expressed mathematically as

New smoothed value = old smoothed value + $\alpha$ (new data value − old smoothed value)

$$(12.1)$$

The term in brackets on the right hand side of (12.1) is the correction needed. Rearranging the terms we obtain the equivalent formula

New smoothed value = $(1 - \alpha) \times$ old smoothed value + $\alpha \times$ new data value   (12.2)

Table 12.1 shows the smoothed sequences obtained for the present example by using 4 different values of $\alpha$ in equation (12.1). Each sequence is started by taking the first data value, 80, as the first smoothed value. Subsequent smoothed values are calculated from

**Table 12.1**  Exponential smoothing for the Trombone Example

| Year | Sales | α=0.05 Correction needed | α=0.05 Smoothed value | α=0.1 Correction needed | α=0.1 Smoothed value | α=0.2 Correction needed | α=0.2 Smoothed value | α=0.9 Correction needed | α=0.9 Smoothed value |
|---|---|---|---|---|---|---|---|---|---|
| 1975 | 80 | — | 80.0 | — | 80.0 | — | 80.0 | — | 80.0 |
| 1976 | 75 | −5.0 | 79.8 | −5.0 | 79.5 | −5.0 | 79.0 | −5.0 | 75.5 |
| 1977 | 82 | +2.2 | 79.9 | +2.5 | 79.8 | +3.0 | 79.6 | +6.5 | 81.4 |
| 1978 | 78 | −1.9 | 79.8 | −1.8 | 79.6 | −1.6 | 79.3 | −3.4 | 78.3 |
| 1979 | 76 | −3.8 | 79.6 | −3.6 | 79.2 | −3.3 | 78.6 | −2.3 | 76.2 |
| 1980 | 79 | −0.6 | 79.6 | −0.2 | 79.2 | +0.4 | 78.7 | +2.8 | 78.7 |
| 1981 | 78 | −1.6 | 79.5 | −1.2 | 79.1 | −0.7 | 78.6 | −0.7 | 78.1 |
| 1982 | 81 | +1.5 | 79.6 | +1.9 | 79.3 | +2.4 | 79.1 | +2.9 | 80.7 |
| Total absolute error | | 16.6 | | 16.2 | | 16.4 | | 23.6 | |

the current data value and the previous smoothed value using equation (12.2). For instance, the smoothed value 78.6 for 1979 with $\alpha$ equal to 0.2 is made up of 0.8 times 79.3, the previous smoothed value, and 0.2 times 76, the current data value for 1979.

The sequence for which $\alpha$ is equal to 0.9 in Table 12.1 is not 'smooth' at all and has the same fluctuations as the original series. Such a large value of the smoothing constant corresponds to correcting the aim of the missile in the above analogy by almost the full amount of the previous error. This results in the generated sequence being unacceptably erratic as it is supposed to describe the overall average behaviour of the data.

On the other hand, the values arising from taking $\alpha$ to be 0.1 are smooth as can be seen in Fig. 12.1. Furthermore they indicate a steady horizontal trend pattern to the data.

In Table 12.1 the absolute errors of the smoothed values have been added together for each value of the smoothing constant $\alpha$. This measures the overall error made by each sequence and we see that the one given by taking $\alpha$ equal to 0.1 has the least such error. Values of $\alpha$ smaller than this result in a larger total error as they track the original series too slowly and take too long to respond to changes in it. Larger values of $\alpha$ track it too closely and respond too quickly and so have as much variability as the original data values, again giving rise to large errors.

Constructing a table like Table 12.1 is a good way of choosing an appropriate smoothing constant for a given time series. Although it is a numerical method and does not therefore give the exact optimal value, we could continue by investigating values for $\alpha$ near to 0.1 to see if they further minimise the error. For instance we could try 0.09 and 0.11 and then attempt to improve on whichever of those is better by further trial and error. In practice this is not pursued and the present example is quite typical in that a value of $\alpha$ equal to 0.1 or thereabouts gives a satisfactory smoothed sequence.

A forecast for 1983 can now be made from the sequence generated by $\alpha$ equal to 0.1. As there seems to be no significant upward or downward trend to these numbers, we shall assume that the latest smoothed value is a reasonable forecast for the next time period's data value. **We therefore predict that 79.3 trombones will be sold in 1983.** The latest absolute deviation from the original data, 1.9, can also be quoted as an indication of the possible error in this forecast.

There are certain advantages in using exponential smoothing rather than simply averaging the given data. Exponential smoothing ascribes more importance to data values relating to the recent past than to those in the distant past. It can be shown algebraically that each smoothed value is a linear combination of all the data values so far. The weight a data value which occurred $t$ time units previously has in this combination is proportional to $(1 - \alpha)$ to the power $t$. For this reason the method is called 'exponential' smoothing and it means that past data is being discounted at the rate of $\alpha$ per time period. This is preferable in many cases to attributing equal weight to all the previous data values.

Another feature of exponential smoothing is that it needs only a small amount of computer store. When forecasts are required for many series, for instance in predicting the sales of all the different items in a supermarket, there may not be enough computer storage space for all the historical data. It would then be impossible to calculate the averages in order to make forecasts. Now the only information needed by equation (12.2) is the previous smoothed value, the smoothing constant and the current data value. It is therefore sufficient to store from one time period to the next only the current smoothed value and the smoothing constant. This represents a considerable saving of computer storage space compared with averaging methods.

Unfortunately, **simple** or **single** exponential smoothing does not give accurate results when the time series has a significant upward or downward trend. In the mathematical justification of the method it is assumed that each data value is a constant to which some random noise has been added or subtracted. If this assumption about the data is not valid then a more sophisticated model of its behaviour is required. In the next worked example we see how exponential smoothing can be adapted to analyse a time series which has a significant trend.

### The Population Example

The population figures for the United Kingdom between 1801 and 1901 were as follows:

| Year | 1801 | 1811 | 1821 | 1831 | 1841 | 1851 | 1861 | 1871 | 1881 | 1891 | 1901 |
|---|---|---|---|---|---|---|---|---|---|---|---|
| Population of the United Kingdom (tens of thousands) | 1194 | 1337 | 1547 | 1784 | 2018 | 2226 | 2453 | 2743 | 3102 | 3426 | 3824 |

We smooth the series and make predictions for 1911 and 1921.

*Solution*　Figure 12.2 shows the data values plotted against time. This indicates a much more ordered state of affairs than the erratic series in the last example and implies that there is a precise relationship between the population size and the year in which it is

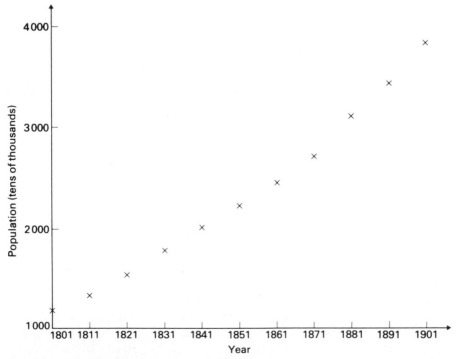

**Fig. 12.2**　United Kingdom Population Example data

measured. The art of analysing a time series is firstly to decide whether it is reasonable to assume that such a relationship exists and secondly, and far more difficult, to decide on the mathematical nature of that relationship, in other words, to build a model.

Now many of the time series found in the social sciences and economics grow or decline in a multiplicative rather than an additive way. This means that their graphs show exponential growth or decay but the logarithms of the values in the series will increase or decrease steadily with time giving a straight line graph. These ideas of growth were discussed in Chapter 1 and the appropriate percentage growth rate in the present example is the excess of the birth rate over the death rate.

Figure 12.3 plots the logarithms to base 10 of the population figures against time. The points are almost in a straight line and there is a great temptation to join them together using a ruler and extrapolating the line to give predictions for 1911 and 1921. In an almost ideal situation such as the present one, fitting a straight line to the data is valid and we shall consider it as a forecasting technique later in the chapter. However, exponential smoothing is preferable as it attaches more weight to recent observations than to older ones and hence adjusts to any change in trend which might occur. There is also the advantage, mentioned in the solution to the Trombone Example, that it is not necessary to have the whole series of data values available in order to make a forecast. In many applications this can represent a worthwhile saving in computer storage requirements.

Conversions of one time series into another, as carried out in this example, are not uncommon in practice. They enable smoothing techniques which detect a linear trend to be used provided that a graph of the transformed series shows this to be a reasonable model to adopt. As for all forecasting methodology, the justification of a particular conversion or analysis lies in the accuracy of the forecasts it produces. This is in

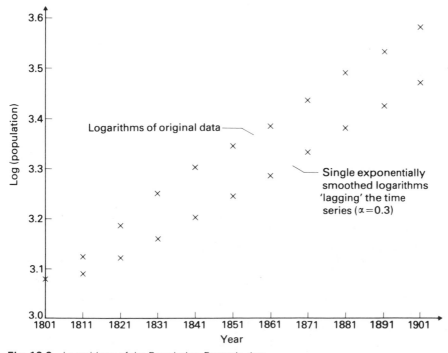

**Fig. 12.3** Logarithms of the Population Example data

accordance with one of the conclusions drawn in Chapter 13, that it is of only secondary importance that we understand why a mathematical model is appropriate in a given situation, the main consideration is that it works.

The model for arithmetic or linear growth is that each data value is the previous one plus a constant called the **slope**. There will also be random noise added to this in any time series observed in practice. Single exponential smoothing will not track such data adequately for in the missile firing analogy used earlier, this corresponds to a target which is always moving in one direction. Correcting the aim of successive missiles by some fraction of the previous error is therefore not a good way of locating the target and the missiles will lag behind it. For a time series, this means that the exponentially smoothed sequence will underestimate the trend, as can be seen for the present data in Fig. 12.3.

There is a technique called **double exponential smoothing** which entails exponentially smoothing the sequence of smoothed values. The argument used, which is quite ingenious, is that the shortfall in the second smoothed value below the first one is approximately the same as that of the first value below the original series. In other words, the error in the first smoothed sequence can be estimated by seeing how far the second one falls below it.

The method we shall use here, however, is a variant of double exponential smoothing called **Holt's method**. It has the advantage that the smoothing is performed on quantities which have direct relevance to the time series itself, namely the current data value and the slope. The working is shown in Table 12.2 and we shall examine it column by column.

**Table 12.2**

| Column 1 Year | Column 2 Population (tens of thousands) | Column 3 Log (population) | Column 4 Smoothed value ($\alpha=0.2$) | Column 5 Increase over previous value | Column 6 Smoothed increase ($\alpha=0.02$) | Column 7 Forecast for next logarithm |
|---|---|---|---|---|---|---|
| 1801 | 1194 | 3.0770 | 3.0770 | — | — | — |
| 1811 | 1337 | 3.1261 | 3.1261 | 0.0491 | 0.0491 | 3.1752 |
| 1821 | 1547 | 3.1895 | 3.1781 | 0.0520 | 0.0492 | 3.2273 |
| 1831 | 1784 | 3.2514 | 3.2321 | 0.0540 | 0.0493 | 3.2814 |
| 1841 | 2018 | 3.3049 | 3.2861 | 0.0540 | 0.0494 | 3.3355 |
| 1851 | 2226 | 3.3475 | 3.3379 | 0.0518 | 0.0494 | 3.3873 |
| 1861 | 2453 | 3.3897 | 3.3878 | 0.0499 | 0.0494 | 3.4372 |
| 1871 | 2743 | 3.4382 | 3.4374 | 0.0496 | 0.0494 | 3.4868 |
| 1881 | 3102 | 3.4916 | 3.4878 | 0.0504 | 0.0494 | 3.5372 |
| 1891 | 3426 | 3.5348 | 3.5367 | 0.0489 | 0.0494 | 3.5861 |
| 1901 | 3824 | 3.5825 | 3.5854 | 0.0487 | 0.0494 | 3.6348 |
| 1911 | Forecast for logarithm=3.6348 | | | | | |
| 1921 | Forecast for logarithm=3.6348+0.0494=3.6842 | | | | | |

Columns 1 and 2 contain details of the given time series. As the suspected growth is multiplicative in this case, the logarithms of the data values should grow additively, or linearly, and these are listed in column 3. The logarithms are taken to base 10 although any base would serve, and 4 decimal place accuracy is used to achieve the 'numerical sensitivity' discussed in Chapter 1. The sequence of logarithms replaces the original data values as the series we wish to analyse.

The remaining columns of Table 12.2 contain the results of applying single exponential smoothing twice. Column 4 has the smoothed data values and its first two entries are taken to be the first two data values in order to start the process. Subsequent values are formed by using equation (12.2) with the smoothing constant $\alpha$ equal to 0.2. As there is a significant trend, however, the new smoothed value is 0.8 times the previous forecast in column 7, not the previous smoothed value, plus 0.2 times the current data value.

Column 5 is self-explanatory and measures the slope of the trend line. It is smoothed in column 6 with $\alpha$ equal to 0.02. This is much smaller than a typical smoothing constant as we do not anticipate as much random noise in the value of the slope as in the raw data and we do not want the slope estimate to fluctuate wildly. As for single exponential smoothing, the most suitable values for the smoothing constants can be found by trial and error on a historical series if this is considered necessary. Hence each entry in column 6 is 0.98 times the previous entry plus 0.02 times the current column 5 value.

Finally, the entry in column 7 is a forecast of the next data value obtained by adding the entry in column 4, the current smoothed value, to that in column 6, the current smoothed slope value. This is smoothed with the next data value to give the next entry in column 4 and the process continues. In summary, smoothed data values are subtracted to give an estimate of the slope of the trend. This is smoothed and added to the smoothed data to produce a forecast of the next time series value. When that number becomes known it is used to obtain the next smoothed data value and the procedure begins again. Forecasting is achieved by adding appropriate multiples of the latest slope estimate, which represents the increase in the series per unit time, to the latest smoothed data value.

The forecast for 1911, which is 1 time period after 1901, is found by adding the slope estimate to the 1901 smoothed value. The resulting logarithm is 3.6348 and the population prediction, which is 10 raised to this power, is 4313.2 in units of tens of thousands. **This is therefore about 43 million and compares with the actual value of 42 million.**

The forecast for 1921, which is two time periods later than 1901, is twice the slope estimate plus the latest smoothed value. This gives 3.6842 as the logarithm and **48 million as the prediction for population size.** This compares unfavourably with the actual figure of 44 million.

It is interesting to note how the model, which consists of assuming that the logarithms of the population sizes obey a particular linear trend, ceases to describe the behaviour of the time series after 1911. Clearly the upward trend was affected by the 1914–18 World War but the model cannot be expected to take this into account using data measured up to 1901 only.

The lesson we learn from this is clear. Even when a mathematical relationship provides an almost perfect description of the past behaviour of a time series, its use in forecasting assumes that it will continue to do so in the future. Apart from catastrophic changes in the real system, like World War I in the present example, there are other reasons why trends in just about any time series cannot continue indefinitely. Certainly any trend exhibited by population figures must level out or become reversed sooner or later. Suppose that the trend identified in the data of this example had persisted uninterruptedly until 1981. The projected logarithm of the population is 8 times the slope estimate plus the 1901 smoothed value which gives 3.9806. This implies a population for the United Kingdom of about 96 million when the true figure was roughly half that!

## Time Series Decomposition

When a time series contains a significant trend together with seasonal variability, historical values can be analysed to isolate and quantify the two effects. The process is called a **decomposition** because an attempt is made to describe the data in terms of trend and seasonal variation components. There may also be a long-term cyclical behaviour to the series which can be incorporated as a component. The next example deals with a highly seasonal demand situation, the sale of sunglasses.

### The Sunglasses Example

A manufacturer of sunglasses divides the year into quarters and records the following sales, measured in thousands of pounds, over a four-year period.

| Quarter<br>Year | I<br>(Jan–Mar) | II<br>(Apr–Jun) | III<br>(Jul–Sep) | IV<br>(Oct–Dec) |
|---|---|---|---|---|
| 1975 | 2.4 | 2.8 | 3.6 | 1.2 |
| 1976 | 2.5 | 3.5 | 3.8 | 1.6 |
| 1977 | 2.5 | 2.9 | 4.4 | 2.0 |
| 1978 | 3.4 | 3.7 | 5.2 | 2.7 |

He wants to estimate the overall trend in the sales and the quarterly seasonal adjustments to that trend. He would like to use these results to forecast the sales figures for the four quarters of 1979.

*Solution*    Figure 12.4 shows the behaviour of the time series in this question. It indicates that the data has an overall upward trend and is highly seasonal with quarter III being consistently above average and quarter IV being below it.

The details of a time series decomposition analysis depend on the type of model adopted to describe the data. The first step with any model is to identify the overall trend and a smoothing technique similar to that used in the last example is required. The smoothed values are then plotted on a graph with the original data so that the nature of the trend and any other long-term behaviour can be recognised.

When a series has seasonal variability it is preferable to smooth its values by averaging rather than exponential smoothing. The latter technique will track all the seasonal peaks and troughs in the data and the results will not be smooth.

A **moving average** of order $n$ is the average of any $n$ consecutive data values. By averaging over a period of time which contains all the seasons appropriate to a given series we hope that their effects will 'cancel out' to expose the underlying trend. In the present example the data relates to the four quarters of successive years and so it is logical to calculate 4th order moving averages because in any period of 4 consecutive quarters all the seasonal variability should average out to zero.

The results of the calculations can be seen in Table 12.3. The first two sets of 4 consecutive quarterly data values have been bracketed together showing how the first two moving averages are obtained. Notice that each one relates to a time which is the mid-point of the time periods on which it is based, in this case between the second and third quarters of each 4 quarter cycle. They are therefore written on a line between those of the second and third quarters and could be plotted on Fig. 12.4 at points half way between those quarters. However we want estimates of the overall trend corresponding precisely to the quarters and not half way between them in order to calculate the seasonal variation of each data value. It is therefore preferable to **centre** the moving averages by averaging them in pairs and this is shown in the 4th column of Table 12.3. For example the entry for quarter III of 1975 is the mean of the two moving averages indicated by the bracket and this pattern of averaging continues down that column. These values are taken to describe the general trend of the original time series and can be seen plotted in Fig. 12.4.

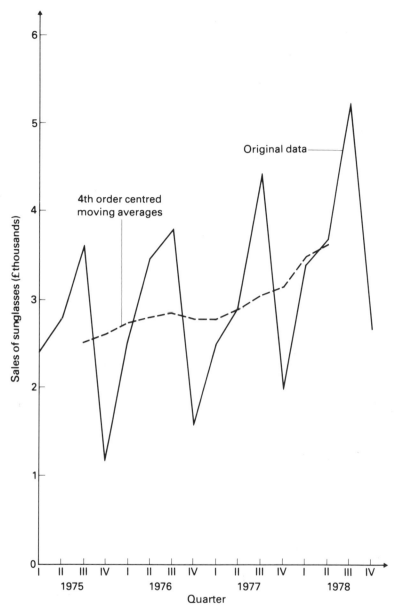

**Fig. 12.4**   Sales graph for the Sunglasses Example

Having calculated trend values for each quarter we come to the second step of the time series decomposition which is the analysis of the seasonal variability about that trend. In general the seasons can be any period of time relevant to the series. This can be days, months or, as in this example, quarters. The variability is modelled either as a multiplicative percentage deviation from trend or else as an additive one. Intuition and the context of a particular situation will determine whether it is appropriate to assume multiplicative seasonality and draw conclusions like 'Saturday's sales are 82% above the average daily sales', or additive seasonality with conclusions like 'March's figures are £50 000 down on the average monthly turnover'. The additive model assumes a degree of

**Table 12.3**

| Quarter | | Sales (thousands of pounds) | 4 quarter moving average | Centred moving average | Percentage seasonal variation of data value over trend value | | | |
|---|---|---|---|---|---|---|---|---|
| | | | | | I | II | III | IV |
| 1975 | I | 2.4 | | | | | | |
| | II | 2.8 | | | | | | |
| | | | 2.50 | | | | | |
| | III | 3.6 | | 2.52 | | | 142.86 | |
| | | | 2.53 | | | | | |
| | IV | 1.2 | | 2.62 | | | | 45.80 |
| | | | 2.70 | | | | | |
| 1976 | I | 2.5 | | 2.73 | 91.58 | | | |
| | | | 2.75 | | | | | |
| | II | 3.5 | | 2.80 | | 125.00 | | |
| | | | 2.85 | | | | | |
| | III | 3.8 | | 2.85 | | | 133.33 | |
| | | | 2.85 | | | | | |
| | IV | 1.6 | | 2.78 | | | | 57.55 |
| | | | 2.70 | | | | | |
| 1977 | I | 2.5 | | 2.78 | 89.93 | | | |
| | | | 2.85 | | | | | |
| | II | 2.9 | | 2.90 | | 100.00 | | |
| | | | 2.95 | | | | | |
| | III | 4.4 | | 3.07 | | | 143.32 | |
| | | | 3.18 | | | | | |
| | IV | 2.0 | | 3.28 | | | | 60.98 |
| | | | 3.38 | | | | | |
| 1978 | I | 3.4 | | 3.48 | 97.70 | | | |
| | | | 3.58 | | | | | |
| | II | 3.7 | | 3.67 | | 100.82 | | |
| | III | 5.2 | 3.75 | | | | | |
| | IV | 2.7 | | Total | 279.21 | 325.82 | 419.51 | 164.33 |
| | | | | Average | 93.07 | 108.61 | 139.84 | 54.78 |

constancy to seasonal change irrespective of the trend whereas the multiplicative approach treats the percentage corrections to trend as being the same from one season to the next corresponding one. For many time series it makes little practical difference which model is adopted.

For either method, a separate set of calculations is performed for each season to find the average adjustment to trend it requires. In our example, the multiplicative deviations are used and the last four columns of Table 12.3 show the percentage variations from trend for those quarters for which a trend value is available. The percentage for each quarter is listed in a column corresponding to the position in the year of the quarter so that the 4 averages can be calculated and these appear at the bottom of the table. If it had been decided to treat the seasonal variability in an additive way, then average additive instead of multiplicative adjustments would be obtained at this stage.

As the trend values represent the average behaviour of the data, the seasonal corrections to it should cancel out over a complete cycle of seasons. In the present problem, this implies that the total of the 4 percentages should be 400 giving an average correction to trend of 100%. In fact they add up to 396.3 and we attribute the discrepancy to random noise in the original data. The seasonal indices can be 'fiddled' to total to 400 by multiplying each one by the extremely useful factor (desired answer/actual answer) which in this case is (400/396.3) or 1.009 336. The resulting seasonal percentage adjustments to trend are Quarter I: 93.94, Quarter II: 109.62, Quarter III: 141.15, Quarter IV: 55.29. It is preferable to quote percentages in reports and other published work which average to 100 as there is always someone who checks them and challenges the author if they do not!

Although the seasonal indices constitute useful management information in their own right, it is usual to quantify the nature of the trend as well. This allows forecasts to be made from the as yet purely historical analysis of the series by enabling the trend line to be extrapolated beyond the range of the data.

It seems reasonable from the graph in this example to assume that the centred moving averages lie on a straight line, allowing for random noise in the data, and hence that the trend is linear. Sometimes a transformation technique is used, possibly involving logarithms as in the last example, in order to obtain a linear trend. As mentioned in Chapter 1, mathematicians like straight line graphs because they indicate a particularly simple relationship between the variables concerned and make all the subsequent working easier.

The trend line can be fitted to the centred moving averages in a number of ways. The regression line approach, which includes the obvious method of drawing a straight line on the graph with a pencil and ruler, can be used but in its simplest form it assigns equal weight to all the points whereas we want later values in the series to have more importance than earlier ones. This can be achieved by weighting the points in a regression analysis or by using exponential smoothing. This was the technique adopted for the same reason in the Population Example and Table 12.4 shows Holt's method applied to the centred moving averages here.

**Table 12.4**

| Quarter | | Centred moving average | Smoothed value ($\alpha=0.1$) | Increase over previous value | Smoothed increase ($\alpha=0.02$) | Forecast for next moving average value |
|---|---|---|---|---|---|---|
| 1975 | III | 2.52 | 2.520 | — | — | — |
| | IV | 2.62 | 2.620 | 0.100 | 0.100 | 2.720 |
| 1976 | I | 2.73 | 2.721 | 0.101 | 0.100 | 2.821 |
| | II | 2.80 | 2.819 | 0.098 | 0.100 | 2.919 |
| | III | 2.85 | 2.912 | 0.093 | 0.100 | 3.012 |
| | IV | 2.78 | 2.989 | 0.077 | 0.100 | 3.089 |
| 1977 | I | 2.78 | 3.058 | 0.069 | 0.099 | 3.157 |
| | II | 2.90 | 3.131 | 0.073 | 0.098 | 3.229 |
| | III | 3.07 | 3.213 | 0.082 | 0.098 | 3.311 |
| | IV | 3.28 | 3.308 | 0.095 | 0.098 | 3.406 |
| 1978 | I | 3.48 | 3.413 | 0.105 | 0.098 | 3.511 |
| | II | 3.67 | 3.527 | 0.114 | 0.098 | 3.625 |

Using the latest estimates for the trend and the slope from Table 12.4 together with the adjusted percentage variations calculated before, forecasts for 1979 can be found as shown in Table 12.5.

The model of a linear trend with multiplicative seasonal variation was prompted by intuition and the scrutiny of Fig. 12.4. This approach to the analysis can be assessed by comparing each forecast in the last column of Table 12.4 with the actual time series value on the next line in the second column. Other models can be developed and a measure like

**Table 12.5**

| Quarter | | Number of quarters after 1978 II ($N$) | Trend forecast $=3.527+N\times0.098$ | Appropriate percentage seasonal variation | Forecast |
|---|---|---|---|---|---|
| 1979 | I | 3 | 3.821 | 93.94 | 3.59 |
| | II | 4 | 3.919 | 109.62 | 4.30 |
| | III | 5 | 4.017 | 141.15 | 5.67 |
| | IV | 6 | 4.115 | 55.29 | 2.28 |

the average absolute deviation of the forecasts used as a criterion for deciding which model is the most suitable.

As we saw in the Population Example, it is an act of faith to assume that a mathematical model will continue to be valid in the future even though it was valid in the past. The accuracy of the forecasts depends on the persistence of both the trend and seasonal patterns and changes in either of these will affect the relevance of the model. Naturally such changes are more likely to occur in the intervening time when models are used to generate long-range forecasts. These should therefore be treated with caution.

## Correlation and Regression

It is sometimes possible to make a prediction about the value of one quantity if we have information about the value of a different but related quantity. Statisticians say that two variables are **correlated** if they can be linked together in this way. For example the size of the skull of a human fetus is correlated with its age. This enables its expected date of delivery to be predicted by taking measurements from a television image of its skull on an ultrasonic scanner.

There is often a mathematical relationship between correlated variables called a **regression** equation. This can be of interest in its own right as it indicates the type of relationship which exists between the variables or it can be used to produce forecasts of one variable from values of the other.

The degree of correlation between two quantities can be seen by plotting a **scatter diagram**. This is a graph whose points have pairs of values of the variables as their coordinates and three examples are shown in Fig. 12.5. These diagrams indicate whether a regression equation exists between the variables and, if it does, what form it will take.

If one of the variables acts as the 'cause' of the other variable then clearly a strong positive or negative correlation will be seen on the scatter diagram. Unfortunately it is often inferred that the converse is true and that an ordered set of points on a scatter diagram implies that there is a 'cause and effect' relationship between the variables. Perhaps an example will serve as a warning against the use of this argument.

Consider the scatter diagram of the number of suicides committed in the United Kingdom plotted against the number of television receivers sold, with each point corresponding to a different year. The graph would look like the example of positive correlation in Fig. 12.5(a) because both variables are closely related to the size of the population and as this has grown over the years they both grow together. However, unless one takes a very morbid view of the effects of watching television, there is obviously no 'cause and effect' phenomenon between them. Such 'spurious' correlation occurs whenever there is a third variable acting as the common cause of the other two. Whilst it upsets any conclusions regarding causality, it does not detract from the value of any mathematical

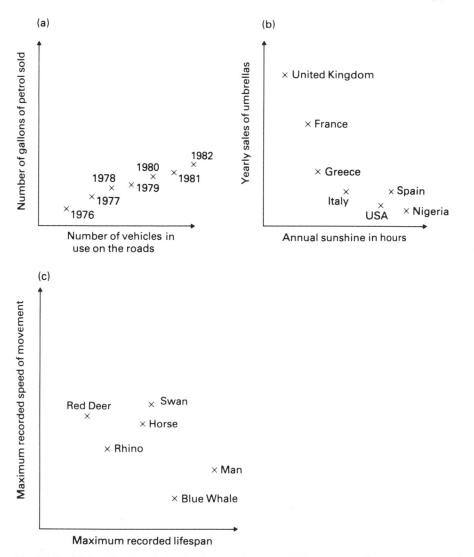

**Fig. 12.5**  (a) Positive Correlation (an increase in one variable corresponds to an increase in the other),
(b) Negative Correlation (an increase in one variable corresponds to a decrease in the other),
(c) Zero Correlation (no relationship between the variables)

relationship we derive. In the above example, although the concept of causality can be dismissed, a knowledge of the number of television receivers sold for some year in the future can be used in the appropriate regression equation to predict the number of suicides which will occur in that year. The existence of a mathematical relationship between two variables, although of practical use, does not provide evidence of causality unless there are other, usually qualitative, reasons for it to be true. These qualitative reasons will originate from the branch of science to which the variables apply, so if there were indications in the theory of psychology that watching television causes suicide, then the regression analysis would support the theory. Notice that this conclusion would require an additional assumption to be made which could itself be the subject of a regression analysis. It is that the number of televisions sold is an indication of the amount of television watched. This use of an easily measured variable in place of a quantity which is perhaps difficult to measure or even to define precisely is common in statistics. The justification for using 'substitute' variables is either that they correlate closely with the quantity of interest or that their use is recognised to be valid by the branch of science appropriate to the problem.

As this is not meant to be a textbook on statistics or statistical inference, we concentrate on the use of regression as a purely mathematical analysis of the relationship between quantities. In the next example we do not concern ourselves with the problem of causality and the variables measured·are not substitutes for other properties. A regression analysis is performed simply as a device for predicting the value of one variable from that of another. We also derive a coefficient whose value indicates the degree of validity that the analysis has.

**The Cosmetics Example**
The profits an international cosmetics company makes from its operations in various European countries are as follows:

| Country | Norway | Denmark | Switzerland | Sweden | Greece | Portugal | Belgium | Netherlands |
|---|---|---|---|---|---|---|---|---|
| Population (millions) | 4.1 | 5.1 | 6.3 | 8.3 | 9.3 | 9.8 | 9.8 | 14.0 |
| Yearly profit (£ tens of thousands) | 3.6 | 3.8 | 4.2 | 9.0 | 7.5 | 9.0 | 10.2 | 15.2 |

What yearly profit can the company expect to make in Finland, which has a population of 4.8 million people?

*Solution*   Obviously there are many factors influencing the amount of money a company will make on any given venture. The population size of the potential market is just one of these factors and may not even be the most important one. However, if a mathematical relationship, a model, can be established to link the behaviour of the two sets of numbers given in the question, then it will form a method of forecasting the profit to be made in Finland. This approach to forecasting assumes that all other factors stay constant. The credibility of that assumption is left to the manager's intuitive understanding of the situation concerned.

A scatter diagram of the data shows whether it is reasonable to expect a mathematical relationship to exist between the variables or not. If such a relationship does exist then the points on the scatter diagram will form an ordered pattern but we are not looking for a curve which passes through every single one of them. The relationship we seek takes into account the incidence of statistical error in the data and describes what is happening on average.

The model assumed in a regression analysis is that the *y* value of a point on the scatter diagram is equal to some function of its *x* value plus or minus random noise. This compares with the models we studied in time series analysis which were either that there was a trend with random noise or a trend and seasonal variation with random noise. The model in all these cases consists of a deterministic part with a stochastic 'noisy' part whose effect we are trying to eliminate from the data, either by smoothing or regression.

It is important to notice that the two variables in a regression analysis are not treated on an equal basis and all the statistical error is assumed to occur in the $y$ values of the data. Often the $x$ variable is a quantity which has no significant measurement error associated with it, like time. It may also be some property which is within our control and we want to set its value in order to achieve a specific value for $y$. For this reason, $x$ is called the **independent variable** and $y$ is the **dependent variable**. The implication is that $x$ values are the 'cause' of $y$ values but as we discussed earlier, this interpretation of correlation can be abused. We shall use these terms simply as technical expressions to distinguish between the variable on the horizontal axis, $x$, and that on the vertical axis, $y$.

The scatter diagram (Fig. 12.6) for the present example has the population figures as

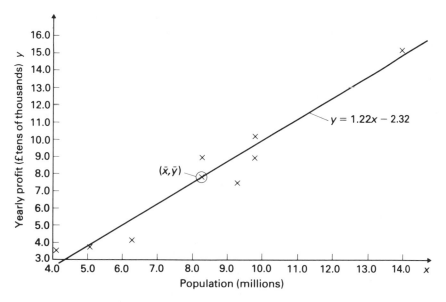

**Fig. 12.6**   Scatter diagram and regression line for the Cosmetics Example

its independent variable and the profits as the dependent variable. This is because we want to predict profit values by using population values and so we treat the former as being dependent on the latter. In some situations it is not clear which variable should be considered as being dependent on the other one and two separate analyses, one for each possibility, can be performed. Each variable could then be predicted from the other by using the appropriate relationship.

Having designated one variable as being 'dependent' on the other and having drawn the scatter diagram accordingly, it is now necessary to decide what type of relationship, if indeed there is one at all, can be fitted to the data. We saw in Chapter 1 the central role that the straight line plays in coordinate geometry and so, not surprisingly, it is the simplest type of regression to perform. To justify such a **linear regression**, we inspect the scatter diagram to see if a straight line on the graph can give a reasonable description of the behaviour of the points. If there is no pattern to the distribution of the points, that is zero correlation, then the analysis stops and no relationship between the variables exists. If there is a non-linear pattern to the points then a transformation procedure is necessary, like taking logarithms as in the Population Example.

There are two ways of finding the 'best' straight line through a set of points on a scatter diagram. Either the line can be drawn by inspection using a ruler and then any predictions read from the graph, or the equation of the line can be calculated from the data values by means of certain formulae. It is helpful when drawing the line by eye to know that the 'best' line passes through the point whose coordinates are the averages of the $x$ and $y$ data values. This point is shown in Fig. 12.6 and should be plotted first so that the line can be drawn through it.

The word 'best' used above has a specific meaning in the context of a regression analysis. As all the statistical error is assumed to be in the $y$ values only, the 'best' line is the one which minimises the sum of the squares of all the vertical distances, which are the $y$ deviations or errors, between the points and the line. It is also true that the eye/brain system in humans perceives vertical distances between points and lines more readily than horizontal ones. This means that a regression line drawn by eye will also minimise the vertical distances of the points from it. The prediction we want would be read from such a line.

It is often difficult to draw the regression line by inspection, even though we know it passes through the average point, as the other points are spaced widely apart. This is the case in the present example. Table 12.16 shows how the equation of the line can be calculated from the given data values. **It predicts the profit for Finland to be $1.22 \times 4.8 - 2.32 = 3.5$ or £35 000.**

**Table 12.6**  Regression Line Calculation for the Cosmetics Example

| | $x$ | $y$ | $x^2$ | $y^2$ | $xy$ |
|---|---|---|---|---|---|
| | 4.1 | 3.6 | 16.81 | 12.96 | 14.76 |
| | 5.1 | 3.8 | 26.01 | 14.44 | 19.38 |
| | 6.3 | 4.2 | 39.69 | 17.64 | 26.46 |
| | 8.3 | 9.0 | 68.89 | 81.00 | 74.70 |
| | 9.3 | 7.5 | 86.49 | 56.25 | 69.75 |
| | 9.8 | 9.0 | 96.04 | 81.00 | 88.20 |
| | 9.8 | 10.2 | 96.04 | 104.04 | 99.96 |
| | 14.0 | 15.2 | 196.00 | 231.04 | 212.80 |
| Total | 66.7 | 62.5 | 625.97 | 598.37 | 606.01 |

Number of data pairs, $N = 8$

Average $x$ value, $\bar{x} = $ (Sum of $x$ values)$/N = 66.7/8 = 8.3375$

Average $y$ value, $\bar{y} = $ (Sum of $y$ values)$/N = 62.5/8 = 7.8125$

$$\text{Variance of } x = \frac{(\text{Sum of } x^2) - N\bar{x}^2}{(N-1)} = \frac{625.97 - 8(8.3375)^2}{(8-1)} = 9.979\,82$$

$$\text{Variance of } y = \frac{(\text{Sum of } y^2) - N\bar{y}^2}{(N-1)} = \frac{598.37 - 8(7.8125)^2}{(8-1)} = 15.726\,96$$

$$\text{Covariance of } x \text{ and } y = \frac{(\text{Sum of } xy) - N\bar{x}\bar{y}}{(N-1)} = \frac{606.01 - 8(8.3375)(7.8125)}{(8-1)} = 12.130\,89$$

$$\text{Slope of regression line of } y \text{ on } x, m = \frac{\text{Covariance of } x \text{ and } y}{\text{Variance of } x} = \frac{12.130\,89}{9.979\,82} = 1.215\,54$$

Equation of regression line of $y$ on $x$: $y = mx + (\bar{y} - m\bar{x})$

so in this case, $y = 1.215\,54x + (7.8125 - (1.215\,54)(8.3375))$

or $y = 1.22x - 2.32$

The regression equation obtained in Table 12.6 can be used to plot the line on the scatter diagram. By putting $x$ equal to some convenient value, say 5 in the present example, we can plot another point besides $(\bar{x}, \bar{y})$ on the graph. The two points can then be joined together using a ruler and the resulting line is shown in Fig. 12.6.

If the regression line is not calculated but drawn by inspection, then its slope can be measured by constructing a right-angled triangle on the diagram as explained in Chapter 1. The equation of the line can be found taking this measurement to be the value of $m$ in the formula in Table 12.6. The process of drawing the regression line by eye is quicker than performing an exact analysis of the data and can be of adequate accuracy if the points on the scatter diagram are sufficiently well in line.

The regression line derived in Table 12.6 is said to be of 'profit on population size' as profit is the dependent variable and population size is the independent one. We argued earlier that this designation of the variables is the correct one in this problem as we want to predict a profit value from a population value. However, the analysis could be carried out to give the equation of the line for population size on profit. This corresponds to fitting the 'best' line through the points when the scatter diagram is turned on its side with the axes interchanged. Both lines pass through the point $(x, y)$ and the better the straight line formed by the data points, the smaller the angle they will make with each other. In the extreme case when the points are in a perfect straight line, the two regression equations will be identical as it then makes no difference how the positioning of the line is determined and the same answer emerges from both calculations. The **correlation coefficient**, defined to be the covariance of $x$ and $y$ divided by the product of their standard deviations, indicates the size of the angle between the two regression lines. It therefore measures the degree to which the points lie in a straight line, that is, the extent of their linear correlation.

The value of the correlation coefficient is always between $-1$ and $+1$ with these extremes corresponding to perfect negative and perfect positive linear correlation respectively. Values around zero indicate a lack of linear correlation but the one we obtain for the Cosmetics Example is $(12.130\,89/\sqrt{(9.979\,82)(15.726\,96)})$ which is 0.9683 and significantly large and positive. It therefore indicates strong positive correlation between the variables and justifies the fitting of a straight line through the points on the scatter diagram.

## Computer Program

Many computerised stock control systems use exponential smoothing to forecast the demand for goods. The programming logic for such a task, as for time series decomposition, is relatively simple. In fact all the techniques we have studied in this chapter are well suited to computerisation and many of them appear in software packages. In particular, statistical analysis packages invariably contain procedures for regression and correlation analysis. Often these programs permit the forecasting of one variable from the values of many other variables, called multivariate regression, and have facilities for transforming the variables so that their relationship is linear.

The program which follows calculates the 'best' regression line passing through a given set of points. It performs the analysis contained in Table 12.6.

```
10 PRINT "REGRESSION CALCULATION"
20 PRINT "----------------------"
30 PRINT
40 PRINT "ENTER X,Y VALUES ENDING"
50 PRINT "WITH 0,0"
60 INPUT X,Y
70 IF X<>0 THEN 90
80 IF Y=0 THEN 160
90 X1=X1+X
100 Y1=Y1+Y
110 X2=X2+X*X
120 Y2=Y2+Y*Y
130 M=M+X*Y
140 N=N+1
150 GOTO 60
160 X3=X1/N
170 Y3=Y1/N
180 X4=(X2-N*X3*X3)/(N-1)
190 Y4=(Y2-N*Y3*Y3)/(N-1)
200 C=(M-N*X3*Y3)/(N-1)
210 S=C/X4
220 K=Y3-S*X3
230 PRINT "REGRESSION LINE OF Y ON"
240 PRINT "X IS : Y = ";S;"X + ";K
250 R=C/SQR(X4*Y4)
260 PRINT
270 PRINT "CORRELATION COEFFICIENT IS ";R
280 END
```

**Specimen Run**

```
REGRESSION CALCULATION
----------------------

ENTER X,Y VALUES ENDING
WITH 0,0
 ?4.1,3.6
 ?5.1,3.8
 ?6.3,4.2
 ?8.3,9.0
 ?9.3,7.5
 ?9.8,10.2
 ?9.8,9.0
 ?14.0,15.2
 ?0,0
REGRESSION LINE OF Y ON
X IS : Y =  1.21554 X + -2.32208

CORRELATION COEFFICIENT IS  0.968298
```

**Program Notes**

**1**   Lines 1Ø to 5Ø print a heading. Lines 6Ø to 15Ø read the coordinates, X and Y, of a point, test it to see whether it is the signal from the user that all the points have been entered, and update the values of the sum of X, X1, the sum of Y, Y1, the sum of $X^2$, X2, the sum of $Y^2$, Y2, the sum of XY, M, and the number of points, N.

**2**   Lines 16Ø to the end of the program implement the formulae in Table 12.6 for $\bar{x}$, X3, $\bar{y}$, Y3, the variance of $x$, X4, the variance of $y$, Y4, the covariance, C, the slope of the regression line, S, the intercept, K, and the correlation coefficient, R. The equation of the regression line and the correlation coefficient are then printed out.

## Summary

**1**   A graph of the data values of a time series should be drawn to determine whether there is an upward or downward trend. It may be necessary to take logarithms of the data or perform a similar conversion so that the trend which emerges is a straight line one.

**2**   If the data does not have a significant upward or downward trend then single exponential smoothing or moving averages can be used to estimate the constant value about which it fluctuates.

**3**   Holt's method is a way of smoothing data values which have a positive or negative trend. It is a form of double exponential smoothing applied to the data values themselves and to their rate of change.

**4**   A moving average of order $n$ is the average of any $n$ consecutive data values. If the time series oscillates because of seasonal effects, then moving averages whose order is equal to a complete cycle of seasons can be used to smooth the data and track the trend. It may be necessary to centre the moving averages.

**5**   Once the trend has been identified, either the absolute or percentage deviations of each data value from the trend can be calculated. Average deviations can be found for each season of the cycle and, possibly after an adjustment to allow for statistical error, can be quoted as seasonal indices.

**6**   Two variables are correlated if their values are linked in some way. Positively correlated variables increase or decrease together while negatively correlated ones behave in an opposite way to each other. Zero correlation is the term given to an absence of correlation when the value of one variable has no connection with the value of the other.

**7**   Regression is the process of inducing a mathematical relationship between two or more variables based on observations of them. The easiest regression analysis to perform is a linear one in which a straight line graph is fitted to the scatter diagram of points representing the data. The line can either be drawn by inspection through the average point on the diagram or its equation can be calculated. It is important to designate one of the variables as being independent and the other as being dependent as interchanging their roles results in a different line being found. The correlation coefficient is a measure of the sensitivity of the analysis to this interchange and therefore serves as a measure of the linearity of the points on the diagram.

## Further Reading

References (40), (41) and (42) are relevant to the work of this chapter with (42) covering an extension of Holt's method to cope with seasonality, called Winter's method. As we have seen, time series analysis draws heavily on statistical concepts and techniques and correlation and regression are discussed in most of the statistics books listed in the Bibliography. Reference (28) contains many worked examples while (27) deals with multivariate regression where there are more than two variables which are inter-related.

## Exercises

**1**   Use single exponential smoothing with a smoothing constant equal to 0.1 to forecast the next value in the series 3.9, 4.5, 4.2, 4.4, 3.8, 4.6, 3.6.

**2**   A company has the following data in its records:

| Month | Jan. | Feb. | Mar. | Apr. | May | Jun. | Jul. | Aug. | Sep. |
|---|---|---|---|---|---|---|---|---|---|
| Advertising expenditure (£,000) | 14 | 15 | 14 | 18 | 13 | 16 | 11 | 13 | 14 |
| Sales (£,000) | 43 | 45 | 46 | 44 | 57 | 41 | 49 | 34 | 42 |

It is felt that sales will lag advertising by 1 month. Plot a scatter diagram of the sales figures for February to September as the *y*-axis against the previous month's advertising expenditure as the *x*-axis. Plot the average point and draw a straight line through all the points by inspection. Predict the sales in a month following an advertising expenditure of £17 000.

**3**   Given the data

| Planet | Mercury | Venus | Earth | Mars | Jupiter | Saturn | Uranus | Neptune | Pluto |
|---|---|---|---|---|---|---|---|---|---|
| Distance from the Sun (Earth = 1) | 0.39 | 0.72 | 1.00 | 1.52 | 5.20 | 9.54 | 19.19 | 30.07 | 39.60 |
| Speed (miles/s) | 29.7 | 21.7 | 18.5 | 15.0 | 8.1 | 6.0 | 4.2 | 3.4 | 2.9 |

(i) Take logarithms of all the data values. (ii) Plot a scatter diagram of the logarithms of the speeds as the *y*-axis against the logarithms of the distances as the *x*-axis. (iii) Calculate and draw the regression line through the points. (iv) Forecast what the speed of a planet would be if it were 25 times further from the sun than the earth is.

**4**   The quarterly averages of the percentage unemployed in a certain industry were recorded as follows:

| Quarter Year | I | II | III | IV |
|---|---|---|---|---|
| 1934 | 22.9 | 15.6 | 16.1 | 19.3 |
| 1935 | 21.2 | 14.2 | 14.1 | 16.5 |
| 1936 | 20.8 | 11.2 | 11.3 | 14.9 |

(i) Calculate the four-quarter centred moving averages and plot them, together with the original data values, on a graph.

(ii) Calculate the percentage variations from trend wherever possible and hence the average seasonal adjustments for each quarter.

(iii) Smooth the moving averages using Holt's method with smoothing constants of 0.2 and 0.02 for the data values and the increases respectively.

(iv) Use your results to predict the percentage unemployed in the industry for the four quarters of 1937.

# 13 Computer Modelling

In Chapter 1 we defined a mathematical model to be a relationship between the variables describing a system's behaviour. Subsequent chapters of the book examined different types of models together with computer programs for some of them. In fact a computer can help in the analysis of all the models we have studied and is especially useful when there are many equations in the model or the algorithm or procedure for solving it is very long. A **computer model** is simply a formulation of a mathematical model which is analysed by computer, usually for reasons of convenience or speed. In this chapter we review the use of computers in general and consider examples of how mathematical models can be computerised.

## Commercial Computing

Applications of computers fall into two main categories, commercial and scientific. A large amount of computer time is spent on commercial data processing operations like the preparation of company payroll documents or customers' accounts. Other commercial tasks involve the retrieval of information from files of data such as bank balances or vehicle registration details. The facility to update and edit files of records almost instantaneously has meant that computers can be used for word processing and in the creation of a completely electronic office.

Commercial applications often entail accessing enormous amounts of stored data with either no calculations being performed at all or else ones of a low level of sophistication. For example, in preparing an electricity bill for a customer it is necessary only to subtract the previous meter reading from the present one, multiply the answer by the unit rate and possibly add or subtract some percentage or fixed charge to the result. However, the memory requirements for storing thousands of customers' names, addresses, previous meter readings and tariff codes are extensive.

As the sorting and searching through of data files is so important in commercial work, computer languages like COBOL, which stands for Common Business Orientated Language, have been developed. They contain instructions which enable the computer to be programmed to organise and handle data files efficiently. The programming itself is usually done by programmers who specialise in commercial computing and they liaise with a systems analyst who designs the system and specifies the programs which are required.

## Scientific Computing

The other main category of computer usage covers all the scientific applications like computer-aided design, manufacturing using robots, and mathematical modelling. Unlike commercial jobs, these tend to be highly specialised and vary in nature from company to company with standard, 'off the shelf' programs, or **software**, having limited value. Whereas the preparation of a payroll does not differ greatly from one firm to another, the computer-aided design of, say, buildings, is significantly different from the design of electronic circuits. Furthermore, scientific computer installations often have pieces of equipment, called **hardware**, like a robot or a graph-plotter, which require programming in a way which is unique to the device concerned. For these reasons there are several computer languages which lend themselves more to scientific than commercial programming, for example, BASIC, standing for Beginners' All-purpose Symbolic Instruction Code, and FORTRAN, standing for Formula Translation.

The use of computers in mathematical modelling ranges from leisure applications like video games through operational research techniques to government models of the economy containing hundreds of equations. The subject disciplines involved in this wide spectrum of models include meteorology in modelling the weather, medicine and biochemistry in modelling the effect of drugs on the body, civil engineering in modelling the behaviour of bridges and other structures, and so on. The models themselves can be statistical in origin like the regression ones discussed in Chapter 12 or obtained from other branches of mathematics, often involving the use of calculus. So widespread has the computer analysis of mathematical models become that the numerical methods necessary for the process are now an important area of study in their own right.

The sheer speed of computer processing allows methods containing many thousands of individual steps to be adopted. Sometimes the method is of a trial and error nature, like deciding on which move to make in a game of chess by laboriously investigating the long-term consequences of each possible move. Trial and error was considered as a method of solution for the Travelling Salesman Problem of Chapter 4 and the Assignment Problem of Chapter 5. Many statistical techniques which are extremely tedious to perform by hand have become feasible because of the computer's speed and ability to store vast quantities of data. **Multivariate regression** is an example of this and is an extension of the regression analysis studied in Chapter 12. It applies when there are more than two variables in the model and results in equations based on observed data which enable the expected values of one set of variables to be calculated from the known values of another set.

In contrast to commercial applications, scientific ones tend to have many calculations performed on relatively small amounts of data. This means that computer installations designed for commercial tasks have lots of data handling peripheral devices like magnetic tape and disc drives while those designed for scientific jobs may have faster and more powerful central processors. The largest computer installations are government-owned and on the commercial side handle public records with others being dedicated to controlling power stations, high-energy particle accelerators and military projects. The net result of the wide range of commercial and scientific applications described above has been the promotion of the computer from the role of a clerk who merely records the details of yesterday's business into that of a working partner who is an integral part of today's operations.

## Computers and Operational Research

There are several types of operational research techniques for which computers are particularly suited. Algorithms like the Simplex method of Chapter 2 and the one in the

Travelling Salesman Problem of Chapter 4 are fairly straightforward to computerise. The programs at the end of Chapters 4 and 5 implement algorithms and there are commercially available **packages**, which are programs or groups of programs, of this nature. There are also statistical packages which are of use in operational research. All the major computer manufacturers market such packages for their machines.

Simulation is another area of operational research in which computers are widely used and the programs in Chapters 6 and 9 illustrate this. The value of computers here has been enhanced by the advent of interactive computing where the user sits at a terminal and communicates directly with the machine. This means that various details of the model can be altered between successive executions of the simulation until the behaviour of the simulated system is satisfactory. The topic was discussed in Chapter 6 and, in the computing context, it can be pointed out that many scientific uses of computers are really deterministic simulations. For example, in meteorology the flow of air and the atmospheric temperature and pressure are simulated in a deterministic way from measurements taken at weather-monitoring stations.

Computers are used so frequently to simulate the action of systems that special languages, like SIMULA, have been developed to facilitate the programming. These languages are usually extensions of an existing scientific one and contain single instructions for implementing commonly used simulation procedures, like choosing an outcome from a given probability distribution.

In the remainder of this chapter we examine some of the ideas involved in computerising a mathematical model. This is usually achieved by a simulation of some sort although the term is misleading when compared with simulations in engineering, for instance that of the fluid flow around the hull of a ship, having no stochastic variables and giving an extremely accurate description of the real system. The first two worked examples are economic models while the last one, presented as a computer program, shows how the population sizes of competing animal species can be modelled.

### The Cauliflower Example

In a certain country, the number of cauliflowers grown by farmers in a particular year is proportional to the selling price of a cauliflower in the previous year. In other words, the more profit a farmer believes he can make, the more cauliflowers he will plan to grow for the following year. However, the selling price itself depends on the number of cauliflowers available to the customers and is low when that number is high and high when the number is low. Hence there are conflicting trends in this model of a commodity market. The higher the price the more items appear on the market and so the price goes down. The lower the price the less items appear on the market and so the price goes up and the cycle starts all over again. Clearly we expect these market forces to create a stable price sooner or later. To see this happen, suppose that in our fictitious country the following relationships are found from experience:

The number of cauliflowers available to customers in a given year, measured in thousands, is equal to 5 times the selling price of a cauliflower, measured in pence, in the previous year                                                                                                    (13.1)

The price of a cauliflower, measured in pence, in a given year is 45 minus 0.1 times the number of cauliflowers available to customers in that year, measured in thousands.                                                                                                    (13.2)

We investigate the behaviour of the number of cauliflowers on the market and their price over several years to determine whether they tend to have limiting or equilibrium values. It is assumed that there are initially 10 000 on the market.

*Solution*   Computer models often have many variables and equations describing their evolution. It is therefore advisable to list their definitions and the equations rather formally so that it is easy to refer to them if necessary. Here is a suitable formulation of statements (13.1) and (13.2) with the initial value of the number given above.

| | The Cauliflower Model | |
|---|---|---|
| *Variables* | $t$ = year number | |
| | $N_t$ = number of cauliflowers available to customers in year $t$, measured in thousands | |
| | $P_t$ = price of a cauliflower in year $t$, measured in pence | |
| *Equations* | $N_{t+1} = 5P_t$ | (follows from (13.1) ) |
| | $P_t = 45 - 0.1 N_t$ | (follows from (13.2) ) |
| *Initial Conditions* | $t = 1; N_1 = 10$ | |

The above formulation is typical of a computer model. The equations are called **recurrence relations** because they relate current values of a quantity to current or previous values of itself or other quantities. The 'playing through' of these equations is really a deterministic simulation and the results can be shown in Table 13.1.

**Table 13.1**

| $t$, the year number | $N_t$, the number of cauliflowers | $P_t$, the price of a cauliflower to the nearest whole number of pence |
|---|---|---|
| 1 | 10 | 44 |
| 2 | 220 | 23 |
| 3 | 115 | 34 |
| 4 | 170 | 28 |
| 5 | 140 | 31 |
| 6 | 155 | 30 |
| 7 | 150  ←Equilibrium values→ | 30 |
| 8 | 150 | 30 |

Stop here as the current values are the same as the previous ones, and will repeat themselves indefinitely.

**Hence the equilibrium values are 150 000 cauliflowers selling at 30p each.**

The approach to equilibrium can be illustrated graphically. Figure 13.1 shows graphs of the equations which govern the model. Both of them are straight lines and can be plotted relatively easily. The arrows indicate how the initial value of $N$, 10, determines the price, 44. This in turn determines the number of cauliflowers available in year 2, 220, which gives the price in that year to be 23. This price means that the quantity in year 3 is 115 and at this point on the graph, the arrows have traced out the outer arm of the spiral shown. The sequence of numbers of cauliflowers and prices for subsequent years is represented by the route taken by the remaining arrows. The path never reaches the point where the graphs cross, which is the equilibrium point, but becomes arbitrarily close to

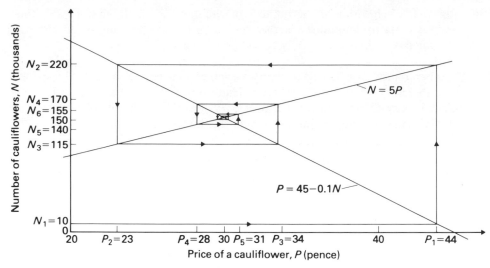

**Fig. 13.1**   Graph for the Cauliflower Example

it. It is also of interest to note that the equilibrium state and the tendency to it are unaffected by the initial value of $N$. The same qualitative behaviour would result if any value for $N_1$ other than 10 were used.

The appearance of the diagram has prompted this type of model to be called a **cobweb** model. Sometimes the path formed by the arrows is a closed rectangle instead of a spiral. In that case the values of the variables oscillate between two numbers and equilibrium is not reached. It is also possible for the spiral to radiate outwards, away from equilibrium, rather than inwards. This represents an unstable system in which the variables concerned will grow without bound. The equations $P_t = 45 - 0.2N_t$ or $P_t = 45 - 0.3N_t$ instead of the one used in our example will give rise to these types of behaviour.

Unfortunately equilibrium is never reached in a real-world economic system. Whenever a trend towards it is established, the factors which underpin the validity of the model may change and the equations no longer apply. It may be that features of the system which were not considered important when the model was formulated have now become important, or effects which were thought to be constant in time turn out in practice to be variables.

Models like the last example which attempt to describe the whole of a country or industry are called **macro-economic**. Those which describe the operation of just one company or other relatively small organisation are called **micro-economic**. Here is an example of such a model.

### The Picture-Frame Factory Example

The model below describes the variables which are considered to be important in the management of a factory making picture frames.

We derive a flow chart to show how the operation of the factory can be simulated and use expectations to gain an overview of it.

## The Picture-Frame Factory Model

*Variables*

| | | | | |
|---|---|---|---|---|
| Time | : | Week number | $t$ | |
| Sales | : | Demand in week $t$ | $SD_t$ | (frames) |
| | | Sales in week $t$ | $SS_t$ | (frames) |
| | | Cash from sales in week $t$ | $SC_t$ | (pounds) |
| Labour | : | Labour used in week $t$ | $LU_t$ | (frame-makers) |
| | | Cost of labour in week $t$ | $LC_t$ | (pounds) |
| Raw materials | : | Timber used in week $t$ | $RU_t$ | (metrés) |
| | | Timber delivered in week $t$ | $RD_t$ | (metres) |
| | | Stock of timber at start of week $t$ | $RB_t$ | (metres) |
| | | Cost of timber in week $t$ | $RC_t$ | (pounds) |
| Frames | : | Production during week $t$ | $FP_t$ | (frames) |
| | | Stock of frames at start of week $t$ | $FB_t$ | (frames) |
| Cash | : | Fixed overheads payable in week $t$ | $CF_t$ | (pounds) |
| | | Cash balance at start of week $t$ | $CB_t$ | (pounds) |

*Equations*

| | | |
|---|---|---|
| Time | : | $t$ increases by 1 each week |
| Sales | : | $SD_t$ has the Poisson distribution with mean 343.6 |
| | | $SS_t$ is the minimum of $SD_t$ and $(FB_t + FP_t)$ |
| | | $SC_t = 8.2\ SS_t$ |
| Labour | : | $LU_t$ has the binomial distribution corresponding to 10 trials each with probability of success 0.86. |
| | | $LC_t = 152.6\ LU_t$ |
| Raw materials | : | $RU_t = 3.5\ FP_t$ |
| | | $RD_t$ has the normal distribution with mean 1187 and standard deviation 85 |
| | | $RC_{t+1} = 0.5\ RD_t$ |
| Frames | : | $FP_t$ is the minimum of $40\ LU_t$ and $(RB_t + RD_t)/3.5$ |
| Cash | : | $CF_t = 800$ |
| Flows | : | $RB_{t+1} = RB_t + RD_t - RU_t$    (timber) |
| | | $FB_{t+1} = FB_t + FP_t - SS_t$    (frames) |
| | | $CB_{t+1} = CB_t + SC_t - CF_t - LC_t - RC_t$    (cash) |

*Initial Conditions*

| | | | |
|---|---|---|---|
| | : | $t = 1$ | |
| | | $RB_1 = 433$ | $CB_1 = 229.66$ |
| | | $FB_1 = 107$ | $RC_1 = 0$ |

*Solution* The above formulation is an important intermediate stage in the analysis of a large system. The list of relevant variables, their relationships with each other and any assumptions about their origin and initial values constitute a precise and mathematical definition of the model.

In the first section, all the variables of interest have been identified, grouped into convenient categories and labelled with letters which reflect the quantities they represent. For example, the fixed overhead cost of the factory is called $CF_t$, the 'C' standing for a cash variable, the 'F' standing for fixed cost and the '$t$' standing for week $t$.

It is crucial to the validity of the model that all the relevant variables are included in this section. For instance, if the company in our problem imported raw materials then the appropriate exchange rate for foreign currency might be a critical factor in the calculation of its cash flow and would therefore be included as a variable of interest.

The relationships which exist or are assumed to exist between the variables are set out in the second section of the model. **Stochastic** variables are described by a probability distribution while **deterministic** ones have formulae from which their values can be calculated. It is important that every variable has a corresponding description or equation otherwise its value cannot be determined when the model is being run. Some models contain only deterministic variables, like the one in the Cauliflower Example, and others have only stochastic variables, like those in the probability distribution chapters of this book. In general, computer models have a mixture of both and it is necessary to simulate the stochastic ones using random numbers and calculate the deterministic ones from their formulae. The latter equations may well be based on a regression analysis as described in Chapter 12.

The relationships listed in the present example are fairly typical. The demand for picture frames is assumed to be described by the Poisson probability distribution as discussed in Chapter 8. The actual sales level which results from this demand is calculated as being equal either to this figure or to the number of frames available, $FB_t + FP_t$, whichever is the smaller. The cash value of the sales, $SC_t$, is equal to the selling price of a frame, £8.20, multiplied by the number sold. Sometimes the values of quantities which are not expected to change very much, like the price here, are simply used in the appropriate formulae without appearing in the list of variables. They may appear instead as a list of **parameters** for the model although there are no hard and fast rules and we have one constant, $CF_t$, disguised as a variable. The important consideration is that the formulation of the model enables it to be readily understood and easy to implement, either by hand or by computer.

The assumption about the available labour in this model is an application of the binomial probability distribution. The factory has 10 frame-makers on its payroll but in any one week each one has probability 0.86 of reporting for work. This means that the number of frame-makers available in a given week is the number of 'successes' in a compound trial consisting of 10 individual trials each with probability of success 0.86. This is the type of situation described by the binomial distribution studied in Chapter 7 and is assumed to apply here.

The model has the cost of labour linked to the number of men reporting for work by a factor of 152.6. This is the cost of employing a frame-maker for a week and, if it is considered to be liable to change, could be listed as a variable. The raw materials equation states that the amount of timber used is 3.5 times the number of frames produced. The equation therefore implies that each frame needs 3.5 metres of timber and this is probably how it was derived originally.

The quantity of timber delivered in a given week is assumed to be normally distributed. This phenomenon may have been observed over a period of several weeks by the factory manager or may indicate a lack of data on deliveries which necessitates an intelligent guess about their distribution. The last raw materials equation defines the cost of timber to be 50p per metre to be incurred a week after it has been delivered. Variables which have a direct effect on the system at time instants after the one to which they relate are said to be **lagged**.

The remaining equations in the model are fairly straightforward. The number of frames produced is equal to the minimum of the available labour times the number of frames each man can produce in a week and the number of frames which can be made with the available stock of timber. Neither of these resource ceilings can be exceeded in any one week, a consideration similar to those contained in Chapter 2 on Linear Programming. The flows which end the section on equations are merely updates of the various balances of timber, frames and cash brought forward from the previous week.

The final section of the model, called Initial Conditions, contains the values in week 1 of all the variables which are calculated a week in advance of the period to which they relate. These have the suffix $(t+1)$ when they appear in their defining equations and cannot therefore be evaluated for week 1.

In order to run the model it is necessary to determine a suitable sequence in which the equations can be processed. Some of them have quantities on their right hand sides which are themselves the results of other equations and so cannot be utilised until those other equations have been processed. Examining the equations in our example we find that, apart from $t$, the quantities $SD_t$, $LU_t$, $RD_t$, and $CF_t$ can be evaluated without referring to the values of any other variables. Three of them require simulation techniques as described in Chapters 6, 9 and 10.

Quantities which do not depend on events within a system but are determined by the conditions prevailing outside it are called **exogenous** variables and are **inputs** to any model of the system. Those which are calculated in the course of running the model are called **endogenous** variables or **outputs**. The classification of a variable as an input or an output depends on the boundaries of the particular model being used. Inputs are often specified stochastically to avoid having to consider their causality in detail. This causality is therefore outside the scope of the model and the input variables are the result of effects which are outside its boundaries. We see this property of input variables in the analysis of a queue where the arrival and service patterns are modelled stochastically as they originate outside the system, which in that case is the queue itself. Similarly in stock control we do not usually attempt to model the cause of the demand for stock but simply follow the movement of the stock items themselves in response to that demand.

Having determined which variables are the inputs to the model, we can organise the logic of the simulation so that their values are generated first when the equations are processed. We see from the list of equations that once the inputs are known then together with the values of any lagged variables from the previous week, or the initial conditions in week 1, the quantities $LC_t$, $RC_{t+1}$ and $FP_t$ can be evaluated. When these are found, the remaining equations for $SS_t$, $SC_t$, $RU_t$, $RB_{t+1}$, $FB_{t+1}$ and $CB_{t+1}$ can all be processed. We have therefore determined an ordering of the original set of equations in which each one has variables on its right hand side which are calculated from equations occurring earlier on in the sequence.

It should always be possible to find such an arrangement of the equations of a model. The method is to rescan the list repeatedly and remove those which depend on variables whose equations have already been removed. The very first scan identifies those variables which do not depend on any others and are the inputs to the model. Subsequent scans show how the outputs depend on each other and the inputs. If a suitable ordering of the equations does not emerge from the use of this algorithm then there is something wrong with the statement of the model and possibly there are not enough equations. As mentioned above, every variable must have an equation or its value cannot be determined when the model is run.

The rearranged list of equations for the inputs and outputs of the model in the present example is shown in the **flow chart** (Fig. 13.2). The diagram illustrates how the model can be run, beginning with the initialisation of the variables for week 1 and continuing with the processing of the equations for as many weeks as required. The various stopping rules for a simulation were discussed in Chapter 6 for the Bakery Example and any suitable criterion can be used in the diamond-shaped box of the flow chart. If the decision is made to extend the simulation for another week, then the week number, $t$, is

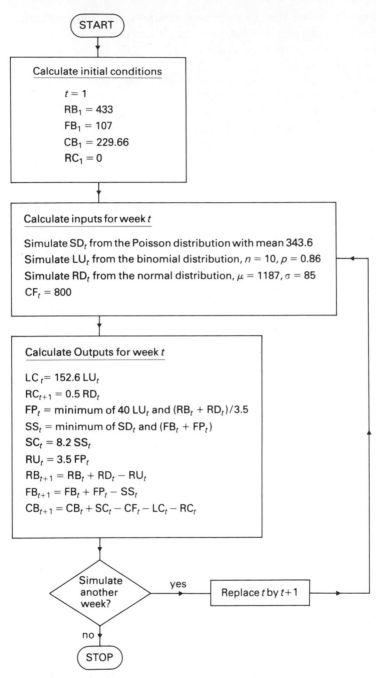

**Fig. 13.2**

incremented and the calculations repeated. A tabulation of the various quantities should be kept so that the progress of the model can be analysed.

Before performing a simulation it is advisable to calculate expectations of the variables involved wherever possible. This was done for the simulations in Chapter 10 on Queues and it gives us an overview of the model which tells us firstly whether it is grossly inappropriate as a description of the real system and secondly how it is going to behave when the simulation is in progress. Taking expectations of the equations in the flow chart we obtain Table 13.2.

**Table 13.2**

| Variable | Expectation | Notes |
|---|---|---|
| $SD_t$ | 343.6 | |
| $LU_t$ | $0.86 \times 10 = 8.6$ | Expectations of the |
| $RD_t$ | 1187 | appropriate distributions |
| $CF_t$ | 800 | |
| $LC_t$ | $152.6 \times 8.6 = 1312.36$ | |
| $RC_{t+1}$ | $0.5 \times 1187 = 593.5$ | |
| $FP_t$ | $\frac{1}{2}(40 \times 8.6 + (0 + 1187)/3.5) = 341.57$ | The expectation of a balance |
| $SS_t$ | $\frac{1}{2}(343.6 + (0 + 341.57)) = 342.59$ | is taken to be 0 and that |
| $SC_t$ | $8.2 \times 342.59 = 2809.24$ | of a minimum to be the |
| $RU_t$ | $3.5 \times 341.57 = 1195.50$ | average of the individual |
| $RB_{t+1}$ | $0 + 1187 - 1195.5 = -8.50$ | expectations |
| $FB_{t+1}$ | $0 + 341.57 - 342.59 = -1.02$ | |
| $CB_{t+1}$ | $0 + 2809.24 - 800 - 1312.36 - 593.5 = 103.38$ | |

The last three expectations are of the net flows of timber, frames and cash occurring in the course of a week. The most important one, that of cash, is positive but the implications of the other two are that the factory eventually loses its stock of timber and frames. Although the figures are small and may be insignificant compared with the variability of the inputs, it may be that production and sales are restricted because of the lack of timber and frames. This would be something to observe in the results of the simulation but it is also possible that the assumptions made in calculating the flows might be false. These were that any balances brought forward are zero and the expectation of a minimum of two variables is the average expectation of the quantities concerned.

Of course one of the advantages of simulating a system is that the various parameters of the model can be altered. It may be that by changing the quantity of timber delivered each week both of the negative flows found above can be rectified. We can estimate the effect of this action by recalculating the expectations for such a change or we can write a computer program to implement the simulation which has the average amount of timber delivered as a user-supplied quantity. The user would then be able to experiment with its value in a way we called the 'what if?' facility in Chapter 6.

## Computer Program

The programs given at the end of every chapter of this book are all computer models of one form or another. In this chapter we have seen how the formulation of a model as a set of recurrence relations helps in its computerisation. These equations describe the evolution of the system from one time period or group of time periods to the next.

A commercially important application of computer modelling is in the design of video games. The position, colour scheme and velocity of any images on the display, like the rackets in a game of tennis, are stored as numerical variables. Subsequent values are calculated from recurrence relations and used to amend the display so that the illusion of movement is created for the viewer.

As the graphics facilities on different computers vary considerably, and a program given here might not run on all machines, we illustrate the ideas by using letters instead of drawings. The following program can therefore be run on any computer which processes BASIC and is not dependent on a graphics facility.

### The Martians and Venutians Example

The inhabitants of the planets Mars and Venus are at war with each other. Each day there is a battle in which one of the two sides captures a unit of territory from the other, the probabilities of victory being proportional to the relative sizes of their existing territories. Hence the larger force is more likely to win the daily battle. The situation is similar to ecological models of competing animal or plant species. The competition there can be for territory or food or the species may have a 'predator–prey' relationship with each other.

```
10 PRINT "MARTIANS AND VENUTIANS WAR MODEL"
20 PRINT "------------------------------------"
30 PRINT
40 PRINT "DAY","TERRITORIES"
50 PRINT
60 D=1
70 M=10
80 V=10
90 RANDOMIZE
100 PRINT D,
110 FOR L=1 TO M
120 PRINT "M";
130 NEXT L
140 PRINT "   ";
150 FOR L=1 TO V
160 PRINT "V";
170 NEXT L
180 PRINT
190 C=1
200 IF RND<M/20 THEN 220
210 C=-1
220 M=M+C
230 V=V-C
240 D=D+1
250 IF M<1 THEN 280
260 IF V<1 THEN 300
270 GOTO 100
280 PRINT "VENUTIANS WIN ON DAY ";D
290 STOP
300 PRINT "MARTIANS WIN ON DAY ";D
310 END
```

**Specimen Run**

```
MARTIANS AND VENUTIANS WAR MODEL
--------------------------------

DAY             TERRITORIES

  1             MMMMMMMMMM  VVVVVVVVVV
  2             MMMMMMMMMMM  VVVVVVVVV
  3             MMMMMMMMMM  VVVVVVVVVV
  4             MMMMMMMMMMM  VVVVVVVVV
  5             MMMMMMMMMM  VVVVVVVVVV
  6             MMMMMMMMMMM  VVVVVVVVV
  7             MMMMMMMMMM  VVVVVVVVVV
  8             MMMMMMMMM  VVVVVVVVVVV
  9             MMMMMMMMMM  VVVVVVVVVV
 1Ø             MMMMMMMMMMM  VVVVVVVVV
 11             MMMMMMMMMMMM  VVVVVVVV
 12             MMMMMMMMMMM  VVVVVVVVV
 13             MMMMMMMMMM  VVVVVVVVVV
 14             MMMMMMMMM  VVVVVVVVVVV
 15             MMMMMMMM  VVVVVVVVVVVV
 16             MMMMMMM  VVVVVVVVVVVVV
 17             MMMMMM  VVVVVVVVVVVVVV
 18             MMMMM  VVVVVVVVVVVVVVV
 19             MMMM  VVVVVVVVVVVVVVVV
 2Ø             MMM  VVVVVVVVVVVVVVVVV
 21             MM  VVVVVVVVVVVVVVVVVV
 22             M  VVVVVVVVVVVVVVVVVVV
VENUTIANS WIN ON DAY  23
```

**Program Notes**

**1**   Lines 1Ø to 8Ø print the headings and initialise the day number and the sizes of the two planets' empires, M and V.

**2**   Line 9Ø scrambles the random number generator so that a different sequence of random numbers is produced every time the program is run. This line may not be necessary for certain machines.

**3**   Lines 1ØØ to 18Ø print the day number followed by a number of Ms and Vs. The number of letters printed indicates the sizes of the empires and in a program with graphics, output could involve the drawing of little spacemen or spaceships to convey this information.

**4**   Lines 19Ø to 23Ø simulate a daily battle. The Martian gain, C, is set equal to 1. A random number between Ø and 1, RND, is then tested. If it is in the range Ø to (M/2Ø) then it is counted as a victory for Mars and control is passed to line 22Ø. Otherwise, it is a victory for Venus and the Martian gain, C, is reversed in sign. In either case, control reaches lines 22Ø and 23Ø where the sizes of the empires are updated by the Martian gain, whether this is positive or negative. These lines are in fact recurrence relations expressing the amounts of territory held on day D + 1 in terms of that on day D taking into account the result of the battle.

**5**   Line 24Ø increments the day number by 1 while lines 25Ø and 26Ø test whether either side has lost the war. If it has then the appropriate victory message proclaiming the other side to be the winner is printed. Otherwise control reaches line 27Ø where it is sent back to line 1ØØ so that another day can be simulated.

## Summary

**1**   Commercial applications of computers are typified by the processing of large amounts of data with relatively few and unsophisticated calculations. Many computerised tasks are the same in all industries and pre-designed packages of programs, or software, can be obtained for systems like payroll and stock control. The most common language used for commercial computing is COBOL. Office automation also comes under this heading.

**2**   Scientific applications cover a wide range including computer-aided design and mathematical modelling. Hardware like graph-plotters or robots may require special programming. In contrast to commercial jobs, scientific ones tend to have little data but complicated and lengthy numerical procedures to be followed. For this reason programs are often written specifically for particular tasks and are not as universally applicable as commercial packages. FORTRAN and BASIC are two of the many languages used in scientific programming. Operational research applications form a subset of both scientific ones and commercial ones, the scientific ones being the implementation of algorithms, simulation and modelling.

**3**   The evolution of a system can often be modelled using recurrence relations. These express quantities measured at time $t$ in terms of other such quantities and values measured at previous time periods. In order to run a model, various initial conditions are required depending on the nature of the equations. It may also be necessary to put the equations into a suitable order before they can be processed. Some variables are classified as inputs and the remainder are outputs. It is helpful to gain an overview of the model by calculating expectations of all the variables although this is not always possible.

**4**   The running of the model may show that the variables within it tend to limiting or equilibrium values. The 'what if?' facility whereby the user is able to run and re-run simulations with different parameters or equations is a powerful aid in designing a system.

## Further Reading

Just as we saw the overlap between operational research and statistics in earlier chapters on probability and regression, we are now examining the common ground the subject has with computing. Most modern operational research textbooks acknowledge this link and many, like (4), (49) and (52), place emphasis on it. This chapter has touched on economic modelling and references (44), (47) and (51) provide further reading on it. The section on Computer Programming in the Bibliography lists some of the many books available on BASIC programming. The other computing topics mentioned in the chapter, like computer-aided design, are developing so quickly that no book can be recommended. Interested readers might consult the numerous magazines on microcomputers for up-to-date information. The Bibliography does include four books, references (43), (45), (48) and (50), which cover the fundamentals of systems analysis and data processing.

**Exercises**

**1**   The following model is thought to describe the economy of Ruritania:

| *Variables:* | $t$ | $=$ year number |
| | $C_t$ | $=$ consumption of goods and services in year $t$ (millions of ducats) |
| | $N_t$ | $=$ national income in year $t$ (millions of ducats) |
| | $G_t$ | $=$ government spending in year $t$ (millions of ducats) |
| | $T_t$ | $=$ taxation in year $t$ (millions of ducats) |
| | $E_t$ | $=$ exports in year $t$ (millions of ducats) |
| | $M_t$ | $=$ imports in year $t$ (millions of ducats) |
| *Equations:* | $E_t$ | $=26$ |
| | $G_{t+1}$ | $=0.8T_t$ (government spending lags its income and there is a 20% loss due to administration costs) |
| | $T_t$ | $=0.3\ N_t$ (tax rate is 30%) |
| | $M_{t+1}$ | $=0.2\ N_t$ (the level of imports is proportional to the national income but not paid until the following year) |
| | $C_t$ | $=N_t - T_t$ (cash flow for people) |
| | $N_{t+1}$ | $=C_t + E_t + G_t - M_t$ (cash flow for companies lagged by one year) |

*Initial Conditions:* $t=1$; $C_1=16$; $M_1=8$; $N_1=96$

(i)  Put the equations into a suitable order for processing,

(ii)  Run the model for the first 12 years keeping your working to 1 decimal place accuracy. Notice that the values of the variables for year 12 are the same as those for year 11. Comment.

**2**   The objective of the following management game is to teach the player some of the considerations involved in the cost of handling stock. It is played by a controller, which can be a computer, and one player, although several players could compete in trying to achieve the lowest score.

*Step 1*: The controller prepares a chart which will always be visible to the player and has columns headed 'day', 'stock level at start of day', 'cost to date', 'delivery' and 'demand'. The 'day' column contains the numbers 1, 2, 3 up to some predetermined value. The 'stock level at start of day' for day 1 is 100.

*Step 2:* The controller chooses a number at random between 50 and 100 but does not tell the player what it is. This will be the average daily demand for stock throughout the present game.

*Step 3:* The controller calculates the stock handling cost to be the stock level multiplied by a holding cost of 10p per item or a shortage cost of £5 if the stock level is zero. The result is added to the previous 'cost to date' and entered on the chart as the current 'cost to date'. The controller asks the player how many items are to be delivered into stock and enters that amount in the column headed 'delivery' on the chart. The controller then simulates the day's demand by choosing a number at random between 80% and 120% of the average demand chosen in step 2. He enters this number on the chart in the appropriate column and calculates the resulting stock level carried forward to the next day. Clearly if the demand is greater than the stock level at the start of the day plus the deliveries then there are zero items carried forward.

*Step 4:* Repeat step 3 a predetermined number of times. The player's score is the 'cost to date' at the end of this time.

# Bibliography

## General operational research

1. Ackoff, R.L. and Sasieni, M.W., *Fundamentals of Operations Research,* Wiley, 1968.
2. Battersby, A., *Mathematics in Management*, Penguin Books, 1975.
3. Bronson, R., *Operations Research*, Schaum Outline Series, McGraw-Hill, 1982.
4. Daellenbach, H.G., George, J.A. and McNickle, D., *Introduction to Operations Research Techniques*, Allyn and Bacon, 1983.
5. Duckworth, W.E., Gear, A.E. and Lockett, A.G., *A Guide to Operational Research*, Chapman and Hall, 3rd edition 1977.
6. Harper, W.M., *Operational Research*, M & E Handbooks, 1979
7. Makower, M.S. and Williamson, E., *Operational Research*, Teach Yourself Books, English Universities Press, 3rd edition 1975.
8. Martin, M. and Denison, R., *Case Exercises in Operational Research*, Wiley, 1971.
9. Moore, P.G., *Basic Operational Research*, Pitman, 2nd edition 1976.
10. Palmer, C. and Innes, A., *Operational Research by Example*, Macmillan, 1980.
11. Sasieni, M.W., Yaspan, A. and Friedman, L., *Operations Research—Methods and Problems*, Wiley 1959.
12. Taha, H.A., *Operations Research—An Introduction*, Macmillan, 3rd edition 1982.
13. Wilkes, F.M., *Elements of Operational Research*, McGraw-Hill, 1980.
14. Woolsey, R.E.D. and Swanson, H.S., *Operations Research for Immediate Application—A Quick and Dirty Manual*, Harper and Row, 1975.

## Introduction

15. Guter, A. and Guter, M., *Financial Accounting*, Teach Yourself Books, English Universities Press, 2nd edition 1981.
16. Murphy, B., *Management Accounting*, Teach Yourself Books, English Universities Press, 1978.

## Linear programming

17. Lev, B. and Weiss, H., *Introduction to Mathematical Programming*, Edward Arnold, 1982.
18. Williams, H.P., *Model Building in Mathematical Programming*, Wiley, 1978.

## Coordinating and sequencing

19. Lang, D., *Critical Path Analysis*, Teach Yourself Books, English Universities Press, 2nd edition 1977.

**20**   Lockyer, K.G., *Critical Path Analysis and other Project Network Techniques*, Pitman, 1984.

## Statistics

**21**   Chatfield, C., *Statistics for Technology*, Chapman and Hall, 1976.
**22**   Clarke, G.M. and Cooke, D., *A Basic Course in Statistics*, Edward Arnold, 2nd edition 1983.
**23**   Cooke, D., Craven, A.H. and Clarke, G.M., *Basic Statistical Computing*, Edward Arnold, 1982.
**24**   Moroney, M.J., *Facts From Figures*, Pelican Original, Penguin Books, 2nd edition 1953.
**25**   Mulholland, H. and Jones, C.R., *Fundamentals of Statistics*, Butterworths, reprinted 1982.
**26**   Siegal, S., *Nonparametric Statistics for the Behavioural Sciences*, McGraw-Hill, 1956.
**27**   Snedecor, G.W. and Cochran, W.G., *Statistical Methods*, The Iowa State University Press, 6th edition 1967.
**28**   Spiegel, M.R., *Statistics*, Schaum Outline Series, McGraw-Hill, 1972.
**29**   Walpole, R.E., *Introduction to Statistics*, Collier Macmillan, 3rd edition 1982.
**30**   White, J., Yeats, A. and Skipworth, G., *Tables For Statisticians*, Stanley Thornes, 3rd edition 1979.
**31**   Williams, J., *The Compleat Strategyst*, McGraw-Hill, 1954.

## Stock control

**32**   Lewis, C.D., *Scientific Inventory Control*, Butterworths, 2nd edition 1981.
**33**   Lockyer, K., *Stock Control: A Practical Approach*, Cassell Management Studies, 1972.

## Queues

**34**   Cooper, R.B., *Introduction to Queuing Theory*, Edward Arnold, 1981.
**35**   Cox, D. and Smith, W., *Queues*, Chapman and Hall, 1961.
**36**   Grassman, W., *Stochastic Systems for Management*, Edward Arnold, 1981.
**37**   Newell, G.F., *Applications of Queuing Theory*, Chapman and Hall, 1982.

## Replacement, maintenance and reliability

**38**   Barlow, R.E. and Porschan, F., *Mathematical Theory of Reliability*, Wiley, 1965.
**39**   Jardine, A., *Maintenance, Replacement and Reliability*, Pitman, 1973.

## Forecasting

**40**   Box, G. and Jenkins, G., *Time Series Analysis, Forecasting and Control*, Holden-Day, 1976.
**41**   Firth, M., *Forecasting Methods in Business and Management*, Edward Arnold, 1977.

42   Wheelwright, S. and Makridakis, S., *Forecasting Methods for Management*, Wiley, 1980.

## Computer modelling

43   Arnold, R.R., Hill, H.C. and Nichols, A.V., *Modern Data Processing*, Wiley, 3rd edition 1978.
44   Beach, E.F., *Economic Models*, Wiley, 1957.
45   Bingham, J. and Davies, G., *A Handbook of Systems Analysis*, Macmillan, 2nd edition 1978.
46   Coats, R.B. and Parkin, A., *Computer Models in the Social Sciences*, Edward Arnold, 1977.
47   Forrester, J., *Industrial Dynamics*, Wiley, 1961.
48   Fry, T.F., *Computer Appreciation*, Butterworths, 3rd edition 1981.
49   Gordon, G., *System Simulation*, Prentice-Hall, 1969.
50   Jeffers, J., *An Introduction to Systems Analysis with Ecological Applications*, Edward Arnold, 1978.
51   Salvatore, D., *Microeconomic Theory*, Schaum Outline Series, McGraw-Hill, 1974.
52   Thesen, A., *Computer Methods in Operational Research*, Academic Press, 1978.

## Computer programming

53   Alcock, D., *Illustrating Basic*, Cambridge University Press, 1977.
54   Forsyth, R., *The Basic Idea*, Chapman and Hall, 1978.
55   Monro, D., *Basic BASIC*, Edward Arnold, 2nd edition 1985.
56   Monro, D., *Interactive Computing with BASIC*, Edward Arnold, 1974.

# Answers to Exercises

## Chapter 1
**1** —.**2** After 3 bad years the donkey receives an eighth of the original food supply, after 4 bad years this will be halved and become less than a tenth. **3** £48 670.41. **4** 36 years. **5** (i) 95 years, (ii) 22 years. **6** 35%. **7** 42.6%. **8** (i) 4 years, (ii) discount rates of 14% and 16% result in 4 and 5 years respectively. **9** £11 487.19, reduced by £1558.11 if the machine is sold. **10** (i) 4000 packets, (ii) 5400 packets, (iii) 2000 packets.

## Chapter 2
**1** 3.75 m of A, 19.5 m of B. **2** 10 4-person tents and 3 8-person tents. **3** (i) 4 Little Big Horns and 3 Big Big Horns, (ii) 4 Little Big Horns and 0 Big Big Horns. **4** 60 refrigerators, 110 washing machines and 0 freezers.

## Chapter 3
**1** Nutwood sends 5 loads to Erehwon and 10 to Oz, Toytown sends 20 to Arkville and 40 to Brobdingnag, Utopia sends 10 to Arkville and 15 to Erehwon. Total cost £235. **2** A sends 200 to Z, B sends 50 to Y and 50 to Z, C sends 200 to Y and D sends 200 to X and 100 to Y *or* A sends 50 to Y and 150 to Z, B sends 100 to Z, C sends 200 to Y and D sends 200 to X and 100 to Y. **3** A sends 100 to X and 50 to Z, B sends 100 to Y and 50 to Z and C sends 200 to X.

## Chapter 4
**1** Reception desk connected to offices A, C and D, office A connected to B, C connected to E, E to F and F to G. **2** Ghost Train to Ferris Wheel to Coconut Shy to Big Dipper to Dodgem Cars and back to Ghost Train. **3** —.**4** (i) Oxford Circus to Bond Street, Piccadilly Circus and Holborn, Bond Street to Baker Street and Green Park, Holborn to Kings Cross, (ii) Kings Cross to Holborn to Oxford Circus to Piccadilly Circus to Green Park to Bond Street to Baker Street and back to Kings Cross. **5** —.

## Chapter 5
**1** Total project time is 24 weeks, critical path is 1, 2, 4, 5, 6. Arranging the music has total float 3 weeks, music rehearsals have total and free float 3 weeks, making the costumes etc. has total, free and independent float 7 weeks. All other float times are zero. **2** (i) expected total project time is 54.5 years, critical path activities are B, C, E, G, H, (ii)—(iii) 0.298, (iv) 0.460. **3** HDBEFCAG or HDBFECAG or HDBEFCGA or HDBFECGA. **4** (i) D to Arthur, E to Bill, A to Charles, B to David and C to Eric or equivalent—time taken is 46 hours, (ii) 2 hours.

*Chapter 6*
1 0.000 337, 3.37 people.   2 2/3.   3 (i) 0.59, (ii) 3/28.   4 £0.027.   5 (i) £4250—accept offer, (ii) expected profit of second product is £8100 so they should market it instead, (iii) first product, (iv) second product.   6 15.17.   7 Aim for the second aircraft.   8 £185.00, £135.00, £210.00, £300.00. Hence they should buy 1 spare with the crane.   9 He has no intention of detonating his 'bomb'. Therefore it does not count as a 'bomb' in any statistical analysis.   10 (i) 4.92 drivers per week, (ii)—.

*Chapter 7*
1 (i) 0.000 003 69, (ii) 0.281.   2 (i) 0.06, (ii) 0.974.   3 The expected journey time by car, 1 hour 27 minutes, is less than that by train, 1 hour 45 minutes.   4 (i) 0.307, (ii) 0.553.   5 (i) 0.011, (ii) 0.675, (iii) 0.084.   6 (i) 0.033, (ii) in view of the low probability of the former event, the latter one seems true.   7 (i) 268 circuits work, probability is 0.67, (ii) 0.011, 0.096, 0.293, 0.397, 0.202, (iii) 1, 10, 29, 40, 20.   8 Probability of 7 or more is 0.090 which is not unduly small. Therefore the observed event is consistent with the shampoos being indistinguishable from each other.

*Chapter 8*
1 (i) 0.157, (ii) 0.690, (iii) 0.392, 0.059.   2 (i) £8.27, (ii) second man loses £4.52 per day on average.   3 0.000 014 7.   4 0.544.   5 (i) 0.352, (ii) 0.346, (iii) 0.560, 0.176.   6 His English mark, as measured by the $z$ score, is better relative to the rest of the class than his Chemistry mark.   7 (i) 0.014, (ii) 0.841.   8 0.000 94.   9 0.405.

*Chapter 9*
1 745 packets every 1.5 weeks.   2 16 arrows every 4 days.   3 (i) 0.167, (ii) probability of demand greater than 3 is 0.0537, greater than 4 is 0.0143—hence it is necessary to keep 4 spares.   4 34 packets.   5 39 ducats per man, 60 ducats per man, 99.6 men, re-order level 102 men.   6 (i) 4.3 days, 55.9 cabinets, (ii) 50.99, (iii) average cost about £1.60 per day.

*Chapter 10*
1 (i) 1.8462 bees per minute, 0.250, (ii) 0.9208, 10.7 bees, 6.8 minutes.   2 (i) —, (ii) —, (iii) about 18 minutes, (iv) about 5 hours, about 50 minutes.   3 (i) 1.16 minutes; the expected service time is 1.9 minutes and hence 2 cashiers should cope, (ii)—, (iii) about 0.52 minutes, (iv) about 0.68 minutes. Therefore the credit card system delays customers.

*Chapter 11*
1 (i) Every 2 years, (ii) every 3 years, (iii) A for 2 years, (iv) A.   2 (i) £2.22 per month, (ii) cheapest strategy is a group replacement every 2 months.   3 0.997.   4 $p^3 (10 - 15p + 6p^2)$ where $p = e^{-t/3.26}$, expected life is 2.55 years.

*Chapter 12*
1 4.0.   2 About £53 000.   3 (i) —, (ii) —, (iii) $y = -0.5x + 1.3$, (iv) 4.0 miles per second.   4 (i) —, (ii) Average percentage seasonal adjustments are 129.9, 80.9, 82.7, 106.5 taking the centred moving averages as the trend, (iii) —,(iv) 18.2, 11.0, 10.9, 13.7.

*Chapter 13*
1 (i) A suitable order is G, M, N, E, T, C, (ii) equilibrium is reached with the variables listed in (i) having the values 24.0, 20.0, 100.1, 26.0, 30.0, and 70.1 respectively.   2 —.

# Index